the WOMAN WHO WOULD BE King

the WOMAN WHO WOULD BE King

THE MADUSA STORY

DEBRAH MICELI

AND

Greg Oliver

foreword by

PAUL HEYMAN

ECW

Published by ECW Press
665 Gerrard Street East
Toronto, Ontario, Canada M4M 1Y2
416-694-3348 / info@ecwpress.com

Editor for the Press: Michael Holmes
Copy editor: Jennifer Foster
Cover design: Michel Vrana
Front cover image: Mickey Fitzpatrick and Anthony Neste
Back cover photo courtesy WWE
Debrah Miceli author photo by Anthony Neste
Greg Oliver author photo by Geoffrey Cole, Shooting the Indies

To the best of her abilities, the author has related experiences, places, people, and organizations from her memories of them. In order to protect the privacy of others, she has, in some instances, changed the names of certain people and details of events and places.

LIBRARY AND ARCHIVES CANADA CATALOGUING IN PUBLICATION

Title: The woman who would be king : the Madusa story / by Debrah "Madusa" Miceli and Greg Oliver.

Names: Miceli, Debrah, author. | Oliver, Greg, author.

Identifiers: Canadiana (print) 20220488827 | Canadiana (ebook) 20220488886

ISBN 978-1-77041-671-0 (hardcover)
ISBN 978-1-77852-141-6 (ePub)
ISBN 978-1-77852-142-3 (PDF)
ISBN 978-1-77852-143-0 (Kindle)

Subjects: LCSH: Miceli, Debrah. | LCSH: Women wrestlers—United States—Biography. | LCSH: Wrestlers—United States—Biography. | LCSH: Monster trucks. | LCSH: Women truck drivers—United States—Biography. | LCSH: Truck drivers—United States—Biography. | LCGFT: Autobiographies.

Classification: LCC GV1196.M53 A3 2023 | DDC 796.812092—dc23

This book is funded in part by the Government of Canada. *Ce livre est financé en partie par le gouvernement du Canada.* We also acknowledge the support of the Government of Ontario through the Ontario Book Publishing Tax Credit, and through Ontario Creates.

ONTARIO CREATES
Canada

PRINTED AND BOUND IN CANADA

PRINTING: FRIESENS 5 4 3 2 1

Dedicated to my mom who absolutely hates the thought of this book.

To my father, a man that never knew I existed.

To the family and friends that stuck around, not wanting a thing.

To careers that nearly killed me emotionally, financially, and spiritually.

To my fans, past, present, and future, you truly are my energy to continue.

To all those that are lost, may they be found and heard.

Most of all, to love, patience, and spiritual healing for helping me always find a way.

CONTENTS

FOREWORD

THE FIRST TIME I EVER MET "Madusa" was in July 1987. We had both just been hired by Verne Gagne's Minneapolis, Minnesota–based American Wrestling Association (AWA), which at the time aired nationally on ESPN. While the promotion had already enjoyed its glory days, it was still one of the Big 3 promotions in the United States, and its

PHOTO COURTESY WWE

Paul Heyman hugs Debrah Miceli at the 2015 WWE Hall of Fame ceremony.

championship was recognized around the world. Getting picked up by the AWA meant you were now working for a big-league promotion.

I was 21 years old and was making both friends and enemies at a record pace. One of the people I knew from my days as a teenaged photographer was Curt Hennig, then the AWA's World Heavyweight champion and a sensational performer who would find greater fame just a few years later as "Mr. Perfect" with World Wrestling Entertainment (WWE). Curt was a second-generation professional wrestler, and his father, Larry "The Axe" Hennig, had a love/hate relationship with the Gagnes for years.

As soon as I got to the AWA, Curt and I started to conspire on how we could get Verne to allow us to work together. The newly minted villainous heavyweight champion and the loudmouth manager from New York seemed like (all puns intended) a perfect combination. On the days we would tape interviews ("promos") in Minneapolis, Curt and I could always be found huddled in a corner, watching everyone else do their shtick, taking notes, and figuring out how to top every single one of them.

At the time, the top female performer in the AWA was their women's champion and sometimes-ringside-manager Sherri Martel, and it was no secret Sherri needed new people to work with. Verne finally hired a Minneapolis-based talent named Madusa Miceli. This was quite the controversial decision, since Madusa was trained by Eddie Sharkey, a long-time rival of the Gagnes, but whose training camp had already produced The Road Warriors, the last big box office attractions the Gagne promotion got to enjoy.

Madusa was different from the get-go. She had the blonde hair and the great looks, but from the moment she walked into the room, you knew this was not some powder puff who learned how to take bumps. This was a fighter. A legit athlete. A badass. Someone to be reckoned with. And someone whose ideas about women in the business were not limited to either "special attraction women's match" or "valet." Madusa walked in determined to be an equal talent to anyone, male or female, and she wanted to compete with them for the top spot — even if it meant competing with me for the top "manager" spot or competing with Curt Hennig for the position of being the number one wrestler in the promotion.

Now, 35-plus years later, the reader of this foreword will most likely say, "Sounds right to me!" But in 1987, the concept of a female competing with men for the top spot, and a manager let alone wrestler in this business, was not even part of the conversation in the professional wrestling / sports entertainment industry. Madusa was not only beyond ambitious, but also she was indescribably ahead of her time.

Madusa arrived already at odds with Sherri Martel, who did not like the forward-thinking vision Madusa had no desire to hide. And Martel had zero desire to partake in a storyline in which Madusa would wind up the AWA Women's champion. Sherri, super popular with everyone in the locker room, was headed for WWE. And Madusa, the new girl on the block trained by local tough guy Eddie Sharkey, with the reputation of working local Midwest indies for five dollars a night just to get the experience necessary to break into the big leagues, was facing a situation where the rest of the talent in the locker room wasn't going to be welcoming.

In case you're wondering, Madusa couldn't have cared less.

She walked into the Gagnes' office / production facility in Minneapolis with her chin up and her chest out. Square-shouldered and fists clenched, a smile on her face that let you know this was not only a strikingly good-looking woman, but also a confident one. Curt decided to have some fun and introduce himself to her and see what all the fuss was about. As he went to talk with her, I was summoned to do an interview promoting our next event in Las Vegas, Nevada; or Green Bay, Wisconsin; or Denver, Colorado; or wherever else the AWA was running an event featuring the talent I was managing at the time. As soon as my interview was over, I darted over to Curt and couldn't wait for the scouting report. "So, how was your first encounter? Is she cool? Is she nice? Does she know anything about the business? Tell me!"

Curt, ever the practical joker ("ribber") said, "You gotta meet her! She's great!"

So, I straightened my tie, popped a breath mint into my mouth, and walked over to her, with my hand extended for our initial handshake greeting. "Hi," I squeaked. "My name is Paul Heyman. People call me 'Paul E. Dangerously.' It's a pleasure to meet you!"

Madusa shook my hand, harder than most men ever had up until that point in my life, looked me straight in the eye, and said, "I'm Debrah. People call me 'Madusa.' Don't fuck with me!"

She didn't let go of my hand. She made sure that eye contact lasted long enough for me to know just how deadly serious she was. Then she broke into a slight grin as if to say, "I think you got the message, right?" let my hand go, and walked away.

I left the AWA at the end of 1987, and Madusa was out the door not too long after I was. I bounced around a little bit until landing at the Ted Turner–owned World Championship Wrestling promotion, while Madusa went out to Asia and not only honed her craft, but also developed a reputation as one of the single toughest females in or out of the pro wrestling business.

So, it was a no-brainer in 1991 when Dusty Rhodes, Jim Ross (J.R.), Jim Crockett (Crockett), and I were putting together a new "Horsemen"-like faction called the Dangerous Alliance. I wanted someone in the group who would play a role that had never been attempted before. We needed a James Bond villain, and that "heel" would be known as the "Director of Covert Operations." There was only one person for the job.

Madusa.

Dusty knew she could be a revolutionary, indeed an evolutionary talent. J.R. loved the idea before I even finished pitching it. Crockett, who wasn't all that familiar with her work, asked, "What's she like?"

"She's too talented for her own good," I told Crockett, at one time the number two promoter in the United States behind Vince McMahon and the owner of the promotion Ted Turner bought and rechristened World Championship Wrestling. "She's got great camera presence, a boatload of charisma, can help us fight our way back to the locker room in case of a riot, can credibly wrestle anyone, male or female, if we want her to, and can take much better bumps and beatings than I can!"

Dusty, J.R., and Crockett heard all they had to hear. Madusa was going to be the director of covert operations for a faction that included top star of the day, Ravishing Rick Rude, and the hottest prospect in the entire industry, Steve Austin, along with their frothing-at-the-mouth manager, Paul E. Dangerously.

I should tell you I'm not much of a drinker, and I especially don't like beer. But when you're sitting with Dusty Rhodes, and he wants you to have a cold one with him, you oblige The American Dream! So, when Dusty reached into his cooler and passed around some Coors Lights, I knew I was going to down one out of respect for WCW's lead writer (then known as a "booker").

"Here's to Madusa!" Dusty exclaimed as we all raised our beer cans for a toast to the decision made and the talent who just got cast in a major career opportunity: "The Director of Covert Operations!"

Dusty guzzled his beer, looked at me, watched me force the beer down my throat, and laughed. "She's going to be a major star, Paulie, and she's got you and me, The American Dream, the super genius, to thank for it!"

"Yes, sir," I replied. "There's just one thing."

"Tell me, kid," Dusty stated, "don't hold back. What do I need to know?"

I straightened out my tie, popped in a breath mint, leaned into Dusty as close as I could get to whisper in his ear, and told him, "She's Madusa. The director of covert operations for the Dangerous Alliance. Don't fuck with her!"

— PAUL HEYMAN, JULY 2022

INTRODUCTION

BEING IN THE PUBLIC EYE for all of my adult life has been both fulfilling and exhausting. The fans have backed and supported me to the top of two remarkably similar industries.

In professional wrestling, I hit the pinnacles both in the United States and in Japan. Then, in one of the most abrupt left turns in history, I entered the testosterone-fueled chaos of monster trucks, taking

It's never too late to change your perspective.

two world championships away from the good ol' boys. Through the process, I traveled the world a couple of times over, finding fame — and incredible pain — in Australia.

Those who clamored for autographs after the matches or waited patiently to talk with me in five-hour-long lines at the Monster Jam pit parties thought they knew me a little bit.

Maybe they called me by my real name instead of Madusa or Alundra Blayze, mentioned my Minnesota upbringing, or brought me a Butterfinger candy bar. Little girls and boys wore their pink tutus, tiaras, and *Queen of Carnage* T-shirts, and gave me tight hugs and said they wanted to follow in my footsteps.

I smiled, laughed, and played nice.

But none of them knew me.

They didn't know the depths of despair I faced growing up; poverty was one thing, but at the extremes, I craved love and attention from a mother unable to give it, and I was sexually abused by the man I had been told was my father.

They didn't understand my fight-or-flight instinct that makes up my very core, an ongoing battle.

And they certainly never knew of my continual heartbreak, my failure. I wanted to be a mom, something I never had myself, really. Desperately. In two male-dominated sports, pregnancy was frowned upon.

But, I tried. Lord, how I tried.

Two separate tubal pregnancies nearly killed me, three IVFs didn't work, I miscarried a few times, and had an adoption fall apart at the last minute.

It tortures me now, and talking about my inability to be a mother openly for the first time for this book has not helped. Nothing will ever help.

Instead, I do what I have always done — throw myself into my work. I cannot sit still, or I think too much about it all. I have overcome the bumps of the ring and track and have evolved. Whether it's public speaking or private life-coaching sessions, I aim to make a difference. I've adapted and can game with the best of them on Twitch, share on social media, and come up with ideas for products labeled with the *Madusa* name, keeping the brand alive.

The title of this book, *The Woman Who Would Be King*, came from Paul Heyman, and it fits. I blazed (and Blayzed) trails, created controversy, defied gender rules, tossed convention — and a title belt — into the trash. I never settled, and nor should you.

I have been working on my autobiography, on and off, for 30 years.

This book is very much like I am — it jumps around like a caffeinated bunny, with the attention span of a kindergartner, who always wants to touch, taste, experience life to its fullest.

Read it with an open mind and imagine yourself in some of the same positions I was in, having some of the same experiences. Let's share this journey. Of course, with a warning label.

This is a story of a girl who experienced life's tragedies and triumphs. There are people I celebrate here, some I vilify, and some whose names have been removed for a variety of reasons.

With great trepidation, letting down my guard for the first time, I invite you to read on. I suspect it will cause the end of some personal and professional relationships for me, maybe even get me canceled in today's overly sensitive society.

So, get over yourself, let your hair down, and enjoy the wild ride. It's time for you to get to know the *real* Debrah Ann Bergman.

1.

GRANNY

ONE OF THE MOST IMPORTANT people in my life has been my motorcycle-riding, tough-as-nails Granny Violet Lewandowski. With her long, jet-black hair, comfortable, stylish homemade clothes, and mischievous twinkle in her eye, she was the antithesis of your traditional old lady grandma; even when her hair finally turned gray in the 1990s, she acted decades younger.

Since my mother was a mess, I got dropped off at Granny Vi's a lot, and she never failed to keep me occupied. She lived in Robbinsdale, Minnesota, only about 15 minutes away from where we lived, first in Minneapolis, and then Crystal.

Granny works on her motorcycle.

Granny always made reference to my nonstop energy and my stubbornness. Darla was the cousin closest in age to me, and we'd often be together at Granny's. One time, Darla locked me outside, and I warned her I'd smash the window on the screen door to get in — and I did. Granny had been working in the basement and came up to bandage me up. I still have a small scar on my right wrist, one of many fond memories of Darla. We didn't know it until we were much older, but Darla and I had similar issues with our parents.

Often, Granny and I would head to a nearby ballroom and two-step — and she'd swing me around, like she knew I needed a break from my mother. My first plane ride as a 15-year-old kid was with Granny. She wanted to go to the Grand Ole Opry, and no one else wanted to go, so I said I would. We saw Mel Tillis, Minnie Pearl, and even rode roller coasters and the Ferris wheel. What a memory.

Her work ethic is one of her traits that I admired and aspired to match. Granny always had two or three jobs going. I can still picture her in her assigned blue dress at the Red Owl grocery store, her hair done up in a bouffant, sneaking me a treat when I'd pop by. For 19 years, she worked as a maintenance supervisor, looking after six different buildings in Brooklyn Center. How many women do you think had similar jobs at that time? Granny also cleaned houses on the side.

And did I mention she also had seven kids? Divorced when the youngest was two.

As I got older, Granny was the one to help me out. She loaned me money for modeling school and for a knee operation I needed early in my wrestling career. And, most importantly, when my second marriage fell apart, she was there to introduce me to my one true love — my pink Harley!

"I'm done. My life's a mess. I need a bike."

"Well, it's about time. I was wondering what took you so long."

"Grandma, I was in Japan!"

As she approaches 100 years young, Granny is still working, sewing for people, upholstering, just making an extra buck on the side.

For all the love I have for Granny, the truth is that she was a big part of the lies, the deceptions, the half-truths that scarred me, and cannot get off scot-free.

My whole life, I was told that Granny, whose maiden name is Pocklington, was part Native American, from the Potawatomi tribe. She dressed the part. The family decided to send away for information on our background through the 23andMe genetic testing. There wasn't a drop of Native American blood in her, but some of the names listed sounded right, and there was a lot of English blood. She didn't know how to explain it. Well, I did: she lied, based on misinformation. And in comparison to some of what you are about to learn, it was a little white lie.

My maternal grandfather, who divorced Granny when I was young, insisted that his side of the family had Jewish origins. Unlike Granny, he *looked* the part of an older Jewish man. But everyone else denied it. The genetic tests showed deep roots in Europe.

Right from the get-go, lies and cover-ups were a part of my life.

Yet I love her and my family. I would do anything for them, despite all that was wrong, all the cover-ups, all the denials.

In retrospect, it's not a surprise that I ended up in colorful professions where I could pretend I was someone else for a little while.

2.

LESSONS LEARNED, STILL LEARNING

SOME PEOPLE AREN'T MEANT to be in school. Back then, I was one of them. Everything I needed to learn was out there, in the real world. Experiences meant way more to me than learning the periodic table or who was the 18th American president. And I was smart, too smart. Give me a test — fuck — I ain't doing it. I could just pass it in a heartbeat, and I didn't have to study (except math, which I refused to do). Every grade just kept passing me, and they shouldn't have because I didn't do

I'd graduate to much bigger trucks.

the assignments; I suspect they did it to both get rid of me and because they knew I could do the work if I wanted.

Consider my track record: expelled from school in kindergarten and again in seventh grade . . . and ninth grade; multiple suspensions; dropped out of high school at the start of 11th grade; modeling school, where I quickly learned I was unable to deal with rejection; then my second nursing training ended midcourse.

But one school did stick, and it was as unconventional as they come — training to be a professional wrestler.

There was a rich history of wrestling in the Minneapolis–St. Paul area, both amateur but especially professional, where a veteran wrestler named Verne Gagne had set up a promotion based in town that promoted throughout the Midwest, and as far away as Las Vegas and San Francisco. But I was oblivious to that.

While I was a girl who loved to have a good time, I was also pretty serious about my gym time. There were days I would teach three or four aerobics classes — and I never studied to be an instructor, either. They just let me lead the classes, on top of hitting the weights.

In the summer of 1984, I was at a beach bar in Minnetonka, a suburb of Minneapolis; it wasn't Venice Beach, but it was our place to hang out and show off. I had run into an old friend named Jenny, and we were all playing volleyball. I had only recently moved back from Chicago, Illinois, where I managed a health club. She introduced me to her boyfriend, Ky Michaelson. We chatted, and I learned Ky was a stuntman and stunt coordinator with extensive major movie experience, including working with the legendary stuntman Dar Robinson, who made Burt Reynolds look so great in so many films. *Hmm.*

Ky was upfront and told me that I belonged in the entertainment industry, that with my look and personality, I'd be a success. He was my "imagineer." Normally, I'd take that over-the-top buttering up as a come on, but Jenny was right there. I dreamed of a life in Hollywood, moving from stunts to an action star. Later, I got a brief taste of it through the connections of Brandon Pender.

Then Ky broke it to me — he meant professional wrestling. At that time, I had never watched wrestling, I never had any interest in wrestling, and had barely caught a few minutes of it on television. I thought he meant mud wrestling.

Ky had a pal named Eddie Sharkey, who operated a wrestling training facility. We arranged to meet down at Sharkey's place. I'll never forget walking in; it was like a dungeon, with old high school gymnastic mats all over, and a bunch of sweaty guys throwing one another around. Eddie and Ky chatted for a bit — they'd known each other for years — and Eddie was upfront with me: "Hey kid, if you're serious about this, you're gonna have to train with the rest here, no different."

"Yeah, I can do this," I replied. With that, my life changed.

It was $2,000 to train, but Eddie owed Ky a favor, so I was never charged — I also wasn't paid to wrestle on shows for a couple of years, either. Ky took a percentage of my pay, as a de facto personal manager, but that never amounted to much. Really, I caught a break getting in with Sharkey, who had shown the ropes to future superstars like The Road Warriors, Rick Rude, Barry Darsow (who wrestled as Repo Man, Krusher Krushchev, and Smash in Demolition), Nord the Barbarian, and Jesse "The Body" Ventura, who would later become governor of Minnesota. I'd often find myself in The Gym — owned by the Road Warriors, and connected to Zubaz — with these local guys when they were home, especially at a gym on the outskirts of town. Ventura liked to work out on the exercise bike and would share stories of his days in the military and from his early wrestling days.

Eddie was always funny, cutting dirty jokes. He was a good trainer, but very old-school. If I wasn't pairing up with the one other girl — I have no idea whatever happened to Danielle Moore, who competed as Wrestling Rose — I would be rolling around with the guys during the evening classes a couple of times a week. A few others would come and go, and no one from my "class" ever really made it in pro wrestling.

Less than two months later, I was in a bar fighting — and it was such a huge rush. I wore the same leotards I'd wear at the gym, and had on a pair of old, worn-in red Reeboks and my 1980s puffy socks. I didn't know what the fuck I was doing. It showed. I knew I was supposed to tell a story, but I didn't know how long to keep someone in a hold or when the big comeback should be. That stuff wasn't taught.

I also wasn't taught that wrestling was a "work," meaning you had to work together for the best performance, so that you didn't really hurt each other. I learned that over time, listening and paying close attention to the guys in the ring.

Right from the start, I was Madusa. Ky and I came up with the idea one day at his cosmetic warehouse. Later, we figured out that it was *MADe in the USA*, but that wasn't the thought at the beginning.

Brilliantly, I trademarked the name Madusa, and it's been in my control ever since.

Maybe I was always meant to beat people up — or later, destroy cars. There was a lot bottled up in me, so much of it tied up in the craziness that I experienced at home, not knowing what "normal" life was like. I was just lost and didn't understand why I felt that way. We were poor, so I had one strike against me just walking in the door. The other kids could tell, like I smelled of welfare.

There was a target on my back from the moment I went to the bus stop by myself for the trip to school at Twin Lakes Kindergarten. All the other parents were there, hugging their sons and daughters goodbye. Not mine. Five years old and I'm on my own. The bullies soon noticed what easy pickings I was, and I'd hide in the bushes waiting for the bus. It didn't work, as they kicked and punched with abandon, but it created a toughness in me. In the schoolyard, I would try to make myself scarce.

The anger built as I was picked on. When you needed to go to the bathroom, you'd have to grab a block attached to a piece of yarn. One time, kids were pushing me out the door, and from another classroom, there was a dorky kid being pushed out. They started in, teasing us that we were boyfriend and girlfriend. I had enough, and I swung the bathroom block and hit the other kid in the forehead. It split him right open, and he fell, blood gushing everywhere. "See what you did!" I screamed, then I continued to the toilet. When I came out, the teacher took me to the office, where I was promptly expelled because I was sticking up for myself. That ability to stand up for what I believed in served me well through the years.

How disinterested was my mom — I call her "Betty" and will throughout the book, since she was hardly a "mother" — in my schooling? I didn't go back to kindergarten, so sat out a year, and entered first grade at Cavanaugh Elementary. (More on Betty to come . . .)

The fighting continued, and, lessons learned, I was the one beating up kids at the bus stop. I tried desperately to make friends, but then something would happen, and we'd end up in a fight, and the other parents would prevent their kids from hanging out with me. It didn't matter, I'd fight anyway — boys or girls, no matter their size.

My first-grade teacher looked like a witch and did not like me. One day she stopped me from going to recess, and I became so angry that I sat at my desk and wet my pants. When the witch returned, she took me to another room and spanked me. When she finished, I just turned to her and said, "Are you done?" That really shocked her, she expected me to cry. Then I got my things and went home. In second grade, I mellowed out somewhat and had a reasonable year. The main reason for this was my teacher, who looked like a perfect doll with an angelic face. She became a surrogate mom, and I wanted to please her, so I behaved.

By third grade, I was probably the biggest girl in the class and the most picked on in the school. There was another kid who was also my competition for being victim number one in the school, Eugene. Sex education classes were just starting after years of public controversy in the state of Minnesota, and kids had been given forms for parental signatures — and Betty refused to sign mine. So when these classes started, there I was, with dork Eugene, our desks moved to the hallway. It was really humiliating, and the embarrassment contributed to my attitude problems. Fortunately, in the fifth and sixth grades, I had teachers who cared, and my marks started to improve.

I also gained some confidence selling books of fundraising vouchers in grade school. There were prizes — simple things like a stuffed animal radio — but I craved the recognition and thrived on the competition. I learned a lot about entrepreneurship and how to work the system and money — and all in a good way. Since I had no parental supervision, I could stay out later at night, knocking on doors, making sales, asking for fifty cents or a dollar. Counting the money was exciting, since we never had money around the house. Similarly, I had no problem hitting up people for work, mowing yards or shoveling driveways for pocket money — and shoveling snow in Minneapolis is serious business. There was a paper route for a time, too.

You know what else is a sales job? Being a pro wrestler. You sell in the ring, you sell yourself to the promoter, you sell your soul to become famous. What's harder is learning who to trust, who to cater to, what to say and when to say it, and what not to say.

Where I lived, there was a junior high school, Hosterman, where seventh, eighth, and ninth grades met. In seventh grade, I was a hellion. I did not want to be there. My life was shit. Betty and my "father," Mike Miceli, had divorced, and I knew I was smarter than either of them anyway. I was so rebellious. I just didn't want to do the work because I was bored, thinking, *Pfft, I don't need this*. That year, we could either take French or German, and I took French. Big mistake. The teacher would always call on me to embarrass me. One day, she pissed me off: she called on me and laughed. This time I was ready. I had brought cherry bombs to school and had some matches. After her class, she went to the bathroom. I threw cherry bombs under the door, and held the door shut. I told her, "Don't you ever, ever do that again. How dare you embarrass me. That's not what teachers do." She was screaming to get out, but I wouldn't let her until she apologized. Kids started gathering, and I was telling them off, too. "Y'all just shut up. You're part of the problem." Eventually, I let the door open. She looked at me and said, "You're gonna pay for this." The next day, I was called into the principal's office and expelled. I had been suspended for a few things before that. I was getting suspended left and right, and I'd just shrug, take the suspension letter, and walk home — which was about four miles, along a highway. And Betty didn't give a shit, and certainly did not reprimand me.

The next year, in a new school, was better, if only because I was introduced to home ec and shop, and I baked, cooked, and did crafty things.

I was really expanding my mind.

It never occurred to me until working on this, but that home ec class was the basis for my love of entertaining, whether it's a beautiful turkey dinner for Thanksgiving, or wine-tasting parties at the house with my eclectic collection of friends — politicians, entertainers, CEOs, military personnel, homemakers, bikers, or just good ol' country people.

In ninth grade, I really started learning about my body. I was strong as fuck, I was an athlete, I was running track and field, doing gymnastics. I was jacked. I was coming into my own as I noticed my body changing — not that Betty ever taught me about the birds and the bees, menstruation, or what to expect as I grew up; instead, I saw some stranger using a tampon and figured it out myself.

I was such a tomboy and was fascinated by others who started wearing makeup or plucking their eyebrows. No one was teaching me that at home, no one was looking out for me, there were no rules, and next to no communication. I really wanted to get my hair feathered, like Farrah Fawcett. I stole some money out of Betty's wallet and sold some food stamps for cash. I actually called ahead to the salon at the local strip mall, and they said they had a spot open if I could get there just before closing. Well, Betty never drove, so she couldn't help. I walked the four miles to get my hair cut. The hairdresser asked where my parents were. I told her they weren't available. She insisted on giving me a ride home as it was dark out. (The haircut rocked, though, and I started getting noticed.)

As in wrestling, later, I had a rival at Hosterman High. Leslie was an athletic, badass mofo, and I always admired her, but also hated her because she was doing cool things that I wanted to do. We would always be head-to-head in competition. In debate class, I was scared to even talk because of what people thought of me and what always happened to me as a kid, and I felt like if I opened my mouth, I'd be an outcast. But as the year progressed, and I watched others, I learned how to do it, and knew I deserved to be heard. I spoke eloquently, I thought, but I was very aggressive. And I remember the teachers saying something like, "Oh my God, this is a future politician." Leslie thought I went too far in one debate and called me on it. After class, I was pissed, pacing back and forth, ranting, and planning my attack. When I saw her, I went right at her, kneed her in the back, grabbed her hair, slammed her head into the lockers, and then dragged her face across the lockers. I told her that if she ever talked to me like that again, it would be worse.

That was the third time I was expelled.

In today's environment, I would have been sent to prison, where shrinks would have had a field day. But, really, why didn't the teachers do anything? Why didn't Betty do anything? Why was I that way?

At the next school, a work–school balance proved to be the solution, until I dropped out in 11th grade (I did get my GED in 1980). At 14, Arby's was my employer, and I stayed there for a few years, starting out at $2.30 an hour and eventually nearly doubling that. It seemed a fortune then. It's odd that I was gladly on time to work the register, but when I got locked up in a desk at school, I was fit to be tied. All those clichés about learning work ethic, how to fit in, and dealing with customers were plusses for me.

The job gave me confidence and it gave me money, so I was able to get the hell out of Betty's house. At first, it was couch surfing, staying at girlfriends' homes — I loved seeing how *real* families operated; honestly, I was hardly ever home.

For a time after the divorce, Betty had a boyfriend named Steve. He complained that she never wanted to go do anything and hardly knew how to cook. Well, duh. I'd come home and change clothes, never really sleeping there. Then one day, I arrived there to find that Betty had moved out, leaving Steve, and she didn't tell me the plan. That was an unspoken indication that Betty was done with me, and I just moved on and did not dwell on her decision; I mean, what would have been the point?

Not long after starting at Arby's, I got an apartment on my own and hung out constantly with a coworker named Kelly. She was my little hippie friend, always smoking weed. I tried it and got so scared and freaked out, and I stayed away from marijuana until I learned about the medicinal aspects of the plant more than 40 years later. (Now, I am a spokesperson for the Küribl line of hemp products.)

Kelly and I took a hit of acid while we were at work, making us high for hours, transfixed by the sound of our cash registers during the lunch rush. Once business calmed down, the manager called us into the office, "What's wrong with you two?" We just laughed. They sent us home, and we hitchhiked around for hours.

Another time, a bunch of us dropped acid in a church parking lot, sitting in my truck. My friends started laughing uncontrollably, and I wondered why my dose hadn't kicked in. Then, *boom*. It was like a horror film, the church steeple started, bending and twisting, and I screamed, "It's alive!" We sped out of there, burning rubber, scared out of our minds.

The Arby's was on a highway, and hitching a ride was our only way to get there. In today's society, that sounds insane, and looking back, it's tough to disagree.

There was actually a regular who picked us up in a beige truck, and Kelly and I would fight about who had to sit next to him. He had one of those '70s mustaches, short, messy hair, and always had jeans on; my memory is very clear on the push-button car radio he had, that I'd fiddle with while Kelly chatted and gave him directions. She'd often just raise her voice and say, "Let us out here!" She'd hop out, and I'd be right behind her, running down the road. The idea was that he wouldn't know exactly where we lived.

One time, Kelly wasn't at work, and, sure enough, he pulled up to offer a ride. I was reluctant without Kelly but didn't see many options. I stayed on the far side of the truck, doing my best to hide my fear. He was talking, but I wasn't paying attention; then I asked to get out like

Kelly always did, and he said no, that he wanted to drop me off. The handle on the door wasn't working, and when he slowed down enough in town, I leapt up through the window and ran like a madwoman. That was the last time I hitched a ride.

Coincidentally, or not, Kelly and I stopped hanging out. I saw her about 20 years ago, and we chatted, and I told her about my book that I was working on — yes, even then — but then we lost touch.

My athleticism was still the key to my future, though I didn't see it. I don't know how to say this without sounding like I'm bragging, but I was good at whatever I tried. The training and pushing myself seemed natural.

But I was not a natural model.

I decided to go to John Robert Powers modeling school, and Granny footed the bill, which was about $1,800 and that I eventually paid back. They taught you everything: how to dress; the makeup; how to walk on the runway; photography and lighting; posing; how to get modeling jobs; putting a press kit together; and all that great stuff. Offered the chance to pick a modeling name, I chose Brittany.

The hustle started out well enough. I modeled for a couple of T-shirt companies, and with All Pro Sports, wearing the hated Chicago Bears gear (Go, Vikings!).

There were a couple of runway jobs, too. I took part in the 1981 Miss Minnesota Teenager Celebrity Pageant, where my bio noted: "Enjoys visiting the elderly at nursing homes. Has participated in arm wrestling competitions." (I kicked ass in those.)

Then I went to a Minneapolis makeup company, located downtown near the First Avenue bar where Prince used to always play. (It was so cool, and I later rented an apartment down there since it was a happening district.) I wanted to model with a makeup company, thinking I'd score free makeup. After some introductions, I was invited to sit with two women, one obviously the assistant to the other. The subordinate flipped through my photos and said, "We can't use you." Her boss looked at her, puzzled, and the gopher continued, "You will never work as a model, or acting. Your nose is huge." My mouth dropped, and she thanked me for stopping by. I grabbed my portfolio, ran out of there, rejected.

Back then, you had to be Twiggy skinny. I was different looking, muscular, athletic, so I kept telling myself that I was unique.

Though I was scarred from the rejection, it also became fuel to work harder. And I did. There were a few modeling gigs intermittently, and it prepared me for future photo shoots in my careers.

In modeling school, I learned the importance of promotional packages, and mine included the usual photos and bio, but also details on my fan club and a *Pin*Her* hanky; I credit it for getting me into the American Wrestling Association, so thank you and fuck you to those bitches at the modeling/makeup company.

The bruised ego from the modeling mistake was nothing compared to what was to come, in wrestling and in monster trucks, but first came dealing with others' bruises.

In the fall of 1980, I enrolled in Hennepin Community College to learn nursing. Finally, an education that I could get into, and I could see an end goal. There was lots of real-life experience during the course to get my degree as a certified nursing assistant. Right away, I found work at Northridge, a retirement home, and started making a decent wage for the first time in my life.

I found myself in awe of the compassion that people had for one another, since I never saw that at home. Even seeing people in deep sadness was moving, and I loved being there to be caring and supportive. My specialty was helping people with Alzheimer's and dementia, and handicapped kids.

The next step was to become a licensed practical nurse, so I enrolled in a course to improve my degree, then, to the surprise of everyone — including myself — I dropped out to focus on pro wrestling.

If I'd stuck with it, I know I would have been a damn good nurse. But who would I have beaten up?

3.

BETTY

THIS IS GOING TO SOUND cruel and harsh, but Betty Jean Lewandowski should never have been a parent. It's not that I don't love her, because I do, but it's not a very normal mom–daughter relationship. She is incapable of showing affection to me, her only child, and is deeply introverted and antisocial, the shades drawn, whereas my default position is to be as outgoing as possible and live life to the fullest. My worst nightmare was to grow up like her, missing out on all the world has to offer.

A rare photo of my mother smiling.

On occasions when she has lashed out, Betty has told me that she regretted having me. From my understanding, her parents forced her to go through with the pregnancy. Relatives have confessed that she tried to abort me, water skiing while pregnant, trying to end the life inside her. Betty got pregnant at age 19 and had me on February 9, 1963, in Minneapolis, Minnesota, not Milan, Italy, as has been reported for years in the magazines and in the monster truck world. Even the spelling of my name has often been wrong: it's Debrah Ann Miceli (though, I added the *h* myself). The man listed on my birth certificate is Michael Miceli.

The story I have pieced together through the years — because no one in my family is ever forthcoming with truths — is that Betty had planned to put me up for adoption, and then Mike came into the picture, and he couldn't have a kid for whatever reason and stepped into both lives when she was very far along. Apparently, Betty actually left the hospital without me, whining I was too ugly to bring home, until her father ordered her back to get me. Did I really break her tailbone, coming out at almost 10 pounds? Maybe. She's just over five foot.

Mike and Betty were both kids having a kid, and nothing was easy. I was too little to remember, but apparently, I spent some time in a foster home — despite being from such a large family. In short, Betty tried to give me away, continually.

Over the years, I was asked a lot about my childhood in interviews, and I had to default to the family trait of mistruths and misdirections. I'd address the poverty we experienced, the low-quality food bought with food stamps, or the closet that served as my room in one tiny apartment — though, it was close to the stunningly beautiful Minneapolis Basilica, where I was baptized. Betty was essentially incapable of working, though she did some odd jobs, cleaning, whatever. When I was young, Mike worked as a baker.

Like flashes of a breaking film, I can faintly remember one night feeling terribly neglected. My parents had friends over, and I was left in the kitchen. I cried and cried on the floor until my mother came and gave me a walloping and stuck me in my closet! That's still better than when I was tied to my crib so my parents could go out — that's a story I heard years later.

There's not a lot that I know about Betty's own youth, as she just doesn't share. My grandfather, Ed Lewandowski, and Granny lived on a huge farm up in Milaca, Minnesota, and had seven kids over the course of a dozen years. Betty is the second oldest. She was always a homebody, didn't do much, and didn't have many friends I know of. One story I have heard is that she had a pet chicken that was blind, and she would torture it by hiding behind trees and calling the name, and the chicken would run into the tree. I'm sure it was just kids having fun. She taught herself how to play the accordion, just out of the blue.

In today's society, she would have been looked at by doctors and probably would have registered on the autism spectrum. Who knows? But when she grew up, in the 1950s, nobody knew about that.

Then Granny and Grandpa got divorced, and Granny moved with the kids to the city, and he had little to do with them, especially his younger four kids. He paid little to no child support, and Granny would have to find out where he worked to get money, and then he'd quit and go someplace else rather than have his wages garnered. Grandpa got a little better as the kids aged and helped with building them houses or other carpentry work. I'd go visit and watch him build, and eventually, he showed me things and let me help, like spreading concrete.

Grandpa was dodgy with his background. He was definitely adopted, he insisted. He told me he was Jewish but told others that we were a German family. You could never get a straight answer out of him. It was pretty cool that he was a pilot, though, and they had a family plane on the farm.

Both Granny and Grandpa remain treasured people in my life, even though they were negligent or less than forthcoming with the truth.

Without brothers or sisters, and with Betty being the odd one of the family, I didn't grow up particularly close to my many cousins. My one aunt and uncle were hard-core Baptists, meaning you couldn't play cards, you couldn't dance, you couldn't watch TV, you had to wear clothes a certain way, you couldn't talk to boys, and I got dumped there occasionally, but that was no fun, even with other kids there.

I can't remember anything great from my childhood. There are pictures from a party when I was young, holding up a *Happy Birthday* sign, but there aren't any kids around, no birthday cake with candles. Only a few pictures of me exist as a kid, and when I complain to Betty about how I was raised, she'll throw one in my face, playing with a truck and a doll, and say, "See, you had a perfect life."

I didn't know that life could be very different. But then, when I finally did see homes where other kids lived, with their toys and nice bedrooms, where the family talked and laughed at dinnertime, it was the spark that lit my rebellious fire.

One evening, I was left with my grandmother while my parents went out. They never came back that night — I thought I was heading for another foster home. It turned out they had been in an accident, asleep in the back seat of a friend's car when a car coming the wrong way up a cloverleaf smashed into them. A day or two later, Mike arrived at Granny's, still wearing his bloody, torn shirt, and his broken leg was in a cast. Betty got it worse, and the head injuries changed her, and she became meaner and even less caring to me. I'm a kid, with two broken parents, in over my head.

After the crash, the arguments between my parents began to get worse and worse. We moved to a very small yellow house (it really was a little shack) with a huge backyard that had a weeping willow and a white birch tree, and a set of swings where I performed all kinds of acrobatics and death-defying tricks, and sang "Jingle Bells" at the top of my lungs year-round. Grandpa built us a garage. It was a real neighborhood, and I ran down the street saying, "Kids, kids, I've got kids to play with!"

Finally, I had a few friends, like Linda, who had a big sister named Debbie, so I was "Little Debbie" around their house. Sandra showed me cool, artsy, crafty things to make, and it kick-started a lifelong passion — I'll make everything from jelly to wreaths.

No doubt, I was a very difficult child for other kids to get along with — my temperament must have been volatile! In fact, one pal,

Kathy, was essentially my personal punching bag. I was very aggressive and, not having had an upbringing based on love and caring, my manners and my method of speaking were really very different from other kids. Essentially, I was a mini adult given all that I had been forced to experience.

Until I moved out at 14, I had a very confrontational relationship with Betty. I can only remember getting the strap once from Michael, and she never spanked me. There were things I'd do to get back at her after she upset me. Betty would rarely make me breakfast, so, in anger, one day I got all my crayons and colored her toenails while she was sleeping. She woke up, started screaming, and that was my cue to hightail it out of the house. Leaving home after a fight became a regular thing.

It made me independent, too. From the moment I started school, I made my own breakfast while Betty stayed in bed. My go-to was two pieces of toast with lots of butter and hot chocolate to dunk the toast into while watching cartoons on our small TV with the adjustable rabbit ears.

I truly believe Betty hung on to me only because she could get money from Michael, as they split when I was about nine. There's no other reason why she kept me, except for the money, because she never worked. She never got her driver's license. She collected government aid — we were on welfare and used food stamps. When I did shoveling or mowed lawns in the neighborhood for 50 cents, I used the money to help with necessities. It was my job to do most of the shopping, which meant that kids my age saw me and I was labeled the "Welfare Kid." She'd write me a note so I could buy her cigarettes, those damn Pall Malls without a fucking filter. Betty finally quit about 20 years ago.

There were a series of men who came by, seemingly a different guy every night. I'd get up in the morning, and there was cash on the counter. That's the shit I had to deal with. I fought back, and not long after the noises started at night, I'd scream, "I'm thirsty!" The guy would freak and leave.

There is no question I grew up fast, learning on my own out in the real world, and I was like a sponge that absorbed the experience of life. Betty never taught me a thing — not how to cook, not how to dress, not even all that puberty shit — and remember, I wasn't allowed to take sex ed, either!

On my own, I threw myself into everything that I could. I wanted to be in Brownies and Girl Scouts, but we couldn't afford the dues or the outfit. I just kept showing up, and, probably feeling sorry for me, they let me stay.

At school, we had opportunities to play instruments, but needed a deposit. First, I tried the viola, and then the French horn. On the way home, I was carrying the monstrous French horn. Betty screamed at me, "I can't afford this!" That was short-lived.

As for the rest of the family on her side, it wasn't much better. Some of my aunts — and Granny — were rumored to have shared boyfriends. And there were tales far darker than I am comfortable sharing here.

One uncle, Michael, was an incredible artist, and I have some of his art at my home. But he was a druggie and even got involved with smuggling all sorts of drugs into Minnesota from some of Mexico's top drug lords. Another uncle told me that, without telling her, Michael once filled up Granny's garage with drugs, and there were apparently helicopters with the FBI when he got busted at the house. In prison, he wasn't allowed to have a proper paintbrush, so he improvised, using hair and coffee grounds. And he was always in and out of prison.

He got into heroin, and it was really bad. As a teen, I remember arriving at Granny's, and he was in the kitchen, his arm wrapped with a rubber tube, about to inject. Uncle Mike just casually offered, "Deb, I can do it to you just one time. It'll be great." I left.

Shall I go on? Nah, you get the picture.

Yet, I know Betty kept little keepsakes, like my first lock of hair or school ribbons. There was love there, under her inability to show it. Or at least I keep telling myself that.

As I moved out and on to my own life, there was never any support or encouragement. We'd go months and then years without talking. And when we did talk, eventually it would get to her standard rant: "All you want is fame, you crave attention, and you're a fucking liar. You're a no-good kid." "Attention whore" is another slight.

One day, I snapped. "If I would have gotten any attention as a child, I may not be seeking it out now! You tell me, Betty."

And yet, I try. Betty lives with Granny, and I'll call, talk with Granny, but Betty, stubborn as an ass, won't talk to me, or will bang pots in the background so I cannot hear Granny. I have made my attempts, like making an organic Thanksgiving dinner at Granny's one year, which only brought complaints and accusations of wanting attention from Betty.

Then May approaches, and I try to buy a Mother's Day card. There's not one damn card that describes her as a mother.

4.

LEARNING THE ROPES

THERE IS NO QUESTION THAT I wasn't ready, but there I was, hoisting the AWA Women's title on December 27, 1987, after beating Candi Devine in a tournament final in Las Vegas at the Showboat Sports Pavilion.

Pro wrestling is about a lot more than just the actions in the ring. There's a psychology to it, there's supposed to be a reason for the

Does it look like it's my first match? I'm facing Wrestling Rose (Danielle Moore).

moves, and it's supposed to take the fans on an emotional roller coaster. The wrestler has to be an actor, a stuntperson, and an entertainer all in one to do things well. Then as a woman, there was the added aspect of sex appeal for the primarily male audience. I had bits of it under control when I became AWA Women's champion, but there was still a long way to go.

There is also no question that I started at the bottom and paid my dues. Eddie Sharkey had me wrestling in front of an audience six weeks after I started training. The time in the gym with Eddie continued, though, and I struggled to make ends meet. I would drive out to South Dakota for no pay. These were small-town shows at armories, VFW halls, high schools. It was not the big time.

It was a feast if I could save up enough to eat grilled chicken breast with baked potatoes and a veggie (restaurants still had real food, not processed, then). I was more broke than broke could get. Eventually, I couldn't keep up my payments on my car — that I had been living in — and crashed with friends, and, on a couple of occasions, on the street.

But, boy, was I ever determined. I kept going, because I did not want to lose everything for nothing.

Eddie saw the drive that I had and sent me to Brad Rheingans for further training — polishing, really. Brad was an Olympic-level Greco-Roman wrestler who had turned pro after the United States boycotted the 1980 Olympic Games in Moscow. He was exactly what I needed. We trained at his place out in Hamel, Minnesota, where he had a ring. He was a workout fiend, and I was, too, but when he got you in the ring, he'd stretch the fuck out of you. Rock-solid but not intimidatingly big, Brad was easily one of the toughest men I have ever met.

The opposite, though, was another woman who had been sent there. She was pretty and had a boyfriend with money and connections, which is the only reason I found myself training with her. She was the one person in this business I just could not stand. Just out for herself, manipulative — wasn't in it for the business. She was doing her own movies and producing them, with the backing of her boyfriend's money. When I got away from the AWA, I never thought about her again, but the fact that she nearly fucking broke my back stuck with me. She didn't know what the hell she was doing.

To get better at my new craft and plan for the future, I devoured all the information I could find about women's wrestling, those who had come before me, and my contemporaries. There were almost no books about wrestling at the time, and the magazines were at least half bullshit — but still I learned.

When I started, women wrestlers fell into two camps: there were independents, like me, who had learned from the various trainers across the country, and then Moolah's girls. For those unfamiliar, The Fabulous Moolah was Lillian Ellison, a sweet Southern Belle from South Carolina, who had controlled women's wrestling for decades, dictating who wrestled who, where they wrestled, how they dressed and lived — all while taking her cut. I dodged a bullet by not ending up in her stable.

I did get to wrestle the "Fabulous" one once, though. I picked up Moolah for an airplane spin, and she just about lost her fucking cookies. She started screaming, "You put me down, damn it! You put me down! Don't you know you don't spin an old lady!" I slammed her down. "There you go!"

Moolah's girls came from all walks of life, which was nice, and the top of them was Wendi Richter, who'd become a mega-star in the WWF, as big as Hulk Hogan at the first *WrestleMania*. Wendi left because she felt she wasn't being treated fairly — she wasn't — and that meant I got to wrestle her. She was a joy, talented beyond compare, friendly, oozing charisma. But as beautiful as she was, she kept to the Moolah style of dressing, which was conservative, way closer to prude than pretty. They would turn their one-piece bathing suits inside out and sew a long shoestring, like from skates, along the leg-hole edges, and then tie them so tight around their legs that the outfit didn't slip up above their ass.

Fuck that. I wasn't wearing a potato sack. I believed that you could be beautiful and still athletic.

Granny sewed my initial outfits out of my ideas. Her basement was seamstress heaven, with a handful of sewing machines, one for leather, one for buttons and buttonholes, and a zig-zag one for elastic. After I went to the store to pick out the material, I'd sketch out what I wanted. I loved the amazing sprinter Florence Griffith Joyner, so she was an influence. "Granny, you've got to make me these outfits. I want to be strong and sexy — but I have to keep my boobs in." She always said yes and would take my measurements, and she'd make my outfits. It wasn't until I got to Japan that anyone other than Granny made my wrestling duds.

By more recent standards, my late 1980s outfits are not racy at all, but for the time, compared to Moolah's girls, it was a revelation. I would have one leg bare, or my midriff showing. My legs were powerful, and I wanted to show them off. I was going for beauty and brawn, but knew enough that I had to let my opponent shine, too.

Out of the blue in late 1986, I got a call from Ed "Wahoo" McDaniel, who was the matchmaker in the Minneapolis-based American Wrestling Alliance. He wanted me to come to Eden Prairie, where the AWA taped portions of its TV show, and meet with owner Verne Gagne. I dressed up and professionally presented Mr. Gagne with my press kit — and remember, I had done exactly zero things of importance to that point. They wanted me to sign a long-term contract on a 60–40 split! Many of the wrestlers signed the contract, but I refused. Verne became really angry, but we eventually agreed to a more flexible contract, which I felt proud of having negotiated.

They promised to start building a women's division, but knew that I needed some experience just being on TV first. The AWA had a national show on ESPN, and then did smaller shows for local TV stations, where the upcoming matches in the area could be promoted. The ESPN deal alone meant that there was exposure for its wrestlers, but the wrestling world was starting to change, and there wouldn't be room for every promotion in the end.

My first paycheck I ever got from the AWA was $800, and I thought I'd won the lottery. Going from fighting on independent shows and rarely getting paid, I started to work my way out of debt.

In the AWA, we generally worked the "five state area," that being the five states around and including Minnesota. We had to pay our own expenses, motel, gas, meals, and everything else. We didn't even get compensated or paid if we were injured. Verne would always say, "But I'm giving you exposure!" Still, working with AWA was a big step up for me — I felt I was in a new world. Unfortunately, there were not too many matches per month, so it didn't work that well, other than Verne's ballyhooed exposure.

We'd drive miles and miles and miles to wrestle, three or four people in a car, and drive all night to the next wrestling location. Every wrestler has road stories, and here's one of mine. Sherri Martel traveled with "Pretty Boy" Doug Somers and "Playboy" Buddy Rose, since they were a bad guy tag team, and she was their manager. I was in another car, and I know Ky Michaelson was along with me, but I can't remember who else. Our two cars stopped at a Dairy Queen, and then left. Doug was driving their car and started mooning us and he got his ass stuck in the window while driving, and they started 360ing and spinning. Sherri popped out of the window and started throwing their milkshakes at us on our windshield — so we couldn't see. And then we started spinning out. Once we settled down, we took off, leaving them in the ditch, Doug's ass still visible in the window.

It wasn't all fun. We stayed in $20-a-night motels to save money. I can remember those days so well. The motel beds would sink in the middle, and the taps ran orange from the rust. The toilets were outhouses where you had to go and squat over the seat! It wasn't an easy life.

By contrast, Verne would have to fly us out to Vegas to the Showboat for TV tapings and put us up in the hotel. The boys loved it because they got to be tramps. There's really no way to sugarcoat it — it was disgusting. I'd come back to my room, and there'd be naked girls passed out in the hallway who had no doubt been fucked by numerous wrestlers, probably drugged or gotten drunk first. Appalled, I'd call down to the front desk and ask them to deal with it. The next Showboat taping, it would be the same thing. I should have done more, spoken out.

You could see the clash happening, as the AWA roster had some older wrestlers, like Nick Bockwinkel and Wahoo, who were respectful to women, and then these new kids, who were monsters, just doing whatever the fuck they wanted.

The Showboat tapings themselves were unique. It was a casino, so the matches were attended by both local wrestling fans and curious tourists taking a break from gambling; for those who brought their kids to Vegas, it was family-friendly entertainment. It had a real old-school feel, like an old classic boxing show, where it seemed like there was only a single light hanging over the ring — that was the feel, if not the reality. There was one entrance, and the announcer's table was right by the ring, and the floor was just concrete and not forgiving at all.

Some of the greatest matches in the promotion's history took place there, like The Midnight Rockers (Shawn Michaels and Marty Jannetty) against Buddy Rose and Doug Somers; they were mesmerizing to watch, four guys who could just *go*.

The Old Guard still had a lot to give. Always a fan of older men, I found myself drawn into the wacky world of Wahoo and Ray "The Crippler" Stevens and their running mates. We'd go over to Crippler's house or we'd go fishing. He was always so fun and was such a prankster.

Wahoo used to have me spray paint on his bald spot before he went out on TV. Like Ray, he was just so personable. And his face, it was lined and worn, and it told a story of perseverance. He'd been a big football star — the New York Jets actually let him have *Wahoo* on his jersey rather than *McDaniel*, and he had some of that memorabilia in his apartment. He was from the generation of football players who had to work in the off-season, and he chose wrestling, and eventually stuck with it, making more money in the ring. Wahoo schooled me on the power of owners in football, how the players association was not strong (at that point), and how a union could work in wrestling.

I was so lucky to be around men like that. They treated me well; they were gentlemen.

I had two roles in the AWA. I was a wrestler, when they had opponents for me, and I was a manager — or "manageress," as I liked to say. Initially, I seconded "Mr. Magnificent" (Kevin Kelly) and Nick Kiniski to the ring, all three of us being beautiful blond(e)s.

Nick and I fell for each other, and even lived together for a time. His father was a former world champion, Gene "Big Thunder" Kiniski. He was such a character. The first time I met him, he shook his head, "Oh my God, another wrestler!" Nick's brother, Kelly, was a pro wrestler, too. Those were some good times, and I enjoyed getting to visit the little corner of Washington State where Gene lived. Neither of the Kiniski boys became big stars, smartly moving on to other careers.

Curt Hennig was also a second-generation wrestler, and I got to manage him. He was amazing to watch, and he sold (made the moves look convincing) like no other — I think I learned to be a bumping mofo just by watching him night after night. He was cute, with his curly blond hair, and had a big smile. The smile often hid whatever rib he was in the process of doing, keeping the dressing room light and fun. Of course, he became a huge name in the WWF as "Mr. Perfect."

"Diamond" Dallas Page was an unknown when he came into the AWA, a bartender who convinced Rob Russen, who booked the tour schedule, that he could be something in the business. They gave him a shot as a manager. You could tell that he had it — he was flamboyant, flashy, and he could speak. I never even thought about his age — he was 32 when he got to the AWA — but, of course, other people always reminded him, which was pretty shitty.

The other relative unknown, at least to a national audience, was Paul Heyman, who was manager Paul E. Dangerously. He'd been around the business for years, as a photographer and writer, so he *thought* pro wrestling. But the first time I met him, he was definitely thinking about something else.

I was managing Curt Hennig. Curt and his fucking ribs, Jesus Jenny.

Paul had just come in. We were at a bar, and they were all sitting at one table, and I was up at the bar getting a drink. At the table, Paul said, "Who the hell is that?" Meaning me. They all started laughing. They're like, "Yeah, good luck with that, Paul." Curt said, "You don't want to mess with that." Paul said, "What the hell could she do?"

Paul sauntered up to the bar, and we said hi, and he asked my name. "My name is Madusa, and don't fuck with me or I will kick your ass." Right off the bat. Paul said he just died. He had no comeback for the first time in his life and went back to the table with his tail between his legs, and the guys were losing it. They went, "What did she say?" He repeated my line and ended with a compliment, "Fuck it. Ultimate respect."

There was some celebrity-ness that came with being on ESPN. On one trip to California, I spoiled myself and stayed at the Beverly Hills Hotel on Sunset Boulevard, where the superstars would go to escape. I always wanted to stay there, and the cheapest room was $375 a night. (Today, it's $1,200.)

I was already in the elevator when this hulking bellhop got in with someone's else's bags. He looked over and said, "Are you Madusa Miceli, the wrestler?" We chatted briefly, and then every time I was in the lobby, heading out to Rodeo Drive to window-shop — though I did buy a Breitling watch at a pawn shop — he and I would talk. We ended up going out for coffee and have stayed friends to this day.

The bellhop, Evan Marriott, ended up being the star of the reality show *Joe Millionaire* on FOX, in 2003. Funny the way life works.

With wrestlers, the matches themselves don't always stand out, and my memory certainly works that way. What we remember are often the things that went awry, the travel tales, the jokes in the back.

Fans will post a clip of a match or segment to Twitter and tag me, and I'll be honest with them — I often don't remember it at all, but I sure appreciate getting to watch my younger self again.

When promoters bring wrestlers in for fan fests, where we sign and take photos with fans, the real draw for us is seeing old friends.

In late 2021, I was at a fan fest. Marty Jannetty was there, and he told a story that I completely don't remember, but that he recounted in bloody detail.

I'd gone to the ring in one of my white outfits, and, during the course of the match, my period started. Some of the white turned red, and fans at ringside started yelling at me about it. Marty said that I yelled out, "So fucking what? It's about being a woman!" Then I finished the match. The boys thought that proved I was a badass bitch.

I stayed with AWA for about 18 months but started to feel that things were not quite right, and I definitely didn't see much future for myself, even as the champ. Talent kept leaving, and despite the ESPN show, Verne couldn't compete with the WWF, which was everywhere, or the National Wrestling Alliance (NWA), which had a huge spot nationally on WTBS. When Verne was mad about something, he stomped around like a kid, hissed through his teeth, and shouted.

Trying to be professional, I gave Verne my notice, which caused some ill feeling when he called a press conference and made some strong statement about my leaving. This led to some closed-door meetings, and soon enough, it was my turn to lose, and Wendi Richter became the AWA Women's champion. A month later, I got the chance to go to Japan to wrestle, which changed my life. (More on that later.)

To my surprise, in the March 1989 issue, I was named *Pro Wrestling Illustrated*'s Rookie of the Year for 1988 — the first woman to win that category, and, even more stunning, the first woman to win *any PWI* Achievement Award since they were launched in 1972. I beat out a couple of future world champions in Chris Benoit and Scott Steiner, and only topped Benoit by 335 fan votes. I was on the cover, bottom right, in a bikini, holding my plaque, and in the issue itself,

I'm slamming Wendi Richter in a full-page photo. At the time, I was thrilled with the award, but when I look back on it, the accomplishment was underplayed, if anything. The world has changed, and women wrestlers are far more celebrated today.

When I started wrestling, there were three big companies: the WWF (later WWE), the NWA (later known as WCW), and the AWA. But there were always other places to wrestle, indies or smaller promotions that often had big (unrealistic) dreams.

The Ladies Professional Wrestling Association (LPWA) was a noble idea, and having survived the ultra-competitive women's wrestling in Japan, I was excited that there was a new all-female group in the United States, after GLOW. LPWA spoke all the right words: dynamic wrestling, emulating Japan, developing the sport of wrestling, and in its early days provided some excitement and opportunity for women's wrestling. The hope would not be a reality. For a number of reasons and primarily, in my opinion, the backwards drift by the LPWA management towards sexual expressive displays and "freak" wrestling, by mid-1991 LPWA had faltered, and the only specialist women's wrestling company in the United States had failed to get off the ground. By May, I was wrestling infrequently with LPWA, hoping it would re-establish Madusa in America after my three-year Japanese adventure.

You'll find me only occasionally in the results of independent shows. Apparently, I was ICW Women's champion in the Northeast, beating Jamie West, but I don't remember much about it. One that does stand out is a match in Colorado with a newcomer in 1999 named Nikita Lafleur. Since I was doing so little in World Championship Wrestling, I was lent out as a favor to one of the promoters. Backstage, Nikita and I were told we had 10 minutes for our bout. After the booker left, I turned to her and said, "Huh, 10 minutes. I'm Madusa. Fuck that." We ended up going about 45 minutes, including our entrances. I was testing her, sure (and she later got a WWE developmental deal), but I was also aching to have proper matches again.

Truthfully, I found more success outside of North America, at least financially.

Wendi and I had a series of matches in Germany that were top-notch, among the best of my career. We were a novelty, sure, but it also meant that we appeared on television talk shows to promote events. The promoter, Uwe Fruth, took us in as a part of his family.

A promoter named John Arezzi booked me and Wendi for a tour of Southeast Asia, hitting Singapore, the Philippines, and Hong Kong, where the matches were taped and aired locally. What really stands out was Jake "The Snake" Roberts locking me up alone in the dressing room with his python, which slithered out of its canvas bag. I jumped, grabbed a pipe, and pulled myself up . . . only to see the snake start going up the wall. Jake came in and collected the snake. Some joke. It was a unique experience.

For every great experience, there are plenty of bad ones, and one stands heads and tails above the rest.

A promoter flew me in for a show, picked me up at the airport, and took me to the hotel. That was par for the course. He insisted on escorting me to my room, and then followed me in and closed the door. Immediately, I was scared and began running the options through my mind: *Okay, how do I manipulate this? How's anyone gonna hear me? I'm dead. Do I just go with it for a while, so I get an exit?*

He'd obviously planned ahead, and the meal arrived in my room. I kept real quiet. And then I suggested we go down to the hot tub. He agreed, but the first time anyone walked by us, he leaned in and threatened, "Don't say a word." In the pool area, there were people, and I said loudly enough that others could hear, "I'm going to go to the bathroom." I hightailed it out of there, just with the stuff that I had in the bag that I took to the pool.

With independent promoters these days, you're able to check up on them online, where other workers will share good or bad experiences.

Through all my years of pro wrestling, Sherri Martel might have provided the greatest roller-coaster ride.

In wrestling terms, we were married to each other in the AWA, meaning that we wrestled each other, often — probably too often. At first, she hated me. In the ring, she never gave me an inch and beat the shit out of me constantly. Knowing it was for the best, I took it with my eyes wide open and my mouth shut.

One time, we were in adjoining hotel rooms in San Francisco, and I knocked on the door between our rooms to go over the match. I heard giggling and could smell pot. I knocked louder, and Sherri opened the door a bit, and as I leaned in, she slammed the door on my hand. I kicked in the door, yelled at her . . . and then taped up the ring and middle fingers on my right hand, and wrestled her that night like nothing happened.

This is hard to explain, but she wasn't a wrestler. She was a grappler, fighting on instinct, not skill. But her psychology was great, and her timing impeccable. Sherri had been an adult dancer before getting into wrestling, so she saw the business so differently than I did. She did what she needed to do to support her son.

The lessons in the ring were learned the hard way with her, and her only real advice she ever gave me in the dressing room was, "Don't fuck with the boys. If you're gonna have a relationship, have a relationship — don't fuck around on them." (Obviously, the boys in the business never heard her lecture.)

The AWA was dying — we could all see it — and she jumped to the WWF, following so many others. She left without dropping the AWA Women's belt to anyone.

Our paths crossed down the road, of course, on the independent circuit a little, but also in WCW. At the Weekend of Champions fan fest in October 1993, we cut a promo against each other, with the idea of feuding in Paul Heyman's revolutionary and violent Extreme Championship Wrestling promotion in late 1993. It didn't happen, as I ended up in the WWF.

Through time, we both grew and matured, and we became actual friends, talking on the phone, or occasionally visiting each other's homes. Wrestler/promoter Jeff Tankersley, from Kingsport, Tennessee, was the key figure in reconnecting us. He and I had a chance meeting in town. I was dating someone nearby, and he introduced himself and said Sherri lived close by. She was out of the wrestling business, and I missed her, so we arranged to go see her the next day, but he wasn't allowed to tell her. We pulled up in her driveway, and Sherri came out to see who it was. I jumped out, and we ran into each other's arms. We told stories for hours.

Sherri died in 2007, at only 49, her fast lifestyle catching up to her. I went to her funeral, holding on to Jeff for support, and actually got to speak a little about her. The memory that sticks with me is that some of the guys, wrestling colleagues, were coked out of their heads.

5.

"DAD"

WHICH CAME FIRST? Learning that Michael Miceli was not my father? Or him raping me? It's all so locked away, pushed to the farthest recesses of my brain, that I honestly can't remember.

But I do know that I still always sought his love and approval after those traumatic events. How fucked up is that?

With Mike in 1973 outside Granny's house.

It's right there on my birth certificate — *Mike Miceli*. It's a hard *c*, so pronounced Ma-chel-li. The clerk at the hospital just wrote his name down as my father, not even checking. I grew up thinking that he was my dad, that his parents were my grandparents, and that I was Italian. Shit, the wrestling magazines wrote that I was born in Milan, and that ridiculousness carried over into Monster Jam.

Mike's parents, Roy and Marcella Miceli, lived in an old house with a big porch in north Minneapolis. I can remember sitting on Grandpa's lap as he told me stories, but that's about all I can recall, as he died when I was only four.

But Marcella was something, your stereotypical large, loving Italian woman, who lived to cook and eat. She had love to share, too, which I was drawn to. Mike had a brother and sister, and Marcella took in foster children, too, meaning there were always different kids coming in and out. I enjoyed going over there, as it was chaotic, vibrant, and so different from my lonely life at home.

Mama Miceli kept a good home for these kids, no matter what their ethnicity was, or their circumstances. We all played together, napped together, and ate together. I was so confused growing up when things started getting weird about racism. "What the fuck? What are you talking about?" That was never a thing in our family.

It doesn't mean it was all sunshine and rainbows. Some of those foster kids were seriously fucked up. There was underage sex, violence, and even a few deaths. Marcella was robbed at home in 1976, tied up with the telephone cord — all for $400. This is all the shit that I saw, knew about, or had to report. It sticks with you.

Marcella played this card game, Kings in the Corner, with these little plastic containers, with dimes and nickels and pennies in it. You'd get excited over winning 20 cents. When I won, I was king.

She was providing a good home life for me, because I cannot tell you one game that Betty and I ever played. I cannot tell you one book Betty ever read to me. I cannot tell you one time we went to a park. It's not much different with Mike Miceli.

I got really close to a girl, Marian, a Native American, and Grandma actually adopted her because her own mother was batshit crazy and didn't want Marian. Though she was a couple of years older, we were like two peas in a pod, always together. She was beautiful and loved ballet, dancing at the Minnesota Dance Theater. I was enthralled to see her in *The Nutcracker*, as the caterpillar that turned into the butterfly.

Marian helped me get started at the same dance studio, but I was trying modern jazz and tap. I loved her, and I was trying to emulate her, expanding my horizons. We'd walk hand in hand to the theater. Everyone was so supportive and loving there, too, which was so amazing. Marian was my big sister. When she was dancing, I'd sneak five dollars out of her wallet, and then announce later, "Look, I found five dollars!" She'd reply, "You're the luckiest kid," knowing full well I stole it.

One positive memory I have of Mike is at the family cabin, in French Lake, Minnesota, where he would put me on his shoulders while water skiing. Safety first? Not in those days.

There was no electricity or running water at the cabin, but Marcella kept all her kids hard at work, including me, as we'd have to lug buckets of water from the lake to the cabin. After you went to the bathroom, you'd flush the toilet with a bucket.

Marcella would take her big old butt and get into an inner tube and float in the lake for most of the day. The kids were allowed to be kids.

I was jealous because Marian knew how to swim, and I was iffy at best. I'd have to have an inner tube when I was in the water. To prove I didn't need the support, I would have to swim across the lake and back like Marian did. That was my goal.

There were a number of boats tied up at the dock, and I would try to swim under them to improve my skills, except one time I got stuck. I got so goddamn scared. I was like, *There's no way I'm going to make it across that lake, ever*. Then one day, I snuck out and I swam the lake by myself. When I was halfway across the lake, I heard, "What the hell?" Marcella came out with her tube, but I kept going. When I came back, she grabbed me by the hair, while I celebrated, "I did it! I did it!" And I was penalized, but then I got to swim on my own.

Mike was at least good for a few bucks, whether he knew it or not. Both Mike and Betty would snore loudly, so I could sneak into their room and slip some money and food stamps out of Mike's wallet. I'd save up the money to buy my own shit and trade the food stamps for stuff from other kids.

Betty and Mike fought and it got worse, and it got to the point where they couldn't stand each other. Mike kept me at the house, while Betty went to Granny's.

But during this time when Mike and I were living there, he fucking raped me. It was bad. And I didn't say a thing. I was scared to death. I didn't know who to tell. I was already a fucked up child — who's going to believe me? So, I kept that in.

I don't know if he was drunk or whatever his problem was. Usually, he was nice. I just never understood.

Betty, ever unstable, changed her mind on me. When Mike was at work one day, she broke into the house, took it over, and he was forced out. We ended up staying there a few months, still on welfare, until we went to Granny's.

One morning, when I was 10 or so, I was sitting on the floor, and I looked at Betty, and she was screaming at me about something. I told her Michael touched me, and what he did to me. She looked at me and slapped me across the face, and she said, "You're a liar, you're such a liar." I couldn't get more words out, and she slapped me again, and just kept telling me I was a liar. "Michael would never do that." To this day, she'll tell you I'm lying.

This is where my timeline becomes a mess.

Was that when Betty slapped me and said, "You're lying. He would never do that. Well, he's not your father anyway"? I can never forget the icy cold feeling that came over my face when she said those words. It was a betrayal, really; and it destroyed me.

Did she hit me because I had told her that Mike had molested me? Or was that later? Dunno.

They divorced when I was about seven. Michael later told me that it was their intention to break the news of my real parents to me when I was about 14. Another small detail — he never actually legally adopted me, even though his name was on my birth certificate.

Though I have no idea why, as a tween, I was forced to live with Michael and his new girlfriend, Mary Jo, and her three kids. By this point, Mike had a better job, at the University of Minnesota, working as an engineer, which he did for 27 years. Later, they moved out to a rural home in Maple Lake, Minnesota, and he drove 60 miles each way to work just to please Mary Jo, because she wanted that house, and it fucking killed him. There were nights he was so tired, he'd pull over on the side of the road and sleep, and then go home. I hated her for making him do that, and she hated me because I was part of Michael's past life.

Mary Jo had three kids, all younger than me. Kim was the oldest and the least welcoming to me, which I get. Jeff was the middle kid, and we were the closest, often talking late into the night. Jenny was the youngest, and there was some hero worship going on towards me, though we were never really pals. In truth, I was upsetting their world when I was there, headstrong and combative.

Around the farm, I would help out, using the tractor, fixing windows, and whatnot. It was a tiny town, and I stood out as a big-city girl. As my life progressed, I'd *really* stand out, zooming into town with a fancy car for a holiday.

Michael tried being a father, and I tried being in his life. I hung on to him as a dad, because I didn't have anything.

When I was wrestling in Japan, I flew him and Mary Jo out to see me perform, and I paid for everything for those two, from the flights and hotel to the food. Yet Mary Jo still found things to bitch about.

No one gets a happy ending.

Marian got married, and she and her husband had a daughter, Katrina. On March 31, 1981, when Donnie was at work, Marian took a rifle and blew her head off. Donnie came home, and the baby was crawling through all the mess. That's how she died. It devastated me.

Marcella eventually couldn't manage the big house and moved to Brooklyn Center, where Alzheimer's took over, and she died in 1986. The newspaper wrote about how at least 50 foster kids came through her home over the years.

When I got my first real check from wrestling, after a big show in San Francisco at the Cow Palace, where I fought Sherri Martel, I bought three tomb markers for the gravesites of Roy, Marcella, and Marian at the Crystal Lake Cemetery. No one else had done it. On Marian's, I wrote, *To the beautiful dancer.*

In early 2005, Jeff called me, and said, "Hey, Debrah, Dad's not doing too good."

I said, "Dad? You mean, like, Mike?"

"Yeah. Why do you do that all the time?"

Then I told him everything that happened. It was uncomfortable, but he appreciated being able to better understand my many issues with Mike.

Riddled with cancer, Mike wanted to talk to me. It wasn't immediate, but I did finally call him.

He said, "I'm so glad you reached out."

The feeling wasn't mutual, and I laid into him something fierce.

"Let's just get one thing straight. I understand what's happening. It's unfortunate. But you raped me as a fucking kid. And you never, ever said a word. You never told anybody, and I lived with this my whole entire life. And now you're dying and you want me to talk to you? Why? So you can feel at peace when you die?

"I'll tell you what; we can talk again, but you need to tell your family, your wife, your kids why I was the way I was, why I upset everything, and why they thought I was an outcast and a piece of shit and a crazy kid. I need you to tell them the truth. And if you do, then I'll call you back. I might find some type of awareness or forgiveness, but you're going to die. And you're the one who's going to have to take it to your grave, and you're going to go to hell. But me? I'm in a better place by not speaking to you."

The first thing that he said was, "I don't remember any of that."

"Oh, then I guess we have nothing to fucking say. You're going to die, alone. You're going to die knowing what you did."

"I'm so sorry. I think it happened. I don't know."

"I don't want your apology. This conversation was enough."

That's the last I heard from him. He died on April 13, 2005, at age 61.

My past has hindered me. People think I'm so strong, so driven, but now that they know the reasons I worked so hard, what I was trying to escape, how will those perceptions change?

6.

THE JAPAN ADVENTURE

CHIGUSA NAGOYA PICKED ME. Out of all the women wrestling in the United States, in 1988 the legendary Japanese woman wrestler requested a match with me. Stunned, I accepted the bout, but there was no way I would have known it would change my life.

AWA promoter Verne Gagne had told me that the All Japan Women's Pro Wrestling promotion had asked about me, but he put them off, saying that I wasn't ready for Japan; "You'll get killed!" he told me. It was a tighter, more high-impact, nonstop style in Japanese rings, especially

All Japan Women's Pro-Wrestling awards in 1990. Clockwise from top left: Manami Toyota, Aja Kong, me, Suzuki Minami, Bull Nakano, Bison Kimura, Bat Yoshinaga, Kyoko Inoue, and Akira Hokuto.

compared to the United States, where it was so much more about the show.

A superstar at home who had trained with and beaten the best, Chigusa wanted to travel and set out on a North American tour. Las Vegas was her first stop, and then she'd hit Dallas, Texas; Memphis, Tennessee; and then up to Calgary, Alberta. She had a reputation as being probably the finest female technical pro wrestler in the world and an awesome, brutal competitor. She showed no mercy. Chigusa was who I aspired to be.

For a little while, the match appeared in doubt. Verne wasn't always forthcoming, or maybe he didn't know what was going on, either. Finally, when the date came, October 15, 1988, I walked into the Showboat Hotel and Casino in Vegas, and Verne said the match with Chigusa was indeed on. The sly old man had purposefully kept me in the dark, keeping it secret for publicity reasons. But it would air on the AWA show on ESPN and in Japan.

There was no time to be nervous. I went down to the dressing rooms and started to prepare. In the cool of that evening I prayed a little, seeking some guidance for the road I knew was ahead of me. I could see Chigusa's face, and the words *Japan, Japan, Japan* were like some kind of drum pounding in my brain. I knew then that in this bout I had to wrestle like I had never wrestled before.

Before the bout, we got to talk briefly backstage, her handlers translating; there was no match-planning as the wrestlers do today, no script. We were almost the same age. I was taller, and she'd been working a few more years than I had. The introductions had me head to the ring first, and the crowd knew me from previous AWA shows that were taped at the Showboat. Chigusa, the All Pacific champion, was new to them, but it wasn't hard to see she meant business, heading to the ring like a prizefighter in her robe, with her belt and entourage.

Her eyes were hypnotic, and the aura she emanated had the fans — and me — totally entranced. Had someone not cried out, "Ya can't fight that — it's a man!" I might have stayed in the trance, awed by her strong red-and-black ninja costume.

The match itself was the most memorable of my career. There is little doubt in my mind that Chigusa could have broken me in half at any time. But she didn't . . . she was a consummate professional and she forced me to seek higher and higher skills and personal targets as the match progressed. I concentrated as I had never done prior. I had to read her every move, to play off her initiatives and gradually I, too, could feel confidence as we warmed to each other in the ring. I lifted my energy level and really started to move around the ring, working the moves and pushing her to new peaks. We both got cheers from the fans. Her charisma was so powerful that she totally captivated the fans, and the match took on a pace and energy level not seen in American women's pro wrestling. The fans responded with gusto, sensing they were participating in an extraordinary event.

To throw her off balance, I stopped suddenly in the middle of the ring and posed like "The Karate Kid" in the famous "striking stork" pose, one foot off the ground and both arms raised over my head, like the fangs of a spider ready to deliver the fatal venom. Chigusa stood baffled for a second, and then we charged each other again. But it was a jump off the corner turnbuckle onto her outside the ring that made a huge impression.

It ended in a double disqualification, but I felt like a winner. I had held my own against one of the world's top stars. Utterly drained and exhausted, I was trying to catch my breath in the dressing room when I was summoned to Chigusa's room. We shook hands, and her eyes reflected both acceptance and satisfaction.

In her limited English, she said, "We meet again soon — Japan!" Her trainers and management filled the room, and I was introduced to them, but they spoke little English. The brothers who ran All Japan Women's Pro Wrestling, the Matsunagas, were in the mix, as was Rossy Ogawa, and as I was about to leave, one of the brothers came to me and simply said, "You come to Japan. We want you in Japan." We shook hands, and I returned to my own room.

From that moment forward, my destiny was set. The match had an immense psychological effect on me. Chigusa became my role model. I wanted to be professional, expert, skilled, and dominant. I wanted to be different, to present an aura and a statement about Madusa and the highest level of wrestling excellence. I needed to get to the next level.

I wanted to go to Japan.

It wasn't immediate, but I soon heard through wrestling magazine editor/ photographer George Napolitano that All Japan Women's Pro Wrestling wanted me to get in touch, and he told me who to contact. (I will add here that there was also the men's All-Japan Pro Wrestling promotion, run by Shohei "Giant" Baba; any time I refer to All Japan, it is a completely separate women's promotion.) We communicated through mail and by fax, setting up my first trip, my generous pay, and the per diem.

There was so much to do. I'd never had a passport, so had to arrange that and the visa. My management company would look after sales of my poster, the fan club, and other various irons in the fire while I was gone. Truthfully, I was on Cloud 9. My flight was actually on New Year's Eve, as 1988 arrived. At the Narita airport, my handlers met me, including Micky Ibaragi, who was a promoter and later a great friend. They all helped get me through customs, and off we went in a van, to my hotel in Meguro City, an inner suburb of Tokyo, where the All Japan facilities are located. That tiny room would be my home base for the next month. They presented me with a schedule for the tour, noting gym time, press events, and the wrestling shows.

There were nerves, sure, but my main feelings were amazement and contentment. I felt at ease in a way it's hard to explain. Everyone was friendly, and I couldn't wait to get in the ring.

That first tour was a total absorption of custom and lifestyle. Again, my experience of life and childhood and growing up became invaluable to me. I listened and looked and asked and took it all in. It also meant I didn't have much attachment or reason to stay in the United States; I left it open with the man I was dating. I had to go through everything tourists do: the language, the food, the currency, the customs. And I had to learn how to survive on tour: bus protocols, watching to see if the other girls put their feet over the seat, how they positioned their belongings, how they washed their underwear by hand and dried it on little hangers from the ceiling of the bus. It was a whole different life. I couldn't get over it. I kept thinking about the sheer discipline and organization of the company, so un-American!

I couldn't get over the fans. Hundreds of them would follow the tours. They would be waiting at each location for the buses to arrive and patiently push forward for autographs at every opportunity. The fans were young and cute, and gave you beautiful little presents. They looked up to the wrestlers with respect and pride. So unlike America. Back at home, the preconception was that to be a wrestler you were some sort of a freak. Here, there were invites to private dinners, media functions, and plenty of television coverage to complete the picture that pro wrestling in Japan was totally different than anything I'd experienced.

No question: I made up my mind on the first tour that I wanted to come back and master Japanese wrestling and become a star, a respected personality.

And the matches — oh my. The crowds threw paper streamers in their favorite wrestler's colors into the ring pre-match, and sang and chanted, but then when the bouts started, they quieted, clapping at moves that they appreciated. All Japan attracted a lot of young female fans, so their reactions were a lot giddier and higher-pitched than I was used to. Soon, I learned to cherish the "Maaadusa, Maaadusa, Maaadusa" chants.

My AWA bout with Chigusa had aired in Japan, making our rematch a really big deal. We fought over her International Wrestling Association (IWA) World title, and this time, I won! It was then that I knew that the Japanese promoters were looking at me as a long-term prospect, and my heart soared . . . then I lost it back to her the next day.

The food in Japan took a little getting used to. At one point, I became very sick from some form of food poisoning. I can never forget Micky Ibaragi sitting up with me all night as the fever took hold, and I suffered through some horrific shivering fits. Ibaragi-san kept bathing my head in cool water. In the morning, he faced concerned members of the team, who wanted an update. By midday I could walk, and without any discussions I indicated to him that we should leave for wrestling. He looked at me carefully and slowly nodded, his eyes fixed on mine and full of admiration. I wrestled that day, and the word went around the company and back to the owners that I was all in. Over the next few days, I was exhausted and continued to get the shakes, but I made it.

As I left from my six-week first trip to Japan, Rossy Ogawa gave me a copy of the video of the Madusa-Chigusa bout. On my return flight, I asked a flight attendant on Northwest Airlines to play the video, and they did! There we were, 35,000 feet over the Pacific, watching me wrestle. It was very surreal.

While home, I took a booking with the AWA, way out in Kennewick, Washington, on February 25, and my knee finally gave out. My knee issues went back to pre-wrestling days, tweaking it while playing volleyball with friends. I iced it and ignored it then. But against Wendi Richter, I tore my left ACL. Granny helped pay for the surgery. My management team wanted me to bail on the Japanese tour, but I knew I'd lose all respect. So, I sucked it up and went back to Japan.

It was only a one-week tour, and I only had one bout — against another great, Chigusa's former tag team partner in the Crush Girls, Lioness Asuka. The Japanese wrestling media was a very real thing, with weekly newspapers reporting on the goings-on in the squared circle. My knee injury was known, so, naturally, Asuka went right at it. My participation was a major success, though no one knew the sheer pain I was in for most of that match.

On this second trip, I learned that Americans — *gaijins* or "foreigners" — were generally perceived as lazy, and that they were more interested in partying than working out. The Japanese wrestlers work out every single day. I wish I'd known that the first go-round, as I would have been in the dojo with them.

My third tour with All Japan coincided with Chigusa's retirement. Her final match (until she unretired in 1993) had five Americans against Chigusa and her allies, and I once again got to battle Asuka. This four-week tour was the last of my short-term stays, as I was offered a formal contract to move to Japan and work full time for All Japan. Hell yeah!

Up until my deal, all the successful *gaijins* who had contracts and had become icons in Japan were men: The Destroyer, Stan Hansen, Bruiser Brody, Terry and Dory Funk, Tiger Jeet Singh. I was the first woman offered a contract with All Japan.

Now, that's not to say that I was the first *gaijin* woman to succeed in Japan. Women's wrestling — *joshi puroresu* — had been in the country since 1954, when Mildred Burke brought her crew for a tour. Many promotions followed, but All Japan Women's Pro Wrestling, established in 1968, rose to the top.

At the time I was there, two competing all-women's promotions were battling it out. All Japan was the bigger promotion, with the biggest stars, treating its wrestlers like pop idols, including the music, magazines, and videos — but forcing them to retire at age 25. Yet I was 26! The double standard wasn't lost on my contemporaries on the roster, and it was almost embarrassing to me, especially given how green and inexperienced I was; I didn't have any knowledge of Japanese at that point to understand the rumblings. Japan Women's Pro-Wrestling (JWP), which started in 1986, had a lesser following, but it was still a major deal; it included some of the All Japan women who didn't want to retire. JWP did more entertainment, movie, and TV crossovers, so it was more Americanized, in a sense.

On August 24, I was back in Japan and settled into a very, very small place high up in a condominium block owned by the promoters, where a number of the wrestlers stayed. It was in Meguro-ku, about a block and a half from the All Japan office, and I had to pay for my own electricity, water, and telephone. I received a monthly fee that was wired to the United States and I was given a small amount in cash on which to live and meet my expenses.

Though I didn't immediately clue in, it became evident that my relationship with the Japanese girls had changed with the contract. I was no longer an import, but true competition. That worked for me, since I took it as a challenge.

My aim was to truly become part of the company and to be treated like any other wrestler. The team was divided into two major groups. The first group consisted of four levels of veteran wrestlers — or the stars. I was one of these but in the case of the others, they all had to spend years as novices in the second group, the "new faces" or "young girls." The novices did everything for the veterans. Each veteran had a special novice dedicated to them, and this helper was responsible for the care of the senior wrestler. They washed our clothes, helped us dress for matches, and unfortunately, as is Japanese custom, received an exceptionally hard time from the Japanese vets. These poor kids also had to put up the ring and take it down after matches, clean the stadium, and, while on tour, complete a whole range of other duties, such as preparing meals, buying lunches, cleaning the bus, and generally serving the veterans hand and foot.

They were the last to bed, the first to rise, and never seemed to stop working. I was assigned a novice, but hardly asked her to do anything. I tried to do everything myself, which caused some waves within the team, as this was not the custom. I enjoyed the company of the younger girls and tried to mix with and work out with them, but a fraternization such as that required the permission of the other vets. I felt it was a custom brought across from the sumo wrestlers, where the apprentices undertake very similar roles. I could never imagine the system working in America.

The training schedules were awesome, and it was nothing to train for three to four hours per day, even on match days. We trained every day except Sundays and usually we were involved with promotional work on the day of rest. They kept us moving. There was so much to learn in terms of new moves and drills. The level of energy was dynamic, and I was forced to lift my own activity rating to that of smaller and lighter Japanese girls.

It challenged me like nothing I'd ever done. We did a 10-mile New Year's run, and I ain't no marathoner. There was a training camp at the foot of a mountain. At the base, we did the usual training and stretching — and I should note that if you couldn't achieve a stretch, the trainer would bend you the rest of the way. Then it was a dizzying collection of knuckle push-ups, running through sand, leaping over other girls, chin-ups with people on your back, jumping rope, squats with others on your shoulders, as well as meditating and martial arts. We'd have to jump into the freezing cold river, climb up the mountain, run, and, where possible, a car would be alongside videotaping us.

You couldn't help but bond with the other girls since you were surviving through a common hell. You helped each other up, quite literally, when you couldn't get up on your own. Through all this, my Japanese improved immensely and I taught them English phrases, but body language was the true common denominator. (All Japan did send me to a Berlitz language school for a bit.) I like to challenge myself and would always walk into stores using the Japanese words I knew. Whenever the bus would stop on tour, I would wander around quite alone and happy. It became an objective for me to learn a few new words every day.

Then there was the shared time on the bus where, again, you had nothing but time together. These weren't school buses, but double-decker Mercedes cruisers taking both the wrestlers and the equipment from town to town. We got it down to a science to pull into a venue, unload, set up, get ready, wrestle, break down, and leave for the next booking, just like a traveling circus. We were each given two seats to stretch out onto, and that was your area, including where you aired out your gear. It was a locker room on wheels, and it smelled like it!

The wrestling coach would always travel with us and became the injury repair man, trainer, and confidant. He would work extremely hard in ensuring the girls stayed in shape. Some nights we were able to stay in hotels, for a glorious sleep. Needless to say after eight or 10 weeks on the road and wrestling every day while living out of a bus, the body becomes totally exhausted, the mind becomes jaded, and the discipline one has to show in forcing performances and simply trying to live with some enthusiasm is incredible.

Given the amount of time together, romantic relationships were formed. And since man-woman relationships were not acceptable while on tour, you get the picture. Always up for something new, I gave it a whirl, too. One of the girls was very handsome, like a guy. The other girls giggled behind me and pushed me into her room. She started talking Japanese, she kissed me on the lips, I kissed back . . . and then I went to town on her, but it was not reciprocated. My world was not rocked by my first lesbian experience.

My world was certainly shaken by a marriage proposal, though!

Back in Minneapolis, I'd been dating Al Noga, a defensive end for the Minnesota Vikings, though when we met I didn't know he played football, only that he was this hunk of a Samoan. He was a romantic at heart and once stood in the pouring rain outside my third-floor apartment and serenaded me. He also bought me a bear-skin coat that was too heavy to ever wear. Knowing I was off to Japan for good, we ended it. Or so I thought.

Out of the blue, I got a call from Granny when I was in Japan. It turns out Al had been interviewed after a Vikings game and told a national TV audience that he was getting married to a wrestler who was in Japan. What the fuck?

A day or two later, I pick up the phone, and it was Al, who proceeded to tell me that he was at Narita airport. I went down on the train to collect him and brought him back to my apartment. It did not go the way he expected. He still wanted to get married, but I had two years left in Japan. We fought, it got heated. All Japan was not happy, either. Having a man was frowned upon, but I got some leeway because I was an American, and it drew some publicity. After all, here was this gargantuan NFLer chasing me down halfway across the world.

Before leaving, Al wanted an answer, whether I'd marry him or not — as he had another prospect. That was a surprise! I told him to go marry her, no hard feelings. Years later, he called — out of the blue — on New Year's Eve; I knew immediately it was him from his voice. We caught up a bit, though he sounded drunk, so maybe he doesn't remember the call.

For a girl from the Midwest, I learned a lot of new things in Japan. Transvestites and transitioning weren't on the radar of Americans in the late 1980s, but in Japan it was accepted. I remember being in a bar with the Jumping Bomb Angels, Noriyo Tateno and Itsuki Yamazaki. I noticed a woman and said, "God, she is gorgeous." One of them said, "Ma-dusa, you don't know?" "Know what?" "That no girl." That was my first experience meeting a transvestite in the 1980s. "Holy shit, she's better looking than half of the women!" We all sat together, drank, and had a great time.

It was nothing for me to go out on my own down to the Roppongi area in downtown Tokyo, bar hopping, dancing. It was good publicity, too. How many other tall, hot blondes were there in those clubs? I was a walking billboard for the matches.

I made some lifelong friends in Japan, too, like Fumi Saito, who was a young journalist. He'd actually done a student exchange and had been at Robbinsdale High School in Minneapolis, but was a couple of years behind me. Fumi therefore had a good knowledge of English. I'd call him for advice — "What does this mean?" He still teases me about 10-minute-long answering machine messages that I'd leave.

Given the amount of shows that I worked in Japan from 1988 to 1990, please forgive me for considering the actual matches a bit of a blur. We did 300 shows a year, easily. I know we delivered monumental action night after night, to crowds big and small, from one end of the country to the other, and even side trips to China, Taiwan, and Thailand. The roster was pretty interchangeable, and you worked with almost everybody at some point, whether in singles or tag teams. In short, they took their turns beating the shit out of me! I gave as good as I got.

Some things do stand out, though.

In November 1989, I won a tag tournament (Tag League the Best) with Mitsuko Nishiwaki, with seven other teams in the tourney. We were given the championship title papers, which is a Japanese custom, and they made a video on both of us. Then in December, there was a major awards night for professional wrestling that's something like the Oscars, but smaller. Olympic-like medals were presented to the wrestlers, and I was awarded the trophy of The Inspirational Wrestler of the Year, which was of real pride to me due the input made to the selection process by other wrestlers, my peers.

Nick Bockwinkel, my old colleague from the AWA, was well-respected in Japan, and he was the referee for a bout where I challenged Lioness Asuka for the WWWA Women's title at Wrestlemarinepiad in May 1989. He made the mistake of getting in my way, and I slapped him. Later, he lectured me, "Madusa, don't you ever touch the ref." And

I replied, "Well, get out of my fucking way. I'm not just gonna tiptoe around you and say excuse me." He was very, very old school.

The real big test came in the summer of 1990, when I did a program with Aja Kong, one of the top All Japan stars. Decked out in bright colors, cropped hair, and face paint on her compact, solid frame, she cut a threatening figure. For whatever reason, the Matsunaga brothers booked us in three legit bouts — boxing, kickboxing, and a street fight. The way I see it, they wanted to get their money out of the American. Without asking, they just did it. I was under contract, and, in their culture, you do what they say. I didn't give two shits; if it wasn't something I really wanted to do, I probably would have fought back.

Aja and I got no direction, no booking instructions about who should win on any of the three, so we just went at it, for real. On some level, we probably held back a little, but there was nothing fake about those bruises. When she had me in a submission and cut off my airway, that was dangerous, but I ended up in that spot, so that's on me.

More than anything, standing up to Aja made me in Japan, and it earned me respect (and financial bonuses). I passed the test. After that, the girls on tour worked with me a little more, rather than outright clobbering me. Small steps.

The Aja-Madusa feud became a wrestling storyline, and we had an epic street fight, where we faced each other in jeans and T-shirts. The fans had truly bought into us by that point, and we belonged on the top of the card.

My kickboxing reputation has been blown a bit out of proportion through the years. All Japan had the bright idea to send me to Thailand to learn Muay Thai, and then fight one of the champions there. I swear someone in the office probably said, "Let's see if she dies!" like I was a *Mortal Kombat* character or something. There were just three of us in the martial arts class in Japan, and I was the only English-speaking person. But I learned what I needed to do soon enough. The instructor spoke loudly and carried a big stick — and wasn't afraid to use it. Fighting pose was key to everything, with your left foot grounded and right leg up for kicks. We had to hold that pose for 10 minutes — though, it felt like an eternity. And if your foot hit the fucking ground, he would take his kendo stick and whack your grounded ankle.

I've still got the scars on my left foot.

Much of the training took place on an island, which would have been a beautiful setting had we not had to take turns running through the stream and up the hill with someone else on our backs, no matter the weather, like a damn Navy SEAL. We were up early in the morning and went until late at night. We would be kicking a tree, punching a fucking pole.

It was all part of me immersing myself in combat sports, getting more in-depth knowledge. Today, that kind of training has all kinds of respect, and people understand it thanks to the mixed martial arts and especially the UFC TV programs that show all the fighters training.

I can't believe I'm the same person as those days. I look back at my younger self: Who were you? Where was your fear? "Okay, you want me to do that? No problem." It's like I had blinders on or something. The word "No" didn't exist for me in Japan, and, in retrospect, it's fucking nuts that I trusted them all so much.

In Thailand, I had a single Muay Thai fight against their champion. I can close my eyes and see myself walking to the ring, my opponent with her headdress on, dancing around to her music, followed by a prayer. I was taller than her . . . and scared shitless.

But then I beat her ass, and they got me the fuck out of there because they didn't know what was going to happen. They're like, "Okay, we go now, we go now, Dusa?" "Okay, let's go." I suspect there was a lot of money bet on the match, and when someone loses big, there are grudges to settle.

My kickboxing match with Aja was the only other bout I ever had.

There were other "imports" who wrestled in All Japan, coming in on short tours. One was the great Esther Moreno, who came from Mexican *lucha* royalty. She was my partner for a long time, and she just had so much talent. I tried to learn some Spanish, but it was tough to try to pick up two languages at the same time. Rossy Ogawa would tease me, "I don't understand; you do Japanese good, but not Spanish. Everyone is the opposite; they get Spanish and not Japanese."

I got to know Reggie Bennett, but she was working for the competing FMW promotion, run by Atsushi Onita. We'd meet up if we found ourselves both with time on our hands in Tokyo. But we were never in the same promotion at the same time in Japan. Our friendship continued, though, and she visited me in Florida over the years. In many ways, she was my successor in All Japan, starting full time after I left and staying until 1997.

Delta Dawn came in from British Columbia, Canada, for a tour in January 1989. But she didn't come alone — she brought a boa constrictor. As two *gaijins*, we were paired in the ring and got to room together, too, and I remember some real giggle fests as we tried to make sense of being strangers in a strange land. Facing Chigusa one night, Dawn was on the outside of the ring, and I acted on impulse. Chigusa had me in a leglock, and I leaned over to Dawn and said, "Hand me the snake!" I grabbed it and I pointed it at Chigusa. She let go of that figure four, screamed, and pushed herself out. There's an amazing photo of that moment that was released as a VHS tape cover — mere months into my time in Japan. That company promoted and marketed me more in three years than any the sum total of all the other places I worked.

The snake traveled with us and stayed in Dawn's room, or in ours if we were sharing. It gets cold in Japan in the winter, and, worried that the snake would freeze, one night Dawn left it on the room's heater. When she woke up, it was dead. Oh my God, that was a horrific deal in Japan. Holy hell, you don't have an animal die in Japan. She was just beside herself, and I think she had borrowed the snake from a friend. The Matsunagas insisted on an elaborate burial for the snake, worried they'd be cursed or some shit. We were all brought out to one of their remote homes, at the foot of a mountain. The ritual seemed to go on and on, and my Japanese wasn't good enough to understand what the other girls were whispering under their breaths. They were probably saying, "What the fuck? We have to go through this just for a *gaijin*?"

I do wonder why Delta Dawn, who was half Carrier First Nation from the Beaver Clan / Lake Babine Nation, was never brought back to Japan. She was a good wrestler, like Monster Ripper. Was it the snake?

Throughout my three years in Japan, I'd periodically head home, sometimes for visa reasons. It was always a culture shock coming back; for one thing, America was so rude compared to Japan. I'd gotten used to living a compact life — a small apartment, few possessions, realizing that I didn't need a lot to be happy — and in the United States, it was all about living large.

But after three years, it was time for a new adventure. There were no hard feelings between the All Japan bosses and me; it was just time. It was pleasing to see Japan opened up for more women to go and live there, train, and get better. Reggie Bennett, Debbie Malenko, Natalya, and LuFisto were some who followed the path I'd set.

Japan transformed me as a person, beyond the obvious great physical shape. No, this was much deeper. There was history around every corner. It's a very spiritual place. They have their own way of worshiping and praying, and I absorbed what I could. While I brought home plenty of trinkets — the best was an alarm clock that would say *"O-hay-ou"* three times until screaming *"O-hay-ou gozaimasu!"* which means "Good morning" — the inner truths I learned about myself and my place in the universe have stuck with me.

After my deal was done with All Japan, I got a chance to appear for JWP, which I'd always been curious about. I worked a series of bouts in August and September 1991 and worked against some notable names who had aged out of All Japan, like Devil Masami.

I made so many friends along the way, that it was great to get to wrestle many of them in the United States over the years, as my career moved there permanently with WWE and WCW. My heart will always be in Japan.

World Wonder Ring Stardom — or just Stardom — was an all-women's promotion started in 2010. I'd become friends with Cheerleader Melissa Anderson, one of those younger, amazing talents who came after me (who also spent time studying in Japan, too), and she'd been working in Stardom and encouraged me to reach out. So, I did. It was like no time had passed, and Rossy Ogawa hired me as the (figurehead) "Commissioner of Stardom," and I did a few trips there. He sold Stardom to New Japan Pro Wrestling in 2021.

The fans hadn't forgotten me, which was pretty amazing. They'd be at my hotel, wanting autographs, some of them with their own kids in tow.

7.

A DANGEROUS ALLIANCE IN WCW

WHILE I WAS IN JAPAN, I had been considering what was next for me back home. In late 1991, I was contacted by World Championship Wrestling (WCW), which was owned by Turner Broadcasting. It had been challenging WWF as the most popular wrestling group in the United States, but had never been the top dog. Signing me didn't put them over the top, and looking back, I rarely wrestled.

I got this vintage photo of the Dangerous Alliance — me, Paul E. Dangerously, Arn Anderson, and Bobby Eaton — all autographed. Miss you, Bobby.

Still, it was a huge opportunity, where I would be viewed on a national stage and have a chance to learn from some of the greatest minds in the history of pro wrestling.

First and foremost was "The American Dream" Dusty Rhodes, who was the booker — or matchmaker — when I arrived. I have so much respect for Dusty. He'd always say, "You could be the new Baby Doll," referring to a famous ringside manager. I'd protest, "But I'm not a valet! We need more talent!" But he was the boss, and you do what the boss says.

My debut came at a *Clash of the Champions* special on WTBS, on November 19, 1991, in Savannah, Georgia, where I came out dressed as a harem girl and distracted WCW's top star, Sting, so that Lex Luger, who was the villainous WCW World Heavyweight champion, could attack him from behind, wrecking his knee. It was all a big scheme, as Sting had been set to defend his U.S. title against Rick Rude, who was managed by Paul E. Dangerously, my old AWA pal. Sting came back before the title would be forfeited, but Rude took care of business, won the belt, and the Dangerous Alliance was formed with Rude, me, "Beautiful" Bobby Eaton, "The Enforcer" Arn Anderson, "The Living Legend" Larry Zbyszko, and some young kid named "Stunning" Steve Austin. Officially, I was "Director of Covert Operations."

Paul really was my biggest advocate, and the "rub," as they say in wrestling, I got from being in his stable kept me motivated. My main job was accompanying Rick Rude to the ring, meaning I'd go from being super athletic for a bout to super sexy as his valet. For someone who played such an egotistical character, Rick was very quiet and private, to the point that you were shocked if he exploded over something. He was very respectful, he never tried anything with me, nothing sexual, not even dirty jokes — making him probably one of the few men who was like that. Curt Hennig was another "perfect" gentleman.

When it was time to do my first interview in WCW, I was so nervous. Remember, I'd been in Japan for a long time and had barely done any promo work in America since my time in the AWA! The Dangerous

Alliance would usually be together, doing our promos as a group or just a few of us. Besides the interview time on the major shows, you would also have to do localized promos for shows in, say, Roanoke, Virginia, or Cincinnati, Ohio; therefore, the interview days could be exhausting. It's nothing like the scripted promos for wrestlers today, either, as we were given freedom to be creative. You listened and learned from the veterans.

I'd messed up probably 10 times, and everyone wanted to leave, so the pressure was on me to deliver. Arn kept yapping about me getting it right, being pushy and annoying, and I snapped. With one fluid motion, I took off a high-heeled shoe, flung it at him, and told him to shut the fuck up!

Then I nailed the promo. Finally.

From that day forward, the men knew *never* to fuck with me, and I gained a lot of respect for sticking up for myself.

Natalya Neidhart told that story again when I was inducted into the WWE Hall of Fame in 2015, and the TV producer cleverly caught a shot of Arn ducking when she said it.

It's important to say that Arn wasn't a dick like that all the time, and we were all tired at that particular moment. I learned by watching him and Larry (whom I didn't really know in the AWA), and from Bobby, who was always quiet. As for Steve Austin, he definitely hadn't found his legs yet, but I had a sense that he was destined for bigger things; in the spirit of honesty, I'll add that I had the biggest crush on him, but never said anything due to the fact he was always with another beautiful, big-boobed blonde.

A few women were brought in here and there for me to wrestle, but the only other regular female on the roster wasn't a wrestler; it was Missy Hyatt, a beautiful blonde who filled many roles through the years, from manager to announcer.

Truthfully, I was more in awe of her than I was any of the male wrestlers. She was so gorgeous, fashionable, and fun, and it made me want to up my game. I absorbed makeup lessons, especially at Center

Stage in Atlanta, Georgia, which was the regular spot that WCW taped its TV shows. There was this back room where they'd throw us girls, and it had one big mirror with lights, and she would spread out her shit all over, leaving me in a corner. At the time, I barely put on any makeup, but I learned.

I was also trying to break myself of some of the habits I'd picked up in Japan. Instead of finding a chair or sitting on the floor, I'd squat against the wall. For years when someone would say something, I would reply "Hai" instead of "Yes" and "Arigato" as "Thank you."

Missy was dating actor Jason Hervey from *The Wonder Years* at the time, and it always looked like they were having a great time. It seemed to be a dream life, lots of travel and riches, like Louis Vuitton luggage and accessories showered on her. Given my upbringing, I hadn't seen a lot of that opulence.

On some level, I think it probably pissed off the powers that be that we got along — we'd trade hair extensions and lots of gossip — rather than being all catty and at each other's throats.

We saved that for the screen.

As the only two women on the roster, it was destined that we would fight. Missy wasn't trained to wrestle — though she secretly wanted to and had done some catfight-type brawls in the ring previously in the Texas territory — but could take a bump. And she had a great mind for the business, the psychology of making the fans want to see the action, to see whomever she was managing get beaten up. It was built to a swimsuit posedown to determine who was the First Lady of WCW at Beach Blast in 1992; she ended up winning, but without a swimsuit — her outfit was Jesse Ventura's scarves strategically tied. Hunt it down if you want, but I'm warning you, it's all pretty damn cringeworthy from my perspective.

The other woman who was around all the time was Janie Engle. Fans won't know who she is, but anyone who ever came through WCW knows her. Essentially, Janie was the right-hand woman to whoever was in charge, rising through the ranks from making notes for the booking committee to making travel arrangements to writing up severances. She's the one who dealt with Steve Austin's termination, so I hope he at least sent her a gift basket years later when he became the biggest wrestling star in the world!

If you know who to look for, she's in a number of WCW skits over the years as an extra. There's a mini-movie that was made to promote Spin the Wheel, Make the Deal from *Halloween Havoc* in 1992, and I got a prominent role, spinning the wheel for foes Sting and Jake "The Snake" Roberts. Janie and I had a blast getting ready for that one, and I'm in a crazy snake outfit, with my hair '80s style with, like, 10 cans of Aqua Net, and Janie's dolled up like some tough chick. (Which she is, but not usually dressed like that!)

My friendship with Janie has continued through the years, from my return to WCW, and then afterwards. No idea how it started, but we still greet each other with, "Hey, SOB." We consoled each other through breakups, and when I needed someone around after an injury, I crashed at her place. That was an unexpectedly wild night, as I took a painkiller she gave me — and I never took pills or drugs while wrestling — and got so loopy that I danced around with her Raggedy Ann doll before falling asleep with it. We had to keep the friendship sort of on the down-low since she was management, and I was talent. Janie has been a confidant, someone I can trust, which is really rare in professional wrestling! I love her so much.

Since wrestling is all about storytelling, it was pretty logical that I would break from Paul E. at some point. At *Halloween Havoc* in 1992, he fired me, though, the disrespect had built and built so much that it should not have surprised anyone who paid attention to the show. I kicked him and beat him up right there live, but there was more coming. Paul E. chewed a lot of scenery in the skits leading up to our bout and spewed some real dated rhetoric, like, "Men were put on this earth for the domination of the female species." Our big Battle of the Sexes match was at *Clash of the Champions 21*, and we fought to a five-minute time-limit draw, but I went after him after with a steel chair post-match. Not long after, he left the company and ended up creating something that revolutionized the wrestling business, Extreme Championship Wrestling.

Me? I ended up injured. My match with Paul E. included Michael "PS" Hayes, a veteran wrestler in his corner. At one point, I was supposed to dive off the top turnbuckle, and Hayes was supposed to catch me but he did not catch me correctly, and I broke my foot. Hayes really lived the whole macho man thing that Paul E. was only pretending. "I'm not gonna let her land on me," is what he apparently told management. That macho attitude towards women was the norm. Years later, I made a joke out of it just to hear Michael's answer. "What the fuck was I gonna do? I don't catch anybody off the fucking turnbuckle," he said. My response? "Well, then, why didn't you tell me that when we were discussing it? Because that was the plan, dickhead."

I didn't spend any time on the sideline and just wrapped my foot nice and tight, usually with duct tape, before going to the ring.

By the end of 1992, I had decided that I wasn't going to stick around. WCW had gone through a ton of behind-the-scenes players even in the short time I was there. Bill Watts, an old-school promoter out of Oklahoma, had taken over, and I just didn't see any future for me with him in charge, and certainly not for women's wrestling. My deal was up in April 1993, and I wrote him a letter. Here's a little of what I wrote: "I have enjoyed myself this past year during my association as a team player with the WCW and hope to continue my career with you. While my prior obligations to WCW have been satisfactory, I feel I need to voice my opinions. Hopefully by expressing myself, I will not be jeopardizing all my hard work."

It was good to have learned how things worked in the big time, but I had stagnated as a wrestler. Hitting the road, traveling the world, was just the solution I needed.

8.

THE QUEEN OF SELF-PROMOTION

THE SMARTEST BUSINESS MOVE that I ever did? No question, it was trademarking Madusa. The forethought has paid off big time through the years, especially as it handcuffed WCW and Monster Jam as far as what it could do with me and my likeness.

And holy shit is my likeness out there.

My first piece of merchandise actually came *before* I had signed with the AWA, so early 1987. It was unheard of for an independent wrestler to

This Pin*Her *hanky was one of my first promotional items, available through my fan club.*

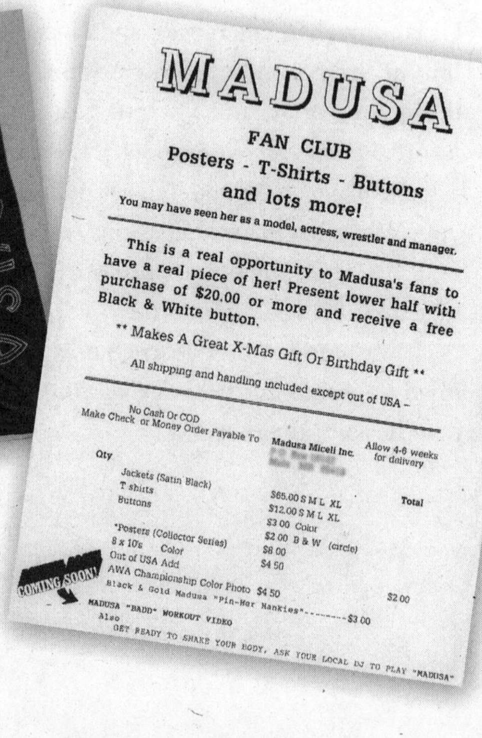

have a product in a store, especially with WWF and all the Hulkamaniacs dominating shelves.

But there I was, sprawling on this chunk of concrete in a bathing suit, my hair done with long extensions, looking like the muscle-bound workout goddess I was at the time. Subtly in the background are my eyes in the sky. It was sold in Target department stores, in one of those old poster frame displays that you flipped through and picked up the wrapped-up poster down below. That was done with a company in Minneapolis, but what I really remember was one of the partners had the hots for me, and he was always hitting on me. He was so much older than me that I just thought it was cute.

With Simitar Entertainment, I did a workout video, distributed on VHS tape in 1994. It was called *Madusa's Championship Workout*, and it promised "10 rounds of a totally new, fun, empowering fitness program," combining boxing and aerobics, and warned, "This video will not make you a boxer or martial arts guru, but women who have used it report a feeling of confidence and physical well-being." There's a segment on it about eating well — we call it "spa cuisine." Then, a few years later, the workout was released on DVD as *Slam! Interactive Personal Trainer* and *Madusa's Tae KickBoxing Workout*.

And who was the first woman wrestler to pose for *Playboy Magazine*? Me. But then I chickened out. It's still a good story, though.

Still early in my wrestling days, I was broke and in debt. Getting naked was a way out. Gathering my nerves, I went into a strip joint and sat in the office, talking to the manager about a job. He was enthusiastic, I was not, and never did dance.

It occurred to me that posing in an adult magazine could work — and this was still a time before porn everywhere on the internet, so the mags mattered. Bravely, I sent my press kit to *Playboy*, and they called me right away and wanted to meet up. They flew me to Chicago, first class all the way; for moral support the night before meeting with them, I went out for dinner with Mike Muzik, a bodybuilder friend whom I knew from the Windy City's gym scene.

The meeting was at The Drake hotel, and next thing I knew, I was posing for *Playboy*. It was a different and really interesting experience, and I was treated with courtesy and respect; it never felt dirty. After the shoot, they presented me with a model release.

I couldn't sign it.

I had reservations about the publicity regarding the photographs and the effect it may have on my career — especially as I was about to leave for Japan — so I withdrew my permission and approval for the photographs to be used. They were surprised. I still have a couple of Polaroids from the shoot.

Around the same time, *Penthouse* asked me to pose, and I declined, and on another occasion, I was flown to Hollywood to be wooed by *Hustler*. After the conversation — I was never going to pose for them, but accepted the flight to L.A. — I went to the *Hustler*-related store and went to pay for a necklace, and I was told that it was taken care of. There must have been cameras watching or something, so I always proclaimed that *Hustler* owner Larry Flynt bought me the jewelry . . . and I still have that necklace today.

Seeing the WWE machine get behind promoting its women in *Playboy* years later was both inspiring — you go, girls! — and left me wondering how my life would have been different had I gone through with it.

Girlie magazines were one thing, the wrestling magazines were quite another — and they weren't as far apart as you might think.

Early in my career with the AWA, I raced to the stores and I bought every wrestling magazine just to see if I was in it. I'd be like, "Grrr, not in this one. There's the GLOW girls. Oh, I'm not sexy enough."

Isn't that weird? Here, I'd posed for *Playboy*, but was still down on my self-image. I could be confident and strut into a room, knowing I'd draw attention, yet wanting to crawl into a corner. Betty always told me that she left me in the hospital because I was so ugly.

With wrestling booming in the late 1980s, there were dozens of magazines on the shelves. There were articles on me, sure, but half the shit they wrote they just made up. I never was from Milan, I never played competitive volleyball, or swam on the high school swim team. I certainly didn't have a black belt in karate. It was easy to get pissed off reading the lies, but, in retrospect, it's still better than the vileness of social media today.

Yet, it was key to anyone's career to befriend the magazine people, like photographer/editor George Napolitano (who was my conduit to Japan), or Bill Apter of the so-called Apter mags, like *Pro Wrestling Illustrated*. "Wonderful Willie" wrote about me in his book, under the provocative title, "Apter's One Night Stand with Madusa" in 1986. We'd never met, and I was dispatched by the AWA office to pick him up at the airport, to bring to the matches. After the show, he accompanied me out to Minneapolis's hopping bar scene. I took him to a place women rarely went, where no one hit on me — an all-male gay bar, called the Gay 90s! Bill being Bill, he played along and made friends . . . and he's remained a treasured pal ever since.

There were also a number of insider newsletters that covered the business far more deeply, and honestly, than the national magazines. They weren't always right, either, but it was good that they were there. When I left WCW the first time, I did a lengthy interview with *The Pro Wrestling Torch* that got a lot of tongues wagging, if only because I talked about some of the people I'd worked with honestly.

If I'd come up in today's wrestling world, I'd have gotten a chance to be on the cover of *Muscle & Fitness* magazine, like so many WWE wrestlers have been. Wrestling-wise, I am on the cover of a couple of magazines, but can I really celebrate *Beauties of Wrestling* from fall 1998? There's a lame-ass *WWF Magazine* where I'm feeding "Diesel" Kevin Nash watermelon to hype *SummerSlam*. There's a whole magazine about me that came out in Japan in 1989, with photos by Minoru Imase. Various motorcycle magazines were enamored by the idea of a wrestler being married to an NFL player (as I was to Ken Blackman), owning a cycle shop, so those were a couple more covers.

The non-existent Milan connection brought Italian fashion magazine *AMICA* out to shoot me and my monster truck at my log cabin in Virginia in 2005. Photographer Robert Erdmann, stylist Anka Itskovich, and their crew just moved right in and made themselves at home, paying for the catering. It was by far the biggest cover shoot of my life, and definitely one time I was okay playing up my kayfabe Italian background. After much fighting on my part, Monster Jam finally agreed to send my monster truck up to the shoot, and there are some great photos of me with the truck, my motorcycle, even with my wolf, Glacier. I even flew Granny in from Minneapolis, and she got her makeup done with me and is in some of the photos, too. When she got to climb into the truck, I could tell that she was itching to drive it! There were moments where I cried during that shoot, like, "I made it, I'm respected for my hard work." I know it sounds silly, but I had fought so hard for exposure, and here it was . . . in Italy, at least.

It seems I get a podcast appearance request every other day now, but when I was coming up in wrestling, there were only a handful of wrestling-specific TV or radio shows. As an independent, you needed to get on some of them, like John Arezzi's *Pro Wrestling Spotlight* radio show out of New York. In Boston, there was a TV show called *Wrestling Talk*, hosted by Paul Fay and Leonard Caplan. In 1988, when I was on their show for the second time, I was on crutches after knee surgery. Somehow, I ended up staying friends with Leonard, even if we are polar opposites in so many ways.

As a WWE or WCW employee, any media had to get approved by the company, so I just rolled with it. But I always knew that it was important to speak professionally and look great.

With so many people wanting a piece of my time now, I am very selective with what podcasts or shows I do, and if you go listen to them, chances are I'm revealing the same things again and again. What really gets me excited are new experiences, like *Drinks With Johnny*, a podcast with Johnny Christ from Avenged Sevenfold.

Books have always been an escape for me, especially with so much time on flights. I'd read just about anything — biographies, horror, historical fiction, whatever caught my interest. Even today, I have a big-ass, 50-pound rucksack full of books, ready for me to hit the road.

When my Japanese adventures came to an end, I knew there was a story there and started on my own autobiography. Again, I was ahead of the curve, as it wasn't until Mick Foley cracked open the wrestling book world with his memoir, *Have a Nice Day: A Tale of Blood and Sweatsocks*, in 1999 that publishers realized wrestling fans could read. I would have been a pioneer had I actually finished the damn thing. In the subsequent years, I spent some more time with various people working on it, and the finished product in your hands is proof that good things come to those who wait!

On a trip home from Japan in February 1989, I was approached by a computer company to produce a video game about me. It was a puzzle-type game for your PC. I doubt anyone ever saw it, let alone bought it, and I'm pretty sure I got stiffed on the pay, only getting half of the $10,000 I'd agreed to. But, hey, maybe you have a copy, if so, hit me up on my website, Madusa.com, which is run by Bill Trevor of WebSmartAdvisor.com.

Like so many things, I was an early adopter of the internet, though it's insane to think about how things changed. Alan Pavlosky and his Sixthman Communications company ran my site when I launched, in 1998, and all it cost me was about $15,000! I'm not complaining, as that was the going rate at the time, and I sure as hell couldn't have done it. You have to remember that they did everything back then, and I couldn't post content myself. Very quickly, colleagues were asking, "Where'd you get that?" Alan was brilliant and saw where the internet was heading, so, early on, I could really interact with people, they could listen to short audio files, and buy some 8 x 10s.

The real find, though, was the photographer. I'd met this dude in California, fresh from Switzerland, and I sensed something special about him. We did a couple of shoots together for the website. Well, he was Per Bernal when I met him, but now he's *Per Bernal*, photographer to the stars. He specializes in athletes, shooting covers for *Muscle &*

Fitness or *Flex* featuring The Rock or John Cena. I am grateful to have discovered him and stayed in touch.

For the longest time, I harbored dreams of being a Hollywood star. Growing up, I wasn't exactly obsessed with TV, but I'd watch early in the morning, while Betty slept. I loved *I Love Lucy* and can remember shows like *Perry Mason* and *The Twilight Zone*. Being on TV as a wrestler was one thing, but I wanted more.

Trudy Adams wrestled as Amy the Farmer's Daughter and had graduated from the all-women's *GLOW* program to actually wrestling in the AWA. (Incidentally, there was a Netflix series revisiting *GLOW*, and I was approached by Chavo Guerrero Jr. to be a part of season four, but the show was canceled.) Trudy and I became friends, and she invited me to crash at her place in Los Angeles, California — well, technically, it was Studio City — and learn the business. She showed me what to do, from looking in the paper for auditions to understanding how the agencies worked.

Her pink convertible Cadillac was one badass fucking car. It was her investment in herself, to show off — because we had no other money. All we could afford were flour tortillas and we'd roll up nothing but Feta cheese with ranch dressing.

When I scored my first audition, she let me drive her car. I thought that was insane. She told me to take good care of it and warned me about parking illegally. I brushed her off, said it would be no problem.

I was told to dress for the position, and I went all out, dressed to the fucking nines, complete with a pair of Carrera sunglasses that I definitely paid too much for. When I saw the other girls, I stood out, having put so much work into my look. It didn't help.

Going in for the audition, I took the sunglasses and laid them down on the little table next to me. I didn't know what to expect. They had all these people sitting at a table. And they said, "Okay, this is so-and-so, and they're going to read the script with you. And you are Miss Molly" — or whatever the fuck I was. I didn't know I was supposed to really prepare before, either, because I thought I could just wing it because of wrestling. That was my mentality — *I got this.*

It took me a moment or two after they counted down to start, and it took me a while to get going, but I started getting into the part, getting emotional. When we were done, they just looked at me and they're like, "Okay, thank you. Have a good day." Or, "Get the hell out!"

Not only was I embarrassed, but also I got a ticket on the car and forgot my sunglasses there, and when I called back, they said they weren't there. I was pissed and knew someone pocketed them, but I couldn't do anything.

We had a great time in that apartment, partied it up with lots of musicians, but I couldn't get rolling with anything, while Trudy continued to get modeling gigs or small roles in stuff. My frustration resulted in me not giving a shit. She started calling me "Pigdusa" instead of "Madusa" because I'd leave the place a mess.

I left after about six months, disillusioned. But I'd be back, just not at Trudy's.

Brandon Pender was one of the people in California who helped WCW promote wrestling shows, and he had some excellent connections in the movie business, and he saw something in me. A personal manager, agent, and a producer, he had worked with all kinds of tough women, martial artists, such as Karen Sheperd and Graciella Casillas, and kickboxers, such as Cheryl Wheeler and "Baby Doll" Bridgett Riley, who had gotten into action films.

We worked out a deal where I used my frequent flier miles to fly to Los Angeles, and he put me up at the Beverly Garland Hotel in Studio City. With Brandon's help, I started meeting the right people — casting directors, producers, directors. I'd grown in confidence, too, another few years as a globetrotting wrestler under my belt. After a few meetings, he brought me to a set in Sherman Oaks, California, where Alan Amiel was filming a movie. Brandon had sent Alan my info, but there'd been no deal; when Alan saw me, he thought I looked great and immediately put me in *Inner Sanction II*. It's a blink-and-you-miss-it moment, and I'm a paramedic, but I'm there! The star was Margaux Hemingway, and she was reading a book when I introduced myself.

Brandon scored me two more roles over the next couple of years — remember, I was fitting in acting around my wrestling commitments, which frustrated him to no end; he always said if I'd gone all-in, I would have had a career in acting. Brandon pushed really hard to get us women in there and do action movies, fight scenes. And that's what I did in *Death Match*, which came out in 1994, and *Shootfighter II*, two years later. The fight scene in *Death Match*, choreographed by Brandon, took three days to shoot. It looks great, but equally important, it got me into the Screen Actors Guild. Watching it now just makes me smile, since they aren't exactly Oscar-worthy films. But I got to experience what it was like to be in the movies.

A few years later, when I was in WCW and my in-ring action had slowed, I approached an agent named Michael Braverman, who had been representing wrestlers, like Bill Goldberg and others. When I called him, he was brusque on the phone, "How did you get through?" His secretary had put me through. "What can I do for you?" Just like that. I said I wanted to do movies, like he was helping the WCW wrestlers. "You're too old." I started, "Why do the guys . . ." and I couldn't finish. I'll never forget that phone call, and I told myself, *Fuck that son of a bitch*. That was horrible; truthful, maybe, but horrible. He could have done something with me, but he chose not to. He could have at least been polite.

Years later, we crossed paths at an event. I was in a business that he wanted a part of. I remember thinking, *This is interesting*. We chatted about how small the world is, and he played like we were old pals. He asked me how I was, and I replied: "I've had my adversities and turn-downs in life. But, you know, I persevered. Do you remember that time you told me that I was too old?" He's like, "Oh, did I say that?" My answer: "You're still a snake." I never spoke to him again.

I bet I would have run into some *real* snakes had I been allowed to appear on *Survivor*. It was the 13th season, *Survivor: Cook Islands*, in 2006. A friend who was a casting agent, Kathy Duliakas, asked if I would be interested in being on the show. Hell yeah, so I sat in a hotel room for two weeks, with no contact with other human beings, waiting for details, and then I was presented with a new provision, which dictated that I couldn't appear on TV in any other role. Huh? I was a fucking monster truck driver! I told them they were out of their minds.

Early in my career, I also ran my own Madusa Fan Club, where I sold not only the workout video, but also black satin jackets, T-shirts, buttons, 8 x 10s, and, of course, my poster.

Contrast that to my first run in WCW, where there was no Madusa merchandise — and I didn't get to be on the 1-800 line, where I know Missy made a pretty penny. In the WWF, *Believe in the Blayze* was my one and only T-shirt, though one more was released to coincide with WWE Hall of Fame induction. I didn't get an action figure until 2017, when I was under a *WWE Legends* deal, as a part of the WWE Elite Collection Flashback from Mattel.

In my second WCW run, after I came in so hot after dropping the belt in the garbage, there wasn't much, either. Recently, I dug up a receipt for my fourth quarter 1997 income for merchandise in WCW — the grand total was $2.32 on Madusa lapel pins; I didn't even bother cashing the check.

Now, there were some trading cards during that time — if you care, my rookie card was a 1993 *WCW Magazine* Collector's Special 3 #17 Madusa.

Chances are if you see any Madusa T-shirts or other goodies, they date from my time driving a monster truck. The Hot Wheels Madusa truck is particularly cool.

With my "Queen of Carnage" and "MADe in the USA" T-shirts, I was always among the top sellers in Monster Jam — and rightfully so.

Heck, there's even a Madusa cornhole game. Since I'd kept the rights to my name, it was a lucrative sideline for me, especially compared to the tiny pay I actually got for putting my life on the line in those beastly vehicles. My Madusa crew shirts, with all the pink-and-white stars, got so many comments that eventually replicas were made to sell to fans, too.

More recently, other companies have evened the playing field for everyone and handle printing and distribution of shirts for me and countless other wrestlers.

One of the most *fun* promotional items I put together was a Motorsport Divas calendar for 2014. Note the title — it's not like Monster Jam wanted to promote its drivers or anything, and they warned the drivers I approached about participating. My argument, which won the day, was that they were independent contractors, and that they couldn't control us away from the track.

This was all my baby. I chose the girls, arranged the location to shoot, and hired the photographer. It wasn't just a money grab, as I gave the girls the rights to their photos beyond the calendar, to do what they wanted with them. All they had to do was fly themselves in.

Since we spent so much time on the road, going in every different direction for the monster truck shows, we had never really just, you know, hung out as girlfriends. It was the kind of nightmare that kept the Monster Jam owners up all night — instead of pitting the women against one another, we were bonding, becoming closer than ever. Grrrrl power!

I told the girls, "Look, I don't want to be sleazy. Anybody can get in a bikini and roll their tits out and show off their ass. What we're going to do is find out more about you and your personality and find out what you love."

Jackpot! One girl had a background as a ballerina, so we shot her with some flowers, leaping in the air. Another had been a surfer, so there was the shot. Now, if you were in publicity for Monster Jam, wouldn't these be great stories to share with the media and the fans? Ha. As if.

There were lots of hijinks, too. Us calendar girls were out for the night, and there was a mechanical bull, which Becky McDonough really wanted to ride — but she was wearing a skirt. With balls as big as any bull, she went up to a dude who was about her size and asked him for his jeans so she could ride — and he agreed, watching while wearing her skirt!

In an ideal world, we would have done another calendar the next year, but some of the girls thought it was a lot of work for little reward, aside from the newfound camaraderie.

Having spent so many years on the road, I never found a lot of time for video games. I first appeared as Madusa in *WCW Nitro* in 1998, and then *WCW Backstage Assault* two years later. Since I was on a *WWE Legends* deal, I have been in a number of WWE 2K games as Alundra Blayze. You can drive me around in a couple of games, too, including *Monster Jam* and its sequel *Monster 4x4: Masters of Metal*.

Then, after finally stepping away from driving, I found myself with some time on my hands and started gaming again. During the pandemic, I launched a Twitch channel and just had a blast hanging out with people. I've even done 24-hour marathons, but not just gaming on Twitch — I showed people how I groom my dog, Daisy, and took questions. My husband, Alan, demonstrated some of his barbecue secrets that he learned from old roommate Barbecue Bob, who encouraged Alan to step up his game with me. With the various levels of subscriptions, Twitch is a great side gig and a fun escape. I don't do it alone. I have my #MadModSquad to keep me running and, of course, the fans.

But I'm still fucking competitive, and while it's tough to win against younger and more experienced gamers, I sure as hell try. There have been times I've thrown my damn controller and broken my screen. The fans are watching your emotions, and they get a sense of your realism, like you are a human. My fans tend to skew older, too, which means it's a bit more respectful — but it's still social media, so you get plenty of trolls.

Down the road, I see this book as a template for a motion picture. Whether it's fictionalized or a documentary, who knows, but through the years, plenty of people have approached me about telling my story.

Or a movie *by* me. I've always had a hidden passion; not only do I want my story made into a movie, but I've also always loved behind-the-scenes production and wanted to learn more. I even took some Lee Strasberg classes on acting.

Jason Brasier is a young, energetic director, and we hit it off. I okayed him to start my life story, and we did a little trailer, a reenactment, for a movie about me, and then we set it aside. The timing just didn't feel right . . . yet.

He moved on to another project, a documentary about Manoli Savvenas, who wrestled as Mike Pappas. The film is called *The Flying Greek*, and it debuted in December 2021, and it tells his tale from Greek immigrant to wrestler to jeweler.

You might recognize the voice doing the narration — it's me!

Self-promotion is a never-ending battle, from small to big. I have special-order Madusa socks that I can give as a present last-minute when meeting someone, and I have plans for a Madusa adult beverage. I started podcasting in 2016, and I am still going strong. My show is called *Five-Minute Mondays, Paving the Way with Madusa*, and is available on all podcast platforms. It can include everything from sports to current affairs to stories from my past. I couldn't do it without my steadfast producer, Marsh. People approach me all the time about appearing on their shows, and, fortunately, I'm in the position to pick and choose.

It all ties into belief in myself, that I have something of value to share with the world. That was not something I learned at home growing up, but it did take hold when I was young.

It started with Anthony Robbins, who knows a thing or two himself about self-promotion. When I was just starting wrestling, I had one of his motivational cassette tapes and darn near wore it out. I'd put the tape on in my car and drive 300 miles and listen, imagine, plan. Honestly, he saved my life in a way, gave me the needed belief in myself that I never got from my shitty childhood. There were others, too. Norman Vincent Peale was a minister and motivational speaker, and he had an event in Minneapolis. At the time, I couldn't afford a ticket, but I drove to the event and listened through a back door.

In recent years, I've started doing seminars on many different topics. I call it "Kick, Wrestle, and Roll." Like me, it is adaptable. If it is a class of aspiring wrestlers, I educate them about out of the ring things like branding, publicity and marketing, trademarks, finances, lawyers, and medical expenses.

When I speak at a school, I change "Kick, Wrestle, and Roll" to be more motivational, and can adjust it to the grade level. No matter the age, they love my props, like my racing suit and helmet and some wrestling gear, and it just leads to so many great questions. Thanks to the generosity of WWE, I can leave behind goodies for them, too, more than just my nuggets of knowledge.

9.

A BLAYZE OF GLORY

THE *SHOWCASE OF THE IMMORTALS*. *WrestleMania*. It's WWE's Super Bowl. I was fortunate to compete at *WrestleMania X*, in New York City at Madison Square Garden, where I defeated my friend, Leilani Kai, and kept my WWF Women's title.

But I can't watch the match now, at least not with the sound on.

At one point, Jerry "The King" Lawler, the color commentator, said that I had "a million-dollar body and a 10-cent face." Even if he was a so-called heel announcer, supporting the bad guys, that still had no place. Remember, I was Alundra Blayze, their fucking champion!

The WWF Women's champion in the middle of the ring at Madison Square Garden for WrestleMania X*, to face Leilani Kai.*

PHOTO COURTESY WWE

Lawler was the worst in the company, and after I left and the Attitude Era slithered in, he was allowed to be even more horrible and degrading to women while they had their Bra and Panties matches and other shit.

It was such a men's club, and I had to fight and claw for everything I got. At the time, Vince Russo was the editor of the *WWF Magazine*. He was supportive of me, making sure the women got coverage in the magazine, but also saw what was going on. Here's what he recalled of that time in the WWF: "Man, back then, and it still is now, no matter what they tell you on the surface, it was the boys' club. I mean, and God forbid a girl or a woman took their spot. It just didn't work that way. And I know [Alundra] was very, very frustrated just because she wanted the opportunity, and she really, really wasn't getting too many. And that's why I always used to try to cover her in the magazine to get her name out there."

Things have come a long way, but it took forever to get to the point where women can be part of the main event at *WrestleMania*. Every era, every woman who has stepped foot in that ring, helped the transition to where it's at today. And I do mean everyone, even in that damn Attitude Era with all the swinging tits and smacking asses. Oh wait, that was me in WCW — damn Russo, making me sound like a hypocrite!

While I am certain I would have ended up in the WWF eventually, it was Greg Valentine who made the call to Pat Patterson, one of the key behind-the-scenes people at WWF, and suggested they hire me. Greg had worked there and his opinion was respected. Through Greg, I had met WWF boss Vince McMahon once previously. (Note, I will keep using WWF, not WWE, since that's who I worked for.)

Not long after, in the summer of 1993, I was invited to fly from Florida up to Stamford, Connecticut, where the WWF offices were (and still are, but in a different building). I was really nervous: *This is it*. Sitting alone in the back seat of the black stretch limo, I said out loud, "I'm actually going to freakin' Titan Tower. This is crazy!" It crossed my mind: *Is the limo driver listening? Is he a spy and going to report this crazy woman talking to herself?* Then it was even more overwhelming walking through the hallways, seeing all the posters and photos of wrestlers on the walls. I tried to soak it all in — the offices, the gym, even the waiting room, though, I was paranoid, wondering whether I was being watched.

Then it was showtime, and I was directed to Vince McMahon's office. He was very friendly and enthusiastic, and seemed to know a lot about me and where I'd already wrestled. The women's division had been nonexistent in WWF for a few years, and the plan was to build it all around me — what a thrill to even think about it. We talked about a movie that I had already committed to, and the deal I had in place for fitness videos. It didn't take long to agree to a deal in principle, though I didn't sign anything and wanted my lawyer to look at it.

We talked about a name and continuing to use Madusa was mentioned. I was honest with him: "I worked so hard for that name, it's trademarked, I really don't want to give it up." WWF has always tried to retain the rights to the names of its wrestlers. I was scared to death that it would be a dealbreaker, and there was a long silence. Finally, Vince said they'd think of another name.

I kept a copy of the thank-you letter — typewritten, so forgive the spelling — that I sent to Mr. McMahon, dated, July 26, 1993:

> It was a pleasure meeting you and thank you for your time. I left very excited and rejuvenated for the outlook you have once again, on women's wrestling. To be employed by the WWF you will have my utmost attention and my 100% teamsmanship. I have enclosed a press kit with a variety of information I hope will be useful. . . . Vince, now that I cluttered your desk with more papers and hopefully got your attention I am willing to see you again and the people that make miracles for new "characters". The name Madusa has been with me for quite some time and everybody needs a change.

In our next meeting, I had an idea. The official name of WWF was actually Titan Sports, and I suggested I become Titania. Oh my God, they loved it. The next time they flew me in, I signed the contract, and we did some vignettes introducing Titania to the world. They never aired, as WWF's lawyers decided that it was too similar to Titan. Well, that was the damn point!

I love the name Blayze, and we added the *y* to be different. Thinking like a business person would, and your company's positioning in the Yellow Pages, I wanted a name that started with an *A*. Together, we came up with the name Alundra. A-lun-dra, again, I was thinking of syllables that people could chant. The surname had to be creative, and, believing that I would be champion one day, *A-B-C* worked — Alundra Blayze, Champion.

Now all Alundra Blayze needed was some costumes and opponents!

One thing that many fans don't realize is that pro wrestlers pay for their costumes, from their boots to their trunks to their elaborate robes. Does the company help? Sure, in some ways, by having designers and seamstresses. Though, I suspect it's not a tried-and-true rule across the entire company deal, as some stars no doubt get perks, but I sure as hell had to buy my gimmicks. The company would bill you back for the material and the labor. As an independent contractor, I could write it off as a business expense, but what a Catch-22 — you had to look good to get ahead, but the more you wrestled, the more worn the gear got, and also the more you were seen, so there's a need for more outfits to stand out. Whatever money I made, I reinvested it back into my brand.

In fact, here's something no one knows: when I had a few days off at home in Florida, I'd take shifts as a waitress at a barbecue restaurant to make some extra money. There were a couple of times people recognized me as a so-called WWE superstar; I'd just laugh, and say, "Oh, I get that a lot."

My idea for Alundra Blayze was that she was ultra-athletic, and the costumes would reflect that. I was a wrestler, and moved around a lot, and wanted to make sure that everything stayed in, if you know what I mean. If anything, inspiration came from amateur wrestling singlets, but starting at my neck. My designers were rock stars, and it was frickin' unbelievable what they came up with. Then I was sent swatches from all of the material I got to choose from, and colors. Each of my well-known outfits, the silver/gray full-body one and the other with the fire, cost me about two grand. Later on, I had others made, including my gear for *WrestleMania X*. For that one, I was instructed to go futuristic, and I chose pink and white, for purity and strength. The white part had a hologram-like iridescent silver color, which really popped. There was a jacket, too, with tails that hung all the way down — a bit of a tribute to my Japanese outfits that were influenced by Prince and Madonna. I even had a separate outfit for the fan fest, and it was all-white leather with knee-high boots, white, silver, and gray, and it was made by the same man who did Randy Savage's clothes.

Just before my contract came into effect, in December 1993, WWF announced a tournament to crown a women's champion. Rockin' Robin Smith — sister to Jake "The Snake" Roberts and Sam Houston, daughter of Grizzly Smith — had been the champion, up until February 1990, when she was stripped of the title for not defending it. (How can you defend it when the company doesn't book you, huh?) Robin and I have circled back in the last few years and are great friends. She is amazingly smart and has a beautiful soul. We have a lot in common. Oh, she's magic on the one-armed bandits in the casino, too!

It was an odd tournament. I actually wrestled for the Memphis-based, WWF-affiliated USWA promotion in the first round, beating Allison Royal, but then I got a bye to the final. I'd lobbied for Heidi Lee Morgan to come in, since we'd worked together in the AWA, and she defeated Black Venus and then Rusty Thomas to face me in the final. I beat her on December 13, 1993, in Poughkeepsie, New York, to win the title, using a German suplex, and the actual match aired on December 26, on the syndicated *All-American Wrestling* show, and then highlights were shown on *Monday Night Raw* the next night, along with taped interviews with Heidi and me.

Heidi became one of my best pals, a frequent traveling partner and opponent. She was a second-generation wrestler and knew instinctively what to do in the ring. Technically, she was not under contract to WWF, so had far more freedom than I did, which is why fans saw her come and go. They continually brought her back, though, because they knew she could deliver, and she lived in the Northeast.

We always found a gym together; we could sniff them out in town when we arrived. Or we'd get to our hotel and check the phone book. Most of the time, they let us workout for free, since we were celebrities, and we paid them back with a few autographs and photos. Heidi always looked like a million bucks, and it was inspiring to train with her. We talked a lot about a proper diet, too, and did our best to eat right on the road — no easy task in the 1990s.

Knowing that we could deliver in the ring, WWF wanted to build us up as a tag team heading into the 1995 Royal Rumble. This is where I have mad respect for Heidi and get mad at the way the business used to be. When WWF called her, Heidi told them she was pregnant and couldn't wrestle, worried about having a miscarriage. Instead of respecting her decision, WWF just completely cut ties with her, and Heidi never wrestled for them again. Could you imagine that today? And her daughter, Adriana, is the light of her life, someone I'd send birthday presents to through the years.

Early in my WWF days, after I'd run through U.S. talent like Heidi, Leilani Kai, Debbie Combs, and Luna Vachon, Vince asked me, "Who do you want to work with?" I was honest with him — I missed the strong style. Why not bring some Japanese girls over? The Jumping Bomb Angels (Noriyo Tateno and Itsuki Yamazaki) had a good run in the WWF from 1987 to 1988.

Keiko "Bull" Nakano was my choice, and the right one. I believe that all of us have that one person in our career that makes us, and Bull Nakano was definitely mine. She came into the WWF in the summer of 1994. We both had grown since our matches in Japan, and she had risen to the top of the card — and that option was never available in the United States for women, though we did wrestle in the first women's match on *Raw*, on August 1, 1994.

Bull wrestled at about 220 pounds and had a crazy tall Mohawk haircut, with her face painted. It worked well against a lily-white babyface like me! (Though I was pretty sassy for a good girl.) The production of her hair pre-match was always something to behold in our women's locker room / broom closet. She'd go through mountains of mousse and Aqua Net hair spray, and she blow-dried it, sprayed it, blow-dried it, straightened it. It was like a layer of lacquer, stiff but still soft. Bull looked like a completely different person out of gimmick — yet you can't disguise being the only Japanese woman on the roster. We were pals and would joke around. I would try to mess up her hair in the middle of the match, and she would call me every Japanese name in the book. It was fun to fuck with her and to get a good laugh in the ring. My Japanese came back to me, and she learned some English. Looking back, she was probably more lonely in America than I was in Japan.

Wrestling-wise, I only improved working with her. I followed her lead, because I wanted a good match. But she totally let me take the reins. I was a great seller, bumping like a mofo. The point was to build to the babyface comeback, so it would be huge and pop the crowd, and that was the key, especially in the United States. In Japan, there was a lot of fast-moving, back-and-forth wrestling, and when you settled into a painful-looking hold, they'd applaud when someone got out of it. In the United States, fans got impatient much quicker.

We fought night after night, from the big lights of *Monday Night Raw* to every arena on the schedule. We had an epic battle at *SummerSlam* that August in Chicago, where I retained my title, but nothing compares to November 20, 1994, in Tokyo. It was ultra-rare for WWF to acknowledge that other wrestling promotions existed at the time, let alone allow talent to participate. But there, Bull and I were facing off at a massive All Japan Women's Pro Wrestling extravaganza called Big Egg Wrestling Universe, at the Tokyo Dome, in front of 42,500 fans. At the time, it was the largest crowd ever to watch a mainly women's show. My entrance was epic, riding out on a Harley, surrounded by another dozen or so bikers, while I waved an American flag. Our roles reversed, and Bull was the hero, but it was a battle, and she came out on top. I wish I remembered more about that show, but

I don't; WWE had me in and out, with not enough time to say hi to old friends.

After the huge show in Tokyo, I have no idea why Bull and I didn't get to fight at *WrestleMania XI* in Hartford, Connecticut. Oh right, boys' club. Instead, the night after Mania, April 3, I beat her on *Raw*. Immediately following my win, I was attacked by Bertha Faye. So I could have some time off, we made it look like she broke my nose. In reality, I had actually busted my nose a few times through the years, and I was having trouble breathing, especially out of the left side. To fix it, the doctor had to chisel through my bone for the deviated septum and whatever else was going on. Since I knew I'd be on the shelf — I recovered at a friend's place in Minneapolis — I figured I may as well get my tits done again . . . returning bigger and better. (Decades later, I still have trouble breathing through that side of my nose.)

The end of Bull's WWF run is shrouded in some secrecy. While I wasn't there, this is what I heard. The boys set her up: they had her try some illicit drugs, and then she failed a drug test. WWE sent her home. I think that put a bad taste in Vince's mouth about women's wrestling in general, and he just said fuck it. Again, that's my take on it, and it had to have factored in on the ultimate decision to drop women's wrestling at the end of 1995. It's unfair, because, again, plenty of the guys got second, third, 14th chances.

Fortunately, that wasn't the end of Bull. She wrestled in Japan for another couple of years, and then slimmed down and became a professional golfer, even living in Florida, trying to make the LPGA tour. She later ran a restaurant in the Nakano section of Tokyo. On her 44th birthday, on January 8, 2012, she was given a proper retirement ceremony, as is the tradition in Japan, and she got married at the same time.

We have kept in touch a little through the years, since our careers will be forever intertwined.

Wrestlers spend so much time on the road that every single one of us has horror stories of travel: luggage getting lost, missed flights, snowstorms, cars that die, accidents. No shit, one year between flying different airlines, I was reimbursed a total of $14,000 for lost luggage. That money had to go into replacing luggage, and all the other things; of course, I learned there was little point in buying nice Louis Vuitton luggage. The valuables you couldn't lose went into the cabin with you.

At least I didn't suffer alone. You realized that you needed your colleagues to manage it, traveling partners, even if you were supposed to stay true to the storyline, meaning the good guys couldn't travel with the bad guys. (It didn't matter when there were only two girls, though.) We learned things like, one would get the rental car, while the other got the luggage at the carousel, and that way we both aren't standing there waiting around like a bunch of dumbasses. You took turns driving, though, and I often bugged Heidi: "You go too slow. Let me drive!"

One time, it was me, Heidi, and Bart Gunn in a car, racing to the airport, and I got pulled over for speeding. Add it to the pile of tickets. Bart finished the drive, as he was extra paranoid about missing the flight. In the shuttle bus, from the rental car drop-off to the airport, Heidi and I were joking around, and he was still steaming. Bart bent over to get something out of his bag, and I saw nothing but opportunity in the space between his jeans and undies . . . and dropped my gum into the crack. Ever the pro, Bart no-sold it, and I never heard about it again, from him at least. Heidi *loves* to tell that story.

My first-ever car accident was while I was with the WWF. I had my beeper attached to the top visor in the rental car, and when it beeped, I looked up to see the number coming across, and at the red light, I hit a stopped car. The airbag came out, it caught on fire, and my sleeves caught on fire. Then, I had to call the office and tell them about the crash. Vaguely, I remember going to a hotel, being told I might have a concussion and instructed to stay awake.

Other things you did were just to kill the sheer monotony of airport rental cars to hotels to show. Rinse, repeat. I'd wander off at the airport to get my shoes shined, just for something to do. Or you'd lay bets over who'd get to the next town first, or other stupidity. Some of the guys were what we called "ribbers," meaning they did practical jokes, like super-gluing your clothes or boots together. I did a few ribs, quietly, but they were not really my thing — I think the guys were genuinely scared of me. I would have beaten the hell out of somebody. I didn't walk around with a corncob up my ass or anything like that, like I'm better than anybody, but I think I had an air of, "Hey, this is my turf; don't fuck with me."

But apparently not. In an interview, Scott Hall — who wrestled as Razor Ramon in the WWF — said that I "came in with a little bit of an attitude, and she got shit ribbed." For those unfamiliar with the "joke," it is simple: when I was not looking or in the ring, someone took a dump in the bag that I brought to the arena.

It wasn't until years later when I was on Sean Waltman's podcast — he was 1-2-3 Kid in WWF and then X-Pac — that I learned who did it, off-air. Sean said something like, "That's why we liked you, because you no-sold it and that's when you earned our respect." Lucky me.

So, decades later, this is still funny to them, but not me. Try that today in a current WWE female superstar's bag and see what happens. Not only would you be fired, but also you might face charges. Or at least that's what should happen; if I'm honest with myself, I'm not sure anyone would lose a job. "Boys will be boys" is always the excuse.

When I came back from the nose and boob jobs, Bertha Faye was my ready-made opponent, with Harvey Whippleman serving as her manager, and, eventually, her storyline suitor. In reality, she was Rhonda Sing, from Calgary, who had become a major attraction in Japan as Monster Ripper just before I got there, a truly monster heel. She was a big girl, probably 60 pounds bigger than Bull even, but could really work, and took the punishment in Japan and dished it out, too. So before we started wrestling, I had a lot of respect for her, but that didn't last.

Rhonda had a lot of demons, as they say, and most definitely had some self-esteem issues. It didn't help that the Bertha Faye character was played for laughs, all dolled up in bright clothing, terrible makeup, straight out of the trailer park. It worked, though, and she threw herself into the character. She pranced, she twirled her hair, she skipped.

Our matches, for the most part, were okay — fans still ask me about some of them — but she'd sometimes show up drunk, and I'd have to carry the match. Having Harvey there — Bruno Lauer was his actual name — meant that there was someone extra in the equation, and they could both gang up on me, or in a similar vein, he could act as a distraction when she was trying to get her shit together. Bertha beat me for the women's title at *SummerSlam* in 1995, and I won it back — for the final time, as it turned out — on October 23, 1995, in Brandon, Manitoba, of all places.

Away from the ring, we did have some nice moments, so it wasn't all bad; though it is tough to shake the image of her jacking off one of the boys under a blanket on a commercial flight. We'd have dinners together, and I can remember a memorable outing at the Hard Rock Cafe in London. I'm trying to stick with those positive memories, as, post-wrestling, she often bad-mouthed me in interviews. She took her own life on July 27, 2001. She was only 40.

Then there was Luna Vachon.

She might just be the most confounding person I've ever known in my life. I loved her. I hated her. And I certainly never had any idea what she'd do next, or which Luna she would be. The gravelly voice that she put on was often a clue that she was going to be unpredictable, but Luna could be equally wacky in her normal tone. She could be so kind and nice, but then two seconds later, you didn't know who you were talking to. It's like, "Wait a minute, Luna, come back!" I don't know if that was a defense mechanism.

We never called her Trudy or Gertrude, though that was her real name, and she was ultra-proud to have come up through the famed Vachon family, even if Paul "The Butcher" was her stepfather, not blood. She could really wrestle in the ring, or beat the hell out of you, and I experienced both.

The worst beating came in the dressing room in Madison Square Garden. She just cracked and attacked me, screaming and waling away. I was half naked, and she left the door open, with people passing by. Bull was shitting herself, trying to stop her: "Luna, no, no, no. You're crazy!"

Since there were so few women, I was seen as a caretaker at times. If Luna needed to be tackled so the airplane could take off, they'd call Deuce — my nickname — to do something. Luna's not on the bus? Send Deuce to go to her hotel room. I knew too much, but yet not enough. She needed medication for bipolar and schizophrenia, but I have no idea if she took it.

One time we were all up in Canada, and I just had it with Vince and WWF's booking of me as the women's champion. "You're not giving anybody their fucking due. You're making me a machine, you're making me go through these girls," I argued. Then I pitched dropping the title to Luna. She deserved it and had a following. Vince said he couldn't trust her and wouldn't let me do it.

I had a different idea. In the dressing room, I told her, "Luna, that's it. I don't care if I lose my fucking job. Just pin me — one, two, three, and you take the title." She didn't believe me. "Do it. What are they going to do, fire me?" But she wouldn't do it. Luna has told that story in interviews, and I will vouch for its legitimacy, as a lot of what she has said is lunacy.

What I wouldn't do to hear her voice again, to cringe as she swore at me again, to laugh until we cried again. Luna died in August 2010 of an overdose. She was 48.

I want to go on the record and say that Leilani Kai is one of the best women wrestlers in history. Period. She blazed a trail in Japan that I was able to follow, going on more than 40 tours there. Plus, she helped train so many greats. It was an honor to get to wrestle against her at *WrestleMania X*; after all, she'd wrestled at the *first WrestleMania*, losing the WWF Women's title to Wendi Richter.

But getting her on the 10th Mania wasn't straightforward. WWF had originally arranged for Debbie Combs, out of Nashville, to face me, but that fell apart. Instead, they turned to reliable Leilani — who took some convincing. She hadn't wrestled in almost two years, and

Leilani hadn't been in the WWF since her Glamour Girls tag team with Judy Martin, who were unceremoniously dumped in 1989, just before a big payday at *WrestleMania V*. She was a little uncomfortable with her physique after her time away, so she wore a full-body suit for our match in March 1994. What she wasn't was shy about speaking her mind. WWF wanted The Fabulous Moolah to referee our match, and Leilani hated her old trainer and booking agent. She refused to let Moolah ref, so, instead, there's the legend, Moolah, who I inducted into the WWE Hall of Fame at ringside, watching, and Leilani whispering under her breath in the ring how much she wanted to go punch Moolah.

My next big opponent was going to be Aja Kong, whom I'd had so many compelling fights with — some real — in Japan. To start it all off, there was an eight-woman elimination tag match at the 1995 *Survivor Series*, where I teamed with Kyoko Inoue, Sakie Hasegawa, and Chaparita Asari against Bertha Faye, Aja Kong, Tomoko Watanabe, and Lioness Asuka. In the end, Aja and I were the two left, and she pinned me. We matched up on *Monday Night Raw*, in a tag-team bout, and she won another match the following week. We were headed for a showdown.

It never happened.

I loved my job and time in WWF, that's why I was so taken aback when I got released. I was told that the women's division was, once again, being discontinued. Sunny, soon to be one of the most popular WWE managers ever, had just started, and I had met another future star backstage, Joanie Laurer, the future Chyna. So they weren't eliminating women — just those who could really wrestle.

The idea was, "We get rid of the women, and we'll focus on what we need." It woke me up, and I knew I was replaceable at any minute, on any given day; it doesn't matter how loyal you are.

Officially, I was told by registered letter on September 14, 1995, that my contract would not be renewed. My contract expired December 13, 1995, and five days later, I debuted on WCW *Monday Nitro*, tossing the WWF Women's title in the trash on live national television.

Out of the blue, WWE tried to get me back. In September 1998, I was approached about returning when my WCW deal expired in December, and then sent a contract to look over. I was happily running Spookee Custom Cycles, our motorcycle shop, with my then-husband, so I thought long and hard about it. (More about Spookee's and *that* husband later.)

I sensed some weird vibe coming from the people at WWE. Though they never outright said it, I figured I would be asked to put over their golden child, Sable, who was being pushed to the moon. After losing to Sable, then what? Chyna? Any legacy I'd established would be gone. Revenge for tossing the title in the trash was likely on the agenda. Luna got that spot. Lucky her.

My lawyer and I found all kinds of things we didn't like, reason enough for both parties to walk away from the deal. More than tossing the belt in the trash, I think not coming back into the fold in 1998 was what distanced Vince McMahon from me for 17 years.

10.

MENTORS, MARRIAGES, AND MISTAKES

"FIGHT OR FLIGHT" IS A phrase I use too often, both as an explanation and an excuse. It comes from my troubled childhood, where it was easier to avoid my mom or dad, and then as I became capable, I battled back.

The same thing has carried through in my relationships. I'm very intuitive, and it's always been my money maker. When I start to feel something is wrong — even a little thing — it's like my mind and body are calculating exit strategies. I always had one foot out the door.

Of course, relationships are hard for anyone. I've been drifting back, thinking about the men in my life, the marriages, the mistakes,

"Oops! . . . I Did It Again" . . . Britney Spears could have been writing about me.

the affairs, the friends I made along the way. The pattern is there. I was attractive and approachable, not an intimidating knockout by any means. Men could see that I was strong, independent, fearless, and didn't give a shit — and that was attractive to many men, at the start at least. I was also loving and giving — probably too much. So many of the guys I dated tried to change me, to tone down what made me *me*, and then it was them controlling me. Fight or flight, and usually I got the fuck out of there.

Right from the start, older men gravitated towards me. I didn't seek them out. They were sexy, knowledgeable, and, though I didn't realize it at the time, they served as mentors, helping me learn about myself and how the real world and the business world worked.

There's no need to name everyone — that would be another whole book — but considering that I'd find myself pursued by successful businessmen, some who would make the *Forbes* list of the richest people in the world, or their heirs, it should not be a surprise that I used them as a chance to learn; it wasn't about their bank account. I'd watch their drive (or how they squandered their gifts), how they operated, how they talked to people, and even little things that I certainly never learned from my parents, like how to tip in a restaurant or use the valet parking.

To this day, I set the table at dinners that I am hosting the same way that I saw at a $2,000-a-plate fundraiser that I went to in Los Angeles — you know, the many forks, the wine and water glasses, and all that jazz. It was an amazing experience, my first red-carpet event. I rubbed shoulders with top celebrities, and one well-known actress eyed me up and down, wondering who this woman was with one of Hollywood's top executives in L.A. Also, Melissa Etheridge sang at the event.

From Steve Schussler, I learned to love birds. It'll make sense when you learn who he is!

We met at JukeBox Saturday Night, a bar that he ran complete with half a pink Cadillac coming out of the wall, and I turned from the guy

I was dating into his arms almost immediately. Steve and I are friends to this day. When we were dating, he had parrots everywhere in his Minneapolis house and dogs. I had my two cats, and then I ended up living with Steve, when I was just starting wrestling. Talk about a zoo!

That menagerie was the start of the idea that would become the Rainforest Cafes; he later sank tons of dough into a prototype of the restaurant in his own home to secure investors. When we were together, collectively, our net worth hardly covered the mortgage, but we each had our dreams — yet the dreams weren't compatible. From afar, I watched him grow into this huge, successful person. People were like, "Oh, you're dumb. You should have stuck with him." Why? Because he's got money, because he's successful? That's not why you stick with someone. I chose my career, and we grew apart.

Well, there was another complication. I went to a Seder dinner with his friends and family, and he was scared shitless to bring me. He actually said, "You know, we probably can't marry because you have a tattoo."

Why weren't men always honest? At a future fiancé's house, he didn't tell me he lived with his parents, and the next morning, his mom was banging on the door, asking why it was locked. He went downstairs and told them about me. Then I went down, and she offered me orange juice. Awkward. Yet she and I remained pals intermittently for years after I broke it off with her son.

Shame on the men who approached me who were married. I beat myself up so many times, thinking it was my fault, because I allowed it to happen and should have known better. But, I trusted them. Isn't that what you do? Oh, silly me, Debrah. Yes, that's what you do. You trust what they say.

As with fight or flight, I built up a trust wall, becoming more guarded. That's a tough balance when your natural state of being is fearless.

Like many women, there were plenty of mistakes. The first real "man" I dated had a Corvette, wore a huge diamond pinky ring, and loved to buy me stuff. It was too good to be true, as he was not only into drugs, but he also hid his S&M fetish from me — a weird thing to stumble across. The gifts he showered on me were put on the company credit card, which he had taken away; I returned everything and never heard from him again.

But that was child's play compared to my first marriage. I had just broken off my first really serious relationship, where we were planning to get married and have children.

I met his guy on the rebound, while I was the aerobics queen from hell. I was teaching aerobics, doing Pilates way back in the '80s, and kickboxing. I had the tightest ass, the nicest fucking body, and I could wear a damn swimsuit without anything jiggling, everything was so tight. We met through a friend, and it went fast — and not just from all the cocaine that was around at the time — as I moved to Chicago to be with him. Then it was off to Hawaii for a wedding, on Kauai Island.

We got back to Chicago, had a celebratory party, and right after, he shared a new detail of his life — he was a fucking gigolo. I freaked and left, moving in with a girl I didn't know to get away. Our communication ended, and I had to put an announcement in the newspaper declaring the marriage over and annulled. I moved back to Minneapolis.

Broken trust came up again in 1990. To deal with my finances while in Japan, I hired a management team in Minneapolis on the recommendation of a friend. There was my poster in stores and a few other irons in the fire that needed tending. My pay from Japan, $5,000 a month, was automatically wired to an account, and they were to handle my bills. I always kept a little money for myself ($1,500) to use in Japan.

But then, all of a sudden, they were flying themselves to Japan, and they were doing other business on my fucking dollar. When I questioned what they were doing, they claimed they were looking into *my* money mismanagement.

When I finally got through to my accountant, he just said there was no money in my account. I lost everything I had, they had taken it. And you know what's really tough? Trying to sue someone in the United States when you're in Japan! It never went to court, I was stuck with a lawyer bill close to $30,000, and I still owed the IRS $70,000. When I was hired by WWF, Vince McMahon gave me an advance to take care of the debt.

God, the shit I went through was heavy duty and horrible. Then a couple of people I knew still went into business with these con artists after knowing all I went through.

And all I wanted to do is wrestle and have a decent life.

Joel Goodhart was a successful independent promoter based in Philadelphia, Pennsylvania, and he had a reputation of putting on some of the greatest wrestling cards outside of the big companies; it was the precursor to what would become ECW years later. For a show on September 21, 1991, he booked me to team with Eddie Gilbert against a young, rising star named Cactus Jack (WWE fans know him as Mick Foley, or Mankind, or Dude Love) and Luna Vachon.

Gilbert was a second-generation wrestler from Tennessee, but he took the wrestling smarts he inherited from his dad, Tommy, and mixed them with the savvy of his mother, Peggy, who was a politician. Many would say that Eddie Gilbert had one of the greatest minds in the history of pro wrestling. He was an amazing matchmaker, creative and able to bring out the best in talent.

The mixed tag match was the first time we'd really spent any time together. By the end of the bout, we were two rocks rolling down a hill, momentarily in sync.

It was so quick — we got together, we hung, we traveled, we got a place in Kennesaw, Georgia, got married real quick by the justice of the peace in Marietta. I wanted domestic bliss, and instead my nursing background came in handy.

Eddie was so into pills it was disgusting. I'd make dinner, and he'd fall asleep, his face falling into the food. He threw up all over himself when

I was taking him to the chiropractor. When I went to change the sheets one time, he had hundreds of pills in between the box spring and the mattress. He'd had so many injuries in pro wrestling and wasn't a big guy, only about five foot ten, but didn't want to give up the in-ring work.

I knew there was a problem, and I asked him to get help. Eddie was wildly unpredictable at this point. He went off one time and just started throwing wire baskets at me. I reached my breaking point: "I'm fucking out of here. You need to clean up, bro. This is bullshit. I am not putting up with your crap." My wrestling successes were a constant reminder to Eddie that his career in the big leagues had seemingly come to an end, and he felt less of a man with his wife in the spotlight. That was his dream, something he had worked his ass off for, and I just fell into my success.

When I told Missy Hyatt — who had been married to him before me — about the breakup in the locker room at Center Stage in Atlanta, she was supportive and took me out for dinner at Houston's Restaurant. We closed that place down, just sharing stories. In recent years, we have become close, calling each other "Sister Wife" for our common experiences with Eddie.

Eddie and I separated, I found my own place, and carried on with my wrestling career. The divorce didn't fully go through until August 1992.

His family didn't see an issue; they sided with him. They also wished he'd stayed with Missy, whom they saw as a beautiful, bright-eyed angel who could never do any wrong.

Eddie was a mess. He showed up unannounced at my place a few times. He asked if I could pay his credit card bills. I said, "Eddie, I'll help you, but I'm not going to pay all your bills. You've got to move on and get help."

I never saw him again.

Eddie died of a heart attack on February 18, 1995, in Puerto Rico. He was only 33. It was Missy who called to tell me. I had one of those big-ass car phones and I was on the road somewhere in Tennessee, getting off a cloverleaf when I heard the news.

There really isn't a word that properly describes how I felt. It was a combination of sadness and not being surprised. I didn't go to the funeral.

Between pro wrestling and monster trucks, I was on the road for almost 40 years. It was inevitable that relationships with colleagues developed. Some of mine were public knowledge, others were not. I've struggled with what to reveal, but in the end, came to accept that if the relationship was known about in the dressing rooms, then it's out in some capacity prior to this. In my professions, you couldn't hide everything — or anything, really.

What you could protect, especially in the pre-internet days, was your *real* life. You'd start getting to know someone, and then they'd break the news that they were heading home to the wife. We were just their piece of ass that they got to use and abuse on the road.

The men no doubt traded their stories. Fuckers. And there's the double standard that has always existed, where a man gets to celebrate his conquests, and the woman is labeled a "slut." Well, I didn't do drugs and only drank sociably, so my ideal evening would be hanging out in the hotel room with someone I cared about, watching an overpriced pay-per-view movie.

I'm sure I was the laughing stock of the fucking dressing room in another way, too, because when I dated a guy, I'd buy him things. It wasn't buying love, I just liked to get people presents, a custom that I picked up in Japan and ran with my whole life.

I should have run far away when another wrestler I dated would use a razor blade to cut my screen door and leave me messages to be careful. What kind of mindfuck was that? But it was a heavy relationship.

Or at least I thought it was.

I heard he was screwing every stripper he could, among others. Yet the woman he had his sights ultimately set on was rich, so he eventually chose her. He was fucking around with me, telling me one thing, and I didn't know about this other life until much later. I missed clues, like when he and a buddy would drive off and say, "See you in a couple of days." I figured they were heading home to Florida to visit friends.

Overall, it's an example of how women are used and abused again and just lied to, not just by their supposed love, but also all the boys in the dressing room who kept their mouths shut, protecting their asshat of a friend.

The Tortoise and the Hare. It's got to be the best nickname ever laid upon a wrestling couple.

Greg "The Hammer" Valentine was slow, methodical, and deliberate both in the ring and outside of it. I was the jackrabbit. People were like, "What the fuck's this hookup?" But we didn't care. It was fun.

We met in WCW, watching matches through the curtain. All we did was talk for the longest time. He was involved with someone, and I wasn't really looking. But we ended up together in 1992, since he told me he'd broken it off with his girlfriend. I gave up my place in Atlanta to move into his house in Florida, which had been in shambles. You could have done a renovation show from all that I did to spruce it up — redoing the kitchen, master bedroom, a bathroom.

Or it could have been a reality show. Since we were on the road so much — he was an independent, and when I left WCW, I joined him, touring around the world — I often had friends crash at our place. One friend managed to wreck Greg's Corvette. In a big open parking lot. She blamed a stuck gas pedal, but how does that result in you damaging eight other cars? When this "friend" told me what happened, Greg overheard the phone call and went ballistic; instead of watching all the pets in the house (a dog, two cats, and a parrot), as we had asked her to do, she fled back home.

It's not a secret that Greg liked his pot, but my parrot, a green-winged macaw named Parador, didn't. I don't know if Greg sat there and got high around the bird and blew smoke in its face, but the bird did not like him. Parador would be in this huge cage, and we'd leave the door open, and he'd walk across the room, but not a lot farther. His vocabulary grew from "What?" to "Mooommmmmy, mooommmmy, oh moooommmmmy."

One time, I was on the road, and the bird came over and climbed onto Greg's wrist and did a little dance, looking at him, going, "Ha, ha, ha, ha." All of a sudden, the bird clamped down on his nipple and would not let go. After that, Greg would not go near Parador.

People were telling me that Greg also had lots of girlfriends on the side. One was so jealous of me dating him that she sent me a FedEx letter telling me that she was dating Greg and she had AIDS. My jaw absolutely dropped. It wasn't true, but the cheating was.

Out of that, Greg and I had our difficulties, and it just went downhill, withering away.

He and I got into it at one point, and he choked me into the couch. We'd been fighting about other women and his ex, and it just got out of control. I thought I was a goner. I think I kneed him as hard as I could and left. Out of spite, I left a note behind on the headboard to fuck with the next person. I'm not proud of that, but I was not in the right headspace. This is the first time I've ever told that story.

The horrible ending of our run is tempered by the fact that it was Greg who called Pat Patterson and the WWF and told them they should take a look at me.

After Greg and I went our separate ways, I bought a house on a golf course in Florida. The house totally rocked, with walls that rolled open to make for a bigger open space in the living room, right to the pool. I could just get out of bed, the walls would open up, and I'd roll into the pool in the morning. I was sleeping naked back then. I never really paid too much attention to how close that damn golf course was, and so they always got an eyeful. Hole number nine was particularly busy in the morning.

The golfers paid the price at the ninth hole, too. One of Parador's words was "fore" and he would scream it unexpectedly, startling the golfers. Parador seemed to get the joke, did his little laugh, and would go, "Fucking bird."

My most significant relationship in wrestling, though, was under the table, during my time in WWF. He was a powerful man then, and is still well connected. From the moment he learned about the possibility of a book, he has threatened to sue, so I will . . . tap dance a bit here.

What I didn't know was that he was married, and when I did learn that, he made all the usual promises about loving me and wanting to stay with me, and that he was waiting for divorce papers to be signed. I believed him, because when you go into a relationship, you trust what the person is saying. He'd be gone from home weeks and weeks at a time, with me, and would never call his wife, so I thought it was legit. I didn't know he was living a double life.

Our run was a good length, and it was mostly kept secret, or at least protected within the business. You won't find stories about our relationship on the internet, but he has bad-mouthed me plenty in interviews.

One day he just came into the dressing room, and Bull Nakano and Luna were sitting there, and he wanted to talk, pulling up a chair. He told me, "I'm gonna stay with my wife." I replied, "I thought you were getting divorced?" He said, "No, we're gonna make it work. Vince called me into his office, and he believes that I need to bring my wife into the fold, to concentrate on making our marriage work. Having you around is going to jeopardize the situation."

I fucking cold cocked him right in the dressing room, and he fell backward off his chair. Bull and Luna saw it.

To my eternal shame, that wasn't even the end of the affair. We spent a weekend together in the Poconos — I thought we were rekindling our relationship or something. I was heading off from WWF to fix a broken boob.

He goes, "Well, that was good. I got $10,000 there for your breast surgery."

I said, "What are you talking about?"

"Well, hey, you gave me a blow job. There's $10,000."

I said, "What? Are you fucking kidding me?"

He said, "No, I took an advance to get the money for you."

While I was recuperating at a friend's place in Minneapolis from the dual breast and nose jobs, he came and stayed over a few days — then went back to his wife.

Not long after, the WWF shut down its women's division — the few of us who were there. This guy and his friends had a lot of stroke backstage and had the ear of WWE owner Vince McMahon — and anyone can see that one and one equals two in this equation. I was gone to protect his spot on the card.

Maybe I'll pause here — give him the space to call me a liar. He's the master of bullshit. He knows it's true. He's called me in the past to threaten a lawsuit if I ever said anything. Who's the one living in fear? He is. Realistically, I don't have the resources to fight a frivolous lawsuit, but he does and would no doubt celebrate bankrupting me and once again causing chaos in my life.

I was told the WWF was going in a new direction, no more women's division, and shortly thereafter I got a courier package saying I was done. The true backstage reason was never mentioned, until now.

It might be hard to understand how fucked up wrestling is behind the scenes. The goal is to kiss the ass of the right people — the owner, promoter, matchmaker, scriptwriter — and convince them that you are a worthy investment. Back then, there was no social media where you could publicly lobby for attention, making your own YouTube show or gathering a Twitter army. Now, it gets complicated even further given how misogynistic wrestling was — and still is. Women have it better than they did, no question, but you can't ever tell me they are on equal footing with the men. It's Harvey Weinstein-ish, the men in wrestling manipulate the women and they laugh about it in the dressing room. Then the women are evil to one another: "Who did you suck off to get that spot on the card?" It's not like you can complain to human resources, since wrestlers are independent contractors.

The #MeToo and #SpeakingOut movements are important and have forced change; however, some people have selfishly taken advantage of the situation and ruined people's lives.

There's so much deep shit, but I choose not to tell all because it's none of your business. But I'm not here to protect anybody anymore. I'm here to just tell my story and the shit I had to go through, hoping to improve circumstances for those in the future. Like, don't date a married man.

There's guilt on my end, too. At various times, this guy and his buddies have said that I was "one of the boys" since I never spilled the tea. What the fuck was I thinking? Oh right, I needed that paycheck.

The story doesn't end there. We both ended up in WCW, and he gained the right ears to pitch storylines. Talk about uncomfortable.

One time, we sat and chatted at the bar in Atlanta's Omni Theater. He told me that he still cared about me. Addressing our past, he said he made an internal decision to stick with whomever he got pregnant first — me or his wife. She "won."

The memory of that conversation is colored by my anger. I know I told him that I didn't want his damn ass, and if I didn't tell him at the time, he'll now know: I was pregnant with his child and miscarried.

Months later, WCW sponsored a race car in NASCAR, and he and I were at a race. He revealed that he and his wife had had a child and named the child the name I had expressed to him that I wanted for my child one day.

So many lessons learned, but they all shaped who I am today. No question I was an idiot with blinders on, and I often floated these guys money, while whatever they were actually earning went back to their wives and girlfriends. I took my relationships that I had seriously, and, of course, you want them to work out. It's really tough being career-driven and successful, and being there all the time for your partner. Plus my spouse needed to be able to accept that I was famous and the object of fascination (and desire) for so many others. I dealt with heartache by jumping further into work, and then, soon enough, another relationship.

11.

TRASH AND TRASHY

WHO'D HAVE THOUGHT throwing a championship belt in the trash would cause such a fuss? Fans often ask about my grand gesture, denouncing the Alundra Blayze name and the WWF Women's title, on *Monday Nitro* on December 18, 1995. It's one of the most talked about moments early in the so-called *Monday Night War*, where WWF and WCW fought for ratings supremacy on cable TV.

PHOTO COURTESY WWE

Dropping the WWF Women's title into the trash live on WCW's Monday Nitro *to the surprise of Steve McMichael, Eric Bischoff, and Bobby Heenan.*

It came about remarkably fast. The man who was running WCW was Eric Bischoff, who was an old colleague from our days in the AWA, where I was starting out as a wrestler, and he was learning to be an announcer. Bischoff was there in my first go-round in WCW as an on-air personality, and, while I had been traveling the world and competing in WWF, he had worked his way into power.

To this day, he will argue until he's blue in the face that I called him about a job in WCW. But no lie, I was sitting on the toilet taking a dump when he called me. I needed work, so it was like a prayer had been answered.

Bischoff asked, "Do you still have the title?"

"Yeah, but it isn't mine. It's WWF's. Why?"

"Bring it. We'll do something."

"Okay, but I gotta have it back."

"I absolutely will give it back."

I showed up at *Nitro* at the Augusta-Richmond County Civic Center in Augusta, Georgia.

He told me to come up on stage with the title and look for a garbage can. I could cut a promo and do whatever I wanted. I let loose: "I am Madusa, I always have been Madusa, and always will be Madusa. This is the WWF Women's championship belt" — then I picked up the trash can and dropped in the belt. "And that's what I think of the WWF Women's championship belt. This is the WCW, I am now in the WCW, and they used to call me Alundra Blayze, but not anymore. Because this is where the big boys play, and now, this is where the big girls play." Mic drop.

Leaving the stage, my belt was returned to me, and I was left to consider what I had done. I really thought that it had been a chance to put myself on the map, get some publicity, maybe even a magazine cover. Regardless, it was going to be a great kickstart to the WCW Women's division that Bischoff had promised to build around me.

Later, I heard that Vince McMahon had seen it and was beside himself.

Did you see the mention of the vaunted WCW Women's division? It never materialized. But there were some good moments.

My first feud was with an old foe. Sherri Martel was set to marry Col. Robert Parker in some silly storyline, and I waltzed into the midst of it and broke up the wedding. Sherri pinning me was the first-ever women's match on WCW *Monday Nitro*. Another old foe, Bull Nakano, was brought in and then only used a couple of times before she returned to Japan.

The next batch from Japan, younger women from the GAEA promotion, stuck around a little longer. WCW had never had its own Women's title, recognizing the NWA Women's title for a while, and, briefly, the LPWA Women's belt. In November 1996, a tournament was held to crown a new champion, with eight spots, but seven women, as Akira Hokuto wrestled twice, once in her Reina Jabuki gimmick. In the end, it was Akira and me in the final at Starrcade, WCW's big annual show. It would be my moment, right? Nope. Hokuto won the title, and I never became WCW Women's champ. The woman they were going to build the division around. Remember that line Vince Russo said earlier about it being a boys' club in WWF? That applied double to WCW. They didn't have a fucking plan for me. Someone didn't like me, but I don't know who it was.

Luna Vachon was back for a bit, and I fought Hokuto often, and then I *lost* a retirement match to Hokuto in June 1997. The truth is that there was some personal stuff going on, and I needed to go away for a bit. I'd only signed a two-year contract, and the deal came up in December 1997.

"Macho Man" Randy Savage was one of the biggest stars in WWF history, and we were pals when we were at the WWF the same time. He really looked out for Heidi Lee Morgan, and, since she was so tiny, considered her his daughter. We had plenty of laughs over that.

Savage had been in WCW a year longer than me and still had plenty of star power. Off TV following knee surgery, he returned in April 1999, and it was the start of Team Madness, and I'd be swept up in it within a couple of weeks. It was a new Macho Man, his hair longer, in a ponytail, new clothes, and with plenty of arm candy — it's not out of line to say that he was portraying a pimp. First up was Stephanie Bellars, who was known as Gorgeous George; she was also dating Savage. Miss Madness / Mona was Nora Greenwood, who'd later gain fame in WWE as Molly Holly. Then there was me.

I drank the Kool-Aid and started wearing different outfits than what I wanted. It was evident where WCW was going, ramping up the sexiness, and I had to adapt or die. Stephanie directed me to Ruby, the woman who made her clothes and outfits for high-end strippers — her former profession. It went the other way, too, as I sent Stephanie to Sonia Peterson, at the Hair Police salon, up in Minneapolis, where I'd gotten my extensions done for years.

My time alongside "Mach" on WCW TV was only a couple of months, but away from the ring, we had some fun. Yes — he saw me as one of the boys.

One time, Mach and I were in a limo on our way to a personal appearance for WCW, and he had it stop at Tampa's famed Venus Flytrap, an all-nude strip joint. Mach asked me, "Do you mind if I get a dancer and have her dance on you, and I watch?" What could I do but laugh? "Okay, Mach, if that's what you want. Sure." This stripper starts doing her thing on top of me, and he was watching, just salivating. I went, "Are we done with this shit show? Can we go? We have a personal appearance to get to." He replied, "Just testing you, Deuce. Oooh yeaah!" I just shook my head at my friend, the weird, kinky fucker. When he finally got away from the wrestling business, and all its temptations, Randy rekindled an old relationship with a woman named Lynn and found comfort and peace in life. Want proof? He let his hair go gray! It hurt to hear that he had died in May 2011.

This is a good place to talk about Elizabeth Hulette, Mach's ex-wife, who also was a WWE superstar, accompanying him to the ring. She'd been brought into WCW, too —the company threw money around, bringing in all the ex-WWE people it could, often paying them just to stay at home. Liz, Janie Engle from management, and I became like the Three Musketeers, always hanging out, and we became really close.

It could be as simple as Liz and I curling our hair in our room and laughing, or, in the evening, having a drink from the mini-bar since we didn't want to face the bar scene. Debra McMichael was a part of our unit, too, but she'd often be out with her then-husband Steve "Mongo" McMichael.

Liz was that sweet girl you saw on TV. That was her. But she kept to herself. With her pals, she was a giver, and I still have this beautiful little beaded purse she bought for me out of the blue.

Liz, Janie, and I relied on one another. We were there for her when she converted to Judaism to marry Cary and then we heard from her how rough things were and encouraged her to get out — and she showed up on Janie's doorstep for protection. Then Liz started a relationship with Lex Luger, and we absolutely were against it. People know about their pill use, but there was violence, too. On May 1, 2003, Luger called 911 to report that Liz wasn't breathing. She died from acute toxicity — too many pills.

Janie broke the news to me. I didn't believe her. "What the hell are you talking about?" And I started looking on the news and there it was . . . one of my best friends had so many pills stuffed into her that she died.

Another WCW friend met a horrible death.

Nancy Toffoloni had been around the wrestling business for years, starting out as a valet in Florida. She was married to Kevin Sullivan, and Kevin had a lot of pull in the office, sitting on the booking committee in WCW. One storyline he pushed resulted in his divorce from Nancy, as she was paired with Chris Benoit on-screen, and they fell in love.

Chris was very quiet and nice to me. Very soft-spoken. Brilliant mind. Great wrestler. I was more pals with Nancy, and we had some laughs backstage. They seemed like a nice couple, and she often spoke about how she loved him.

In 1999, Chris left WCW, went to Japan, and then went to WWE, and we all sort of fell out of touch. It was a shock to everyone in the industry when we learned that Chris killed Nancy, their 10-year-old,

Daniel, and then himself in June 2007. In a marriage, we never know what goes on behind closed doors.

The double-murder suicide turned a harsh spotlight onto the wrestling industry, and the use of both steroids and painkillers, and the many concussions suffered by wrestlers. Wrestling had to clean up its act, and it did, to a certain degree, with wellness programs and banning headshots with chairs and other stupidity. But wrestling still has a long way to go.

In the category of "If you can't beat 'em, join 'em," I took a couple of months off for the boob job and came back way bigger in October 1999. What a mistake, both the comically big boobs and returning. The storylines were going into the shitter, and it is embarrassing to look back on now.

At one point, when I had the red, white, and blue hair, and outfit to match, "Diamond" Dallas Page pulled me aside and said, "Deuce, you look like a clown." I told him to fuck off, but he had a point. I wasn't a wrestler but a showpiece, albeit an original one, with my colored hair extensions and clothes to match. Now, no one blinks twice when someone has colored hair.

Whether it was an Evening Gown Match with Mona (who was way better than this shit), where I ended up in my shorts and sports bra, or shilling WCW cologne in a bikini, I wasn't happy. But the worst times were when Vince Russo's buddy, Ed Ferrara, was portraying "Oklahoma," a direct shot at WWE lead announcer Jim Ross. Ferrara, one of the scriptwriters, was in no way a wrestler, but I had to get in there for "matches" where I'd end up with barbecue sauce poured all over me.

Oklahoma actually challenged me for my WCW Cruiserweight title belt — yes, I had won a men's title. They had me aligned with a young up-and-comer named Evan Karagias, and we played up the romance on TV. It was a big break for him to get so much screen time, and post-wrestling he went into acting, so it was good advice when I told him to think of our fondling, kissing, and other silliness to be exactly that: acting. First I was his manager, and then I dumped him and beat him for the Cruiserweight championship, and I had Nitro Girl Spice as my manager for about a month.

If it sounds convoluted and stupid, it was. It was also a slap in my face. I had spoken my mind again and again to the writers, and I was punished. They also knew that I was a married woman, and my then-husband, Ken Blackman, was a 320-pound, six-foot-six fucking linebacker who could beat up most of the WCW roster. Ken and I did talk about what they wanted me to do, and he just shrugged; nothing ever seemed to bother him. It was a real laugh coming home one day and finding him goofing around with my belt — like he was a cruiserweight!

Evan had been a part of a group called Three Count, with Shane Helms and Shannon Moore, and they were all exceedingly talented, but smaller. Those guys tried so hard. They were lit. But the other dudes on the booking committee would all sit there and laugh at them. It wasn't just Three Count, either. There was a massive pecking order in WCW: the powers that be thought their shit didn't stink and that everyone else didn't deserve a chance. The top dogs had these massive contracts where they hardly had to work, and all kinds of young, hungry talent filled out the TV time.

They did not think much of women, either. The Nitro Girls were a dance team that was brought in to add some sexiness to the show, which is great, but they got more screen time than women's wrestling did; for the most part, I liked them but I was like, "Hey, I'm right here! Use me!"

WWF was tons more professional. In WCW, it just seemed like a damn cat house filled with beautiful women with big fake tits. And I was one of them.

Behind the scenes, I fought, I complained, I lobbied. They just didn't know what to do with me. I think the mindset became, *Let's slowly push her out and see if she quits*.

Since they had nothing to do with me, I was assigned the role of trainer at WCW's Power Plant facility. I was employed. I was getting a paycheck. I'd had it with them and knew I was on my way out, eventually. Other trainers included "Sarge" DeWayne Bruce, Paul Orndorff, Jody Hamilton, and Bill DeMott, and they mostly had me working with the young women.

While I did my best with newcomers Torrie Wilson, Stacy Keibler, and a few others, it was tough. They had been models and were hired to wrestle without qualifications — and were being paid three times what I was, on a trail that I blazed. So much for paying dues.

In the non-nonsensical booking that WCW excelled at, we built a match between Torrie Wilson and Shane Douglas against Billy Kidman and myself. On a scaffold, 20 feet in the air. Torrie was *not* ready. I remember thinking, *This poor girl is scared of her own shadow, but she's trying hard. But why a scaffold?* Ellis Edwards was WCW's stunt coordinator and worked with us. Ellis and I practiced the fall into brown cardboard boxes, leaping off the scaffold into them to ease any fears.

The match was billed as a Pittsburgh Plunge Scaffold Match at the *Fall Brawl* pay-per-view, and the goal was to climb down the ladders on either side to win. It was strange, because the scaffold was designed to rise, so we sorta stood there idle as it lifted us. There's not a lot you can do on a scaffold, and we certainly could feel it shaking whenever someone was slammed. I took the plunge first, and I was about a quarter of the way down the ladder when Shane kicked me, and I fell back first onto the padding. Billy got a nut-shot from Torrie (at the time his real-life girlfriend), and then Shane threw him from the actual scaffold down — the bump looked great, probably 10 feet higher than mine, but, really, what was the purpose?

I didn't even get paid a bonus for it, when all these fuckers are making millions. I was pissed off about it. Hell, I was so over wrestling at that time. I gritted my teeth, *This is what you're gonna push? Fine, fuck you.* I was a team player, though. You always wanted to take care of the other person, make sure they were safe.

One cool thing that happened was when the A&E show *Behind Closed Doors with Joan Lunden* came by to shoot at the Power Plant. In the segment, I'm interviewed, and I show the ropes to some of our trainees — and to Joan herself! Not long after, she was in the ring on an episode of *WCW Thunder* in Wilkes-Barre, Pennsylvania, talking with announcer Mean Gene Okerlund, and I came down to interrupt. "Wait one minute, Joanie Lunden. Journalists like you give pro wrestling a bad name."

"That's not true."

"You know, I love what I do. You know what? This is serious business. This is *WCW Thunder* live. You need to get out."

Then Joan tossed me — just like I'd taught her.

More than 15 years later, I ran into her at *WrestleMania*, and Stephanie McMahon was with her. Joan recognized me, and she yelled, "Madusa, oh my God!" and ran over for a hug. We exchanged pleasantries, and then Steph grabbed her, "We need to go." I was disappointed Joan was rushed away. It doesn't change the way I feel about Joan. She's amazing, because she's been through so much, and she's a great role model for women, for strength, perseverance, and overcoming adversities.

WCW was always trying to make it into mainstream culture, as WWE had through the years. Given its backing of its owner, Time Warner, this should have been a cinch, but it wasn't — in part because of things like the December 1999 episode of *Politically Incorrect*, hosted by Bill Maher on ABC. On that show, the guests were me, Roddy Piper, Bobby Heenan, and a rare, out-of-gimmick, Sting. No idea how I was a part of the panel, but I held my own — but nothing in nature could stand in the way of Roddy when he was raging. Maher's questions were mocking, Piper took offense, and he lashed into Maher to protect the business he loved. In the first commercial, Maher heard it from us. He tried to calm the situation, "Guys, I'm just asking questions. And I'm not here to put your profession down." Realizing he couldn't get out of the hole he'd dug, he ignored us in the subsequent breaks, his nose in his notes or asking someone to fix his hair. I admire his work ethic and have grown to love what he does today.

The corporate structure of WCW never made a lot of sense to me. You had Eric Bischoff being able to hire his buddies on huge contracts for the longest time, and he had higher-ups, but they never tried to rein in the spending — or the boorish behavior, which should never have flown when the company was publicly traded and a part of one of the biggest media companies in the world. Harvey Schiller was Eric's direct boss as president of Turner Sports, and he was as guilty as the rest. Schiller sent me a bunch of fucking flowers, trying to woo me — and I was married. He invited me upstairs to his office, and we had a conversation about how my career could go, him implying how I could go further. That is exactly how I took it because that is how it was implied. Why in the fuck would Harvey Schiller be asking me to come to his office in the Turner broadcast studios?

"Come sit here near me."

"I'm quite comfortable where I'm at. I don't understand this meeting. We're talking about my career, right? I'd like more wrestling."

He wanted a different kind of wrestling. *Ugh*. I hightailed it out of there, with a trail of choice words. I'm guessing I wasn't the only woman there he tried that creepiness with.

Being transparent, I was paid peanuts in comparison to others. On my first two-year contract in WCW, I made $75,000 per year. Now, remember that we paid many of our own road expenses, so take out taxes and the cost of being out there for hotels and restaurants, and it wasn't much. WCW would fly you to a starting point, and then back home from an endpoint, and everything else was your responsibility. My second two-year deal doubled my salary, and I negotiated that my hotel and rental car would be paid for.

Not only did I have to see all these others get better contracts than me, but also many of them started getting these damn Lloyd's of London insurance policies, a result of a loophole somewhere in their contracts, and they'd "get hurt" and take a settlement of millions — and they were still getting paid under their WCW contract! What did they do with all the money? Fuck, I just wanted a damn decent paycheck.

Now, the contracts made it tougher to get rid of people. Someone sure tried with me, but I have never figured out exactly who set me up.

Imagine getting a letter like this sent to the house:

July 19, 1999

This letter is to notify you that WCW's Medical Advisor has reported a positive test result from your recent urine sample. This test result evidences the existence of banned substances in your system. Pursuant to the WCW Substance Abuse Policy, you are hereby instructed to attend and cooperate in clinical evaluation and rehabilitation counseling with Dr. Robin Armenia-Cope (404-768-3351). You will need to contact Dr. Cope within seven (7) days of receipt of this letter to schedule an evaluation and retesting.

Dr. Cope's office is located as follows: 3580 Atlanta Avenue, Hapeville, GA 30354.

Please be reminded that pursuant to the Policy, a second positive test may subject you to suspension without pay until you complete further rehabilitation and counseling at your own expense, and that any return to WCW will be conditioned on continued negative testing thereafter.

Sincerely,
Diana L. Myers
Director of Legal and Business Affairs

Fuck, the guys used to ask *me* to pee for them, because they knew I was clean and they weren't. I didn't even take painkillers — and I didn't pee for them, in case you were wondering. I truly believe that someone had tried to get rid of me rather than pay the rest of my contract. When I got the letter, I stormed into the legal department's office, livid. "Y'all are fucking wrong. And I'll piss right now, and I'll prove I'm clean." They knew they were wrong and never fired me.

Yet you had these jacked-up freaks walking around in WCW who you knew were pumped up to dangerous levels with all kinds of chemicals. Why would they always have me take a piss test? Oh, right, I spoke my mind, and I was always the one they wanted to get rid of. I did not fit into their narrative, an outsider. I had to turn away when I saw them with "ring rats" and not say anything to their wives or kids. I didn't take drugs or steroids, showed up on time, and did my job. I liked to have fun, sure, who doesn't, but I valued my relationships. Not playing the victim, but the truth is the truth.

Some of this might seem repetitive, but I want to stress why I knew that I was done with pro wrestling.

Imagine being in a profession for years, the most respected woman wrestler in America, and being treated like an afterthought. The disrespect was both overt — no storylines or idiotic ones — and behind the scenes. I had my sources telling me what was being said about me. WCW was such a messed up place anyway, and we all sensed we were on a sinking ship. Everyone was only looking out for themselves.

There were countless times where I rejected an idea, like Bra and Panties matches, yet I was still involved in some pretty racy stuff. The new women coming in, often out of modeling or cheerleader squads, had no problem doing it, and were years younger than I was. So not only did I have to help train them at the Power Plant, but also then they were put on TV. Later, I learned how much more lucrative their contracts were than mine. As an example, one girl was making $5,000 a day, with limo service, without any wrestling experience.

I didn't like being bitter towards the other women, but it was hard not to be — it was not their fault. It was bullshit, the women coming in getting bigger contracts than a person who was supposed to be the center of the women's division.

It still boggles my mind that I was never the WCW Women's champion, but they gave me the damn Cruiserweight belt — fuck them, circle jerk motherfuckers who didn't know how to book women. I'm only as good as my writer, my opponent, my skills, and marketing.

I was destined for other things, though.

Michael Weber had been around wrestling since 1986, when he worked at WWF in public relations — he's the guy who had to circulate the fictional attendance number from *WrestleMania III* of 93,173, when it was closer to 70,000 — and had moved to WCW. He ended up in marketing at WCW in the glory days of the promotion and was a key player in so many of the mainstream deals that the company made. One of his ideas was to have WCW-sponsored monster trucks; he was so good at his job that the people at Monster Jam hired him away from WCW.

One guess who he called to drive a monster truck.

12.

A NEED FOR SPEED

IF DESTINY IS A THING, from the start, mine was to ride, to go fast. From my Harley-riding Granny to my championship days in monster trucks, it was meant to be. Wrestling may have been a little slower, but I had plenty of time on the road, going from town to town, to earn those speeding tickets.

Mike Miceli had a motorcycle, a 750 Honda, and he'd take me on long motorcycle rides up to the cabin on French Lake. It was a few hours' ride,

I'm in the jeans, third from the right, watching Elliott Sadler.

and I was pretty little, so he figured out a way to keep me on, for when I would inevitably fall asleep — he wrapped a bungee cord around me and attached it to the sissy bar at the rear of the bike so I wouldn't fall out.

His bike was one factor in my love of motorcycles, but nothing compares to Granny. She was the one with a Harley, while Grandpa didn't ride at all. They also had an airplane, and both could fly it. I remember her sitting down talking to me, "Someday, you're probably going to want a Harley or a motorcycle." "Yeah, Grandma, I want to be just like you." As a young adult, I took out her photos, and there was this awesome one of her, on the back of a camper, leaning back, laughing and smiling, with a fifth of whiskey.

When I was little, I don't remember ever riding with Granny, though — it was my Uncle Roger who took me out. He is married to Granny's sixth kid, my Aunt Arlene, who is only nine years older than I am, so she served as an older sister at times. On my first ride with him, I was scared to death and held on for dear life.

Then, when I was older, Uncle Roger let me drive *his* Harley, which was a long bike, with a sissy bar in the back. It was like I was born for it. We left the house, and I just cut the throttle real naturally. He knew what he was doing, challenging me from the start. Uncle Roger had me go down the road, and then had me take a left up a hill. There was a stop sign, and I had to stop for the first time. I was freaking out because there were cars behind me, and I started screaming, "No, I can't do it." And I kept killing the bike, and then had to start it, just learning to work the clutch and the brake at the same time. I kept rolling back, and he kept laughing behind me. That's how I learned.

I really learned to drive by watching Mike; he never truly taught me. With my Arby's money, I saved up enough for a Chevy K5 Blazer, three speed on the column, with a back that came off, like a convertible. Mike drove me to the dealership, signed whatever paperwork he needed to; I made the down payment and the monthly payments. "Are you sure you want this? It's a three-speed shift," he asked. "Yeah, I know how to do that." Following him on the drive back to Maple Lake, there was a lot of grinding of gears as I figured out what to do. When there's no one around, with big open roads, you're going to learn quickly. Like most things, I just jumped right in with both feet.

I loved that truck, and I drove it to about 300,000 miles, and then I sold it to my Aunt Arlene and Uncle Roger for $500, and they drove it till it died. In Minnesota everything gets rusty because of the salt they have to put down to deal with the ice, and I had plywood on the bottom as the floor rusted right through. Often, I'd drive it off road, too, through the woods and the muck, unknowingly prepping for my future career driving a monster truck.

I also associate Mike with snowmobiling. There were snowmobiles at Grandma Miceli's cabin. I was just an adrenaline junkie as a kid, and I'd hop on one by myself and just go, and they'd get all pissed off and run after me. I was so young and I was out there on this snowy field on the snowmobile.

When I was older, snowmobile poker was a thing. As you go bar to bar, you're given a playing card, and at the last stop, you play your hand. Again, a different time, and having a few drinks and operating a vehicle was fairly common. Later, we played the same game going place to place on our Harleys.

Minnesota in the winter is a wasteland, so you need to find things to do. I skated when I could and got pretty good at it, and broomball — essentially hockey while wearing boots and using a broom — was a fun way to bust your ass. We didn't do any skiing — cross-country was popular, as there aren't many big hills in the state.

Somehow, when I was 17, I learned about this "Ice Racing, Blindfold" competition. The driver's eyes were covered, and the passenger could see. My mom had numerous boyfriends or husbands through the years, not that I was close to any of them, but at the time, she was dating Steve, from Wisconsin, who was kind of fun and adventurous, and encouraged me to sign up.

The race was on a wide-open frozen lake, surrounded by side hills. As the driver, I got to see the course beforehand. Roughly a dozen trucks were there, and there were two heats. When it was my turn, and I heard the go signal, man, I hit that fucking gas, and Steve yelled, "Holy shit!" Then he gave me some directions. I told him to slow down, just tell me a little bit ahead of time. "I got this." And he was panicking. Since I'd gunned it, I was so far ahead of everyone else that I didn't crash into the other trucks and actually won the race.

As great as that Chevy Blazer was, it doesn't compare to the *real* love of my life, my 1992 Heritage Softail Harley, which I still have today.

I'd been to Japan, came home and married and divorced Eddie Gilbert, and needed something better in my life. Granny knew what I really needed. She took me down to the Twin City Harley dealership, asking me on the way how much I had to spend, which was about $1,500. As I was walking around the showroom, I spotted her — the custom paint job, magenta pink, already done.

"There it is, Grandma!"

"That? That's a big bike."

"I've got this."

Granny and I sat down to arrange for payment, for some extras, and adjustments, and to come back for pickup.

That was the part I hadn't thought through: I was living in Florida with Greg Valentine, and the bike was being modified in Minneapolis. Fortunately, a close friend at the time volunteered her and her brother to drive it down in their truck.

The bike came in the evening. I was so excited and happy, and wheeled it out of the truck. Now, remember that I hadn't been on a bike since my uncle took me out. The sun was going down, but I really wanted to ride, and I didn't want to look like an idiot, so I just acted like I knew what I was doing. I fiddled with this and that, got on the bike, and started trying to figure out the toe-heel click. I really didn't know what the hell I was doing. It started up, and I went, "Fuck, yeah!" I rode it around the corner, and thought, *Great, I've got a big block. I can rev it up. Whirggggg.* I missed all the gears. So embarrassing. I slowed down, coasted, got my bearings, went back to first, second, third, and drove around the block, came back, and told them everything's good.

Here we are 30 years later, and she's still a beauty, an old bike that rides hard, lacking all the bells and whistles of motorcycles today. Hell, I put on a windshield for the first time just a few years ago.

For Granny's 80th birthday, I rode from Florida to Minneapolis, and then we went cruising around town on our bikes. She rode until she turned 88. How awesome is that?

Now, one of the reasons that my Harley has lasted is that I co-owned Spookee's Custom Cycles in Homosassa, Florida. That was with my ex-husband, Ken Blackman, who loved Harleys, too.

I guess this is as good of a place as any to talk about that marriage, because we shared a common love of going fast, whether it was on our bikes, jet skis, dirt bikes, ATVs, horses, whatever it was.

On June 2, 1997, WCW held its *Monday Nitro* show in Dayton, Ohio. The post-show scene was in the bar at the Marriott hotel. I know Elizabeth was there, and the couple Steve "Mongo" McMichael, who'd played in the NFL, and his wife, Debra. We were off to the side, and a beer appeared in front of me. I looked across the room, and I saw this guy who was cute as hell. He looked at me and smiled. Debra, in her Southern voice, saw me check him out. "Oh, yeah. Oh, he's cute. He's big. Mongo, he's a football player, right? Oh, you need that. You need to hook up with that."

I grabbed my beer, Miss Cocky, and walked over to his table to say thanks. His back was to me, and his friend's eyes got really big. I said hi, and he turned around. "Hey, thanks for the beer." And he started laughing. I'm like, "You bought me a beer." "I didn't buy you no beer." I'm like, "Okay, hi." He looked at me, and went, "Oh, that's how you do it." I'm like, "What? No, my friend egged me on and said that you did buy me a beer." Flustered, I said goodbye and started to go back to my table. He grabbed my arm and said, "I didn't buy the beer, but, yeah, I'd like to talk to you."

We started talking and had a good time. Next thing I knew, Mongo, Debra, and Elizabeth were laughing. And, sure enough, I found out he was a football player, a six-foot-six, 320-pound linebacker for the Cincinnati Bengals. He had his Harley with him, and with me on the back, we hauled ass all over Dayton, Ohio. I barely got back in time for my flight.

From there, Ken Blackman and I were inseparable. We were 15 years apart in age, but it didn't matter. We had the world by the balls and seven months later, we were about to get married. His family was against it, and his mother had many ailments. When I could, between my wrestling gigs, I'd fly in to help the family take care of her, and then be off again.

We didn't want anybody at the wedding, and I found this really cool place in Jamaica. It was called the Ciboney. Our room came with a personal butler and a pool. For the wedding announcement, I put together a small little Ziploc, not even an inch tall, and I filled it up with white sand, glued it inside the card, where it said, *Wish you could be here, we know that you can't, throw this on the floor, sprinkle your toes in the sand, and wish us luck.*

It was still a time of physical phone answering machines, and a week later, after being away somewhere, we came home to about 100 messages. Tons of people said, "We're coming to the wedding!" They all wanted a vacation. So much for our plan. We had about 50 people come to the damn wedding on February 14, 1998, and it ended up being a lot of fun. Since the plan changed, I relented, and flew in Granny — Betty doesn't fly — and Aunt Arlene and Uncle Roger came in, too.

It was an insanely fun few days, with paddleboarding, jet skiing, beautiful dinners, and just hanging out on the beach. What made it even more special was Merry Beth, one of my very best friends, decided to get married in Jamaica, too, three days after our wedding, and I was her maid of honor, and Ken served as the best man.

Ken had a place near Cincinnati, and I had my place in Florida, with all the various pets. Since the NFL season was a little more than half the year, it made sense to set up shop in Florida.

Spookee's Custom Cycles was on a highway, and it kept us busy. Ken had many friends in the NFL, and we custom built or modified plenty of bikes for those giant men. He was hands-on and loved working on the bikes. We also had a full-time mechanic. My job was to meet with customers and do the bookkeeping when I was home — which wasn't that often. I helped the guys with tires and smaller things, and often heard, "Hey, Deb, can you come and help?" I had no problem getting dirty.

Then Ken hurt his knee, and the Bengals released him. I turned him on to Alabama's Dr. James Andrews, who so many of the wrestlers had gone to. He chose surgery, and I'll never forget watching some of it; because he was so big, they needed a few surgeons and special equipment to hold up his massive leg. While it was technically a successful surgery, his knee was never the same. Wanting to stay in Florida, he first tried out for the Jacksonville Jaguars, and then made the Tampa Bay Buccaneers — but then got injured again. The NFL money had been good, but not like today's players make. Early on, I realized that his insurance policy was woeful, and we upped it to a million-dollar policy, knowing that the careers of football players were not long. (Ken's was 35 games, total.) About a year later, he got to collect it. We invested much of it, but we had a little spending money. On a flight, I looked in a magazine and saw this custom-made log home, like I always wanted.

The house was in Virginia, $250,000, on 200 acres, on top of a mountain; even the driveway was nearly a mile long. On the way to a viewing, he made me promise not to overreact and offer to buy it immediately. After we bought it, I ripped out all the carpets and put in hardwood floors throughout the whole thing. We redid everything.

I built a brand-new horse barn and had a whole separate well dug for the barn just for the horses. Through the contractor we hired, I met one of my best friends, Sheila. Her husband, David, was as Southern as Southern gets, and when he was telling me about drilling for the well, he kept asking about where I was going to get *peaarr* for the equipment. Huh? I must have asked him to repeat himself a half-dozen times. "You want a pear?" Sheila started laughing. He meant "power."

In retrospect, the house was the turning point. He was out finding new things to do in Virginia and meeting new people. Ken was at loose ends without football. Video games didn't fill that void. He made the call to close the motorcycle shop; we could have kept it going, but been less hands-on.

Our split after nearly 10 years was the most amicable divorce ever. We basically went, "Do you want the jet skis?" "No." "I'll just take one." "Okay." "Do you want this?" "No." That was it. After our divorce, and we signed the papers, I never heard from him.

Until he showed up on my doorstep in Florida, that is. About six years ago, out of the blue, in our place well off the beaten path in Florida, Ken knocked and said he was "in the neighborhood" and wanted some old tax returns. I sent him on his way. I suspect there was more to the story, but never learned it. Ken returned to his high school sweetheart, and they have a son and a daughter.

I kept the house in Virginia for a few years, but I sold it as it was too much upkeep and I ended up back in Florida.

An ongoing project is trying to restore Granny's 1972 Harley-Davidson Electra Glide. With my crazy-ass relationship with my mother and distant family, it took some cajoling to actually get it in my possession, but I did. In the end, I was the only one who wanted to preserve it and not sell it off for cash, and Granny recognized that. All the kids and grandkids have memories of riding around, holding on tight to her. When we brought it by trailer from Minneapolis to Florida, it was held together in spots with duct tape, bungee cords, electrical tape, wire, chain, whatnot. Sourcing vintage pieces, like the seat which Granny changed at some point for improved comfort, takes time — and money. I'm keeping an eye on the great-grandchildren in the family to see who might be the best fit for it once I can no longer ride.

I wish I could be talking about my stardom from *Deuce's Wild* here. Eric Bischoff and Jason Hervey made up a whole pitch for a TV show built around me, like *American Choppers*, which was hot at the time. It was going to cover my monster truck driving and the Harley shop, but I had to say no because Clear Channel / Monster Jam wouldn't let me.

Actually, Monster Jam promised me something similar, and then never delivered. Think of the late racer and TV personality Jessi Combs, who holds the land-speed record for women; that was me then.

There's a definite kinship with other Harley riders. Bikers have got to be the most generous, amazing people I've ever met, and they probably have more rallies for charities than any other group. They have runs for veterans, for abducted children, for cancer patients, for abused pets, toy runs to collect gifts for the holidays. It's incredible. Obviously, there are a few rotten apples who make others look bad — I've met a few myself. Ken loved it, and I swear he got a hard-on from the crazy lifestyle. However he knew he could not get fully immersed while in the NFL, so when he retired — oh boy, did he ever dive in headfirst.

In 2003, a writer named Kathy Duliakas from *Woman's Own* magazine came out to interview me about life in monster trucks, and we became friends. She and I both participated in part of America's Ride 9/11, which was a charity run from Los Angeles to New York, to raise money for those affected by the terrorist attacks on 9/11. You did 500 to 700 miles on your motorcycle every day, stopping at a hotel for the night, though people came and went from each leg — including celebrities —and very few of us did the whole trek. One of the celebrities was Cris Judd, who had been married to Jennifer Lopez. It was already pre-mapped by the organizers, listing places for gas, food, scenic stops, and, most importantly, where you could get your bike serviced. Kathy just hopped from bike to bike, riding with other people, and she started getting bandannas and little fake tattoos. It was so cute. And we got to know each other for the article along the way.

She saw it all, including me cutting loose, swinging from a chandelier after a few beers too many. We were all sunburned, and we looked like raccoons because we had sunglasses on all day. One wild night, there was no way I was getting my bike back to the hotel. In walked the unexpected solution. This woman comes in, she sees the crowd well into the party, and she just took off her top and bra. Her tits are all tattooed, including her nipples. When I asked, she insisted it hadn't hurt. She heard me lament not being able to drive, so she said, "You can just park it in my store." It turned out she owned the porn shop next to the bar. "You want me to ride it into your porn shop? Hell, yeah! You guys had better get good pictures of this!" Sure enough, I got the bike into the store, and we all had lots of laughs in our drunken state checking out all the goods. In the morning, I groggily retrieved my bike and kept riding.

Since I was a "name" rider, I was assigned a pseudo-bodyguard, like a road cop to make my life a little easier. Mark Gajewski — "Ski" is what we called him — became an amazing friend. The events of 9/11 were scarred into him, as he was one of the people who worked on cleaning up the World Trade Center site. He told horrible stories of the bodies, the smell.

There'd be people gathering at each town, a podium where we would speak on behalf of what we were doing, the money we raised. Sometimes we were presented with gifts or a key to the city. We all had these vests made, with a big flag on the back and it said *Never forget*. Unbelievable.

There was a close call, where I almost bit it really bad. We got to Pennsylvania, where United Airlines Flight 93 went down in the field. It was horrible. I was almost sick right there. Just before the speech and moment of silence, we went over some gravel, and my bike started going, and I went in the ditch, about four feet down. And I flew through the air and somehow I saved myself and just gassed out — when in doubt, gag that bitch and put the pedal to the metal, baby. The bike spun out, and everyone's looking, "Holy fuck, Deuce!" They thought I was being silly and having fun — and so I played it up that way. I was saying to myself, "be cool." I'm like, "Yeah, just having some fun," while I'm shitting myself. So now everyone knows that I felt like an idiot.

Ski's other nickname was "Roadkill." You rode staggered, but Ski would always come up to fuck with me. We were always trying to talk above the sound of the Harleys, which is almost impossible, but you have a lot of sign language riding a bike. I look ahead when I ride a bike, you try not to look right down in front of you — but you always

LEFT: *My favorite picture as a kid . . . a true redhead.*

BELOW: *Teenage me was a bit of a mess.*

With my friend Marion, the beautiful dancer.

Modeling, even in Chicago Bears gear. I'm a Vikings girl. Skol!

Sitting outside with my mother, age three.

Granny and I in June 1976, before a parade.

My father, Clyde David Bergman.

My new family: Inger with her daughter, Gemma, David, and me.

My self-promoted poster, sold at Target, before I'd even signed with the AWA.

I styled Freddie into a perfect little pumpkin in my grooming salon, KoolKats and HotDogs.

The motorcycle shop I owned.

IWA Japan champion.

AWA Women's champion.

PHOTO COURTESY WWE

I was the first woman to be WCW Cruiserweight champion.

And still . . . WWE 24/7 champion (according to me).

Could I be more of a badass?

PHOTO COURTESY WWE

PHOTO COURTESY WWE

I'm most associated with Bull Nakano and she was a great opponent, whether in Japan or in North America.

My fights with Aja Kong gained me respect.

I've got Lioness Asuka all tied up in Japan.

I owe a lot to Chigusa Nagoya, though you wouldn't know it from how I'm treating her.

In midair with my jump instructor, Tom Buchanan.

Though this is a promo shot, I'm no stranger to guns.

Getting fixed up during the shoot for my exercise video.

The toughest trails result in the best views.

I'm third from the right in this group shot from the initial WCW Hog Wild ride. Who else can you identify?

This was my first ever ride in a monster truck.

While I wasn't the first woman to drive a monster truck, I quickly became the best known.

I would not have become World champion without RL Arace.

ROBIN ARCHIBEQUE

Doing another death-defying backflip at the 2011 Monster Jam World Finals in Las Vegas.

CHRISTOPHER SAWICKI

Being on fire was always a scary experience, and this one happened at the Carrier Dome in Syracuse, NY, in March 2015.

With my "Sister Wife" Missy Hyatt in WCW.

You never knew what you were going to get with Luna Vachon.

Heidi Lee Morgan was a workout buddy, a frequent opponent, and is still a great friend.

Time to mess up Wendi Richter's hair.

Bending Bertha Faye.

PHOTO COURTESY WWE

With Karl Malone, the NBA star who wrestled in WCW and sponsored his own monster truck.

With tennis star Martina Hingis.

Proof I knew Evan Marriott before he was "Joe Millionaire" — he's the tall, smiley one! We're with Greg Nolan and "Ski" Mark Gajewski.

With football legend and WrestleMania XI headliner Lawrence Taylor.

Hanging out with the Misfits in WCW.

Backstage at a concert with Joe C., Dale "The Demon" Torberg, Kid Rock, and Asya.

Somehow, Regis Philbin pinned me, and Kathie Lee Gifford calls a timeout.

STEVE FRIEDMAN

Casually posing with Glacier during an Italian magazine cover shoot at my home in Virginia.

It was easy to love my wolves, like Silver.

Glacier with her litter of pups from Stroker.

Had I followed through with more training, perhaps I would have been the Tiger King.

Meet Shyanne and Freddie.

have your head on a swivel. So we're riding, and I noticed this dude, like, three bikes ahead of us, hit something, and everyone swerved. I saw it, and Ski was trying to talk to me, and I was paying attention to the road more than he was. Etiquette is you point down to whatever is on the road for riders behind you. I noticed the warning; Ski didn't. Whatever it was, it was dead and bloated, and he hit it just right for the roadkill to pop up over his windshield and land right in his lap, splattering all over him, guts and blood from the carcass. I looked back, and he was spitting out whatever he'd inhaled. I was laughing so hard along with everyone else. When we found a place to stop, here's this six-foot-five beast racing to get cleaned up while we're howling in laughter. He came out, and I went, "How's it going, Roadkill?" The nickname stuck. We could not leave with all of us rolling around in laughter so hard.

They found out that Ski's lungs were polluted with all of that fallout from the 9/11 site, and he died from lung cancer in 2011. I was living in Germany at the time, and the first snowfall of the season happened the day he died, and I went out to do a snow angel in his memory. He was one of my best friends. We'd been through a lot together.

Not sure what compelled me to do it, but I bought a book during the trip, *America's Heroes: Inspiring Stories of Courage and Sacrifice and Patriotism*, that had just been published about 9/11. I made it a mission to get as many of the riders as I could to sign it: "To the coolest chick I know." . . ."Mama cita, diggin' you so much." . . . "You are certainly one of a kind." . . . "Proud to be your friend." . . . "We'll never forget this movie we are in."

There's this flower that Ski picked on the road, and I kept it in my Harley until I put it in my book, right where Ski signed it:

> 9-11-01 has a different meaning now that you've come into my life. You are the wildflower I've been waiting for! No goodbyes 'cause I'll be seeing ya soon! Happiness & love always & forever.
>
> Mark W. Gajewski, "SKI," Roadkill — Go on, keep laughing!

Another great friend I met because of my Harley was Jeff Turner. One time, a bunch of us were out riding, and at some point Jeff volunteered his wife to make me a jacket. We stopped at their house, and I met Gail Chovan, who was a chill chick, rock 'n' roll, but also Gloria Steinem-ish. We chatted about my wrestling outfits, then I left and forgot about the offer. Months later, I got a delivery, it's this huge cape — WWF fans will remember it, as it was white, with red flames, rhinestones, glitter, and sequins. I got to show it off again at the WWE *Evolution* show, where I was in the battle royal. Gail went on to become an internationally renowned designer and educator. Jeff remarried, and remained one of my best friends until his death in January 2018, and his wife, Shannon, is one of my best pals.

Not all my need for speed took place on a Harley.

I've been skydiving twice. The first time was actually organized by WWE, when I was wrestling there. The company filmed us each doing tandem dives at Ranch Parachute Club in Gardiner, New York, and Sean Waltman and Shane McMahon (son of Vince and Linda McMahon) both jumped as well. One of WWE's photographers, Tom Buchanan, was actually licensed to jump with others, so he took us out and looked after the photos. What a rush.

For my second jump, I did all the training that you had to do so that you could go solo. Now, they are still super-protective and monitor your every move in case something goes wrong, so you're never really on your own. It was worth it.

Less successful was my one and only time surfing — that might surprise some people given all my time living in Florida and my constant thrill-seeking.

My pals Rosie and Carl are big-time surfers, fascinating people who love to sail their big-ass sailboat everywhere. They convinced me to give it a try early in my days as a monster truck driver — there was a lot of off-time when Monster Jam was starting. We were surfing near St. Petersburg, and Carl went out farther in the ocean, Rosie was closer to shore, and I was in-between. Next thing I knew, I was caught in a break. That was a spot in the ocean where it was near impossible to move, the water pushing-pulling at the same time. Thank God I was in great shape and could swim. I fought and fought, for well more than an hour, until I clued in that I needed to swim alongside it, not going in or out. When I eventually reached shore, I was puking. Rosie and Carl said, "We seriously didn't think you were gonna make it." I never surfed again . . . but I did ride Harleys with Rosie.

For a while, WCW sponsored a car in NASCAR, driven by Elliott Sadler. Somehow, I ended up being the WCW rep down in the pits all the time, in my WCW firesuit, waving the flag to let Elliott know where to pit — it was a long, heavy metal pole, so a good workout, too. It was fine with me, because Elliott himself was pretty fine. We kind of had the hots for each other, though nothing ever happened — but it made work fun! What a thrill it was being down at track level, just so intense. Let me tell you, I wanted to get in the car badly, but never asked.

Through the NASCAR connection I met Gary Bechtel, who was part of the money behind Sadler's car. His (much younger) girlfriend and I became fast friends — every pun intended — and he would fly us in his private jets to events. At the time, Gary lived in North Carolina, and one weekend, we were up there, and he asked, "Deuce, how would you like to drive?" I'm like, "Fuck, yeah, I'll give it a try."

Next thing you know, I'm at Charlotte Motor Speedway. He'd set me up to drive a Busch-level car — the level just below the top in NASCAR — and my heart was pumping wildly. I got geared up, and they told me everything to do. *Vroooommmm!* They radioed me to pull over. They're like, "Deuce, did you ever drive?" "No, but I'm fucking high right now. My adrenaline is through the roof. I need to keep going." Instructed to "Drive it like you stole it," I got to do a few more laps. I ended up beating the time from the previous week's practice lap by the pro drivers.

While I never got to actually drive one — though it was offered — I called speed boat racing a few times in 2004. They brought me into the races, and I was a talking head on the TV broadcasts. It was pretty cool, but not especially my thing, and when the checks started bouncing, I bounced, too.

Through speed boat racing, I developed a friendship with Nick Carter of the Backstreet Boys, who had a boat and lived in the Florida Keys. "Madusa?! What's up?" He was a fanboy, and we hung out a bit. His little brother, Aaron, was cute as a button, and would stand and stare at me. Love those kids. Rest in peace, Aaron.

I also did pit reporting for the International Hot Rod Association in 2004 and was an announcer for the *2018 Outlaw Monster Truck Drags* on Fite TV.

Being on the road for so much of my life, it was tough to keep in touch with any old friends, especially before the internet was a big thing. To compensate, and to get some much needed girl time after all the hours working, I set up "Chica's Forever," where various female friends from my past came together for a weekend. It started when I was living in Virginia. I would plan something, send out invitations, tell them how much it would cost, and figure out who was in. There were childhood pals right through to recent friends. Often, I helped foot the bill for those who needed the boost.

At the first one, we just had it at my log cabin, a pamper fest. I hired a chef, a masseuse, someone to do our nails. Later, the trips were more adventurous: white-water rafting, parachuting, a health expo, and even one in Florida at the Don CeSar Hotel, because I love hauntings and I love horror flicks. It was a chance to let our hair down, but also bond, work on our mental health, and challenge ourselves to do something new and exciting.

My bike has so many stories. It was nothing for me to hop on my bike and ride 500 miles by myself. However, being a woman on my own, I needed protection. Once at the border heading into Canada, we realized that the switchblades we were carrying were actually prohibited, so we found a place to bury them and come back for them later.

Growing up, I had no exposure to guns, but it was suggested that I get one to protect myself while riding, so I did. About 25 years ago, I went to the classes and I got my license to carry. I bought a little pistol and just kept it with me in my boot. There was only one time where a couple of guys had the wrong idea of why I was out in a field with my bike that I had to even show it to anyone — and it worked, as they left pretty damn quick.

As with many things in my life, I don't go halfway. Guns just interest me, and I graduated from there, and I've got Glocks, I've got Kimbers, I've got Smith and Wessons, all locked up. One home I owned had enough space for a homemade outdoor shooting range.

Naturally, people ask about accidents. One on my Harley stands out above the rest.

Being young and invincible, it wasn't uncommon for me to head out to ride in a tight tank top, shorts, wearing a badass bandanna, and sunglasses.

WCW filmed its TV shows at Disney/MGM Studios down in Orlando, Florida, and I lived in Largo, so it was a great ride on my bike there. This particular time it was your typical Florida pouring rain out of nowhere, then back to sunshine. When it rained, I was under a bridge, and then headed out again; this happened three times. When it rains, all the oil and other junk sits on top of the water, so it's very slippery, dangerous as hell.

For some reason, on this trip, I had a helmet on, just a half shell. Good thing, too. The sun was beating down, it was muggy, and I was going slower than normal, but then out of nowhere, my ass-end of the bike came out, slid underneath me like if you're thrusting your hips forward. The wheel came out from underneath me and did something like a 360 in the air. There was no warning or indication that the bike was going. "Oh, shit!" *Boom!* On a Heritage Softail, they have these little crash bars — motor guards — and you put your foot pegs on the inside or the outside; my foot pegs were on the inside. When my bike went down, my feet were on the inside, the crash bar caved in, and pinched my foot in there. *Wham!* I slammed to the ground, legs trapped, and scraped along the highway. I had shorts on, and a halter top. I felt a burning down my side and my legs, my butt, my back, and my head. Somehow, I held my head up, the helmet still on, and my adrenaline kicked in. *HONK! HONK!* "That's a fucking semi!" Bending back, I could see how close it was. I got one foot loose, shaking, flipping, just trying to get out of it. I knew I'd be split in half by the semi or the guardrail, or the truck would roll over me. All this went through my head in seconds. I turned my body, and the momentum slid me all the way across I-4 into the grass, and the semi just missed me. My bike bounced off the guardrail and shot over to the grass. Now I didn't see that happen, but it ended up there.

I was lying there in the ditch, on my back, and it started drizzling. I wondered, *Wow, I'm dead. Is this what it's like to be dead?* All of a sudden, I started feeling pain. I sat right up like The Undertaker does, and I looked over to my left, and there were people who had pulled over, screaming, "Ma'am, are you all right?" "Yeah, yeah, I'm fine." They wanted to call somebody, and I insisted I was good.

My halter torn, with my boobs hanging out, I managed to stand up. I retied my top and tried to pull up my shorts. I was just road-toasted. *Where's my bike?* That's the first thing I thought about, and managed to walk over there. I'm like, "Fuck, I'm gonna be late for work." So stupid — damn wrestling mentality.

The wheel on the motorcycle was still spinning around, smoking. Now, this bike is 850 pounds, but with my adrenaline strength, I just lifted it up, crouching down, my whole ass under it. Right away, I tried starting it. Then I noticed there was a little gas leak, so I popped the gas line back in there, fixed a few things with what I had in my emergency kits — electric tape saved the day. I went to start it, and she started right up. I looked at everyone, I said, "I'll be good," and left.

I can still picture getting to the cloverleaf off the highway to Orlando Harley-Davidson, and I pulled up to their big garage. Everything stopped,

I could hear tools dropping by the mechanics as they all came running out. Some lady came out of the office, "Oh my God!"

I'm like, "Can you help me? I crashed on the highway. I think I need to call my insurance company."

"Ma'am, you need to come with me." So she walked me over to the back and had a hose and she picked all the pebbles out of my skin — and I mean everywhere.

I called WCW and said, "I'll be late." Yes, I made the show, my backside looking like ground-up hamburger. Yes, I did wrestle that night.

Eric Bischoff, who ran the show, decided to have a live wrestling pay-per-view in Sturgis, South Dakota, at the Sturgis Motorcycle Rally. He called the first one, in 1996, *Hog Wild*; subsequent shows were called *Road Wild*, because Bischoff never cleared it to use "Hog" or something. Those of us who rode met at the Mall of America in Minneapolis. Naturally, Granny came down on her Harley to see us off, and there's photos of her with all the boys, and her favorite, Sting.

Ellis Edwards, who set up stunts for WCW, was on the ride, and I had to watch out for him. He was always full of fucking funny ribs and jokes. But he wouldn't do it to you unless he knew that you could handle it — and he wouldn't have done this to anybody who wouldn't know what to do. We were about 100 miles into the ride, we're just cruising, 90 or 100 miles per hour down the highway. Ellis came up from nowhere on my right side. I was on the white line and I had other riders to my left. Ellis came up on the damn shoulder, beside me, and flipped a switch while riding by to shut off my bike. All natural instinct, I pulled in my clutch and clicked the "On" button, and that bitch started right up. That's not even thinking, that's just knowing what to do. He's lucky I'm not dead. That is crazy-dangerous. The practical jokes after that were funny, but not as homicidal.

There wasn't much thought about the condition of the wrestlers to actually compete when we got there. Me? I was sunburned pink. Fortunately, I was scheduled to wrestle my old pal, Bull Nakano.

The rally itself was a sight to see, bikers surrounding the ring, where we wrestled outside. The coolest thing was, I got to ride my Harley to the ring. Bull was with her manager, Sonny Onno, and they came out with a Japanese-made bike, which made them ultra-villains in that crowd; I mean, I've seen nutbars wreck Japanese bikes out of some misguided principle.

The noise was incredible. Every time I did a move in the ring, they'd rev their motors. When Bull did a move, they'd boo — and the stipulations of the match meant that the loser's bike would be destroyed.

Here I was, over with my people, a crowd that I understood intimately. Naturally, WCW being the mess that it was, never used me again on one of the Sturgis shows.

13.

SIT DOWN, STRAP IN, AND CRANK IT UP

IT WAS LOVE at first jump.

My foot was shaking over the gas pedal, and I was scared shitless, but I gunned it, and it nearly scared the piss out of me. The power of the monster truck was awesome. I hit the gas again. *Whoopa!* I hit the throttle, gagged that bitch up through the air, throttled, *ba, ba, ba,* landed — *ughhhhh* — and then aimed for another small hill and hit it.

I could see Dennis Anderson — we were at his estate, doing my test drive — waving me down. I pulled over, and once the noise subsided, it became clear to me the Monster Jam people were stunned. "You've really never driven one before?"

It was 20 years before they got me out of that seat.

I'm getting to know my first monster truck.

I owe my second career to Mike Weber, who'd been a part of my first career. Mike had been with WWE in public relations, and then in WCW, where he was a marketing guy, but he'd never just done wrestling and had some other neat jobs along the way, including at SFX Motorsports.

At WCW, Mike was the guy who made the deal to create WCW wrestler-themed monster trucks. There was a Bill Goldberg truck, Hulk Hogan, and Sting; they each had one, and there was even a truck for the New World Order faction. SFX Motorsports had hired Mike back and away from WCW. One day, they were talking about getting a woman driver, and Mike told them he had just the gal.

It was sure as hell a call out of the blue, though he was familiar enough with both me and how frustrated I was at WCW to know I'd be open to a new idea.

The pitch went something like this: "I was in a meeting, and this company needs help. We want to build this company, we want women and little girls. And I don't know where you're at, what you're doing, or what your contract is. But do you think you'd be interested in driving a monster truck?"

"What?"

"No, really. This is a shoot. This isn't a rib."

"Are you fucking kidding me? I've never seen one. I've never been to a show."

"Deuce, please just consider it. You're an adrenaline junkie, you ride Harleys, four-wheelers."

I filled him in on what was going on at WCW, and Mike said, "Maybe it's time to change."

Dennis Anderson is perhaps the most iconic figure there is in the monster truck world. He created the Grave Digger truck, which became a power both on the circuit and merchandise-wise. But at the time, in late 1999, I had no idea who he was.

I was flown up on a Thursday, and then Friday, I was driven to the small town of Kill Devil Hills, North Carolina, where Dennis had his garage — Digger's Dungeon — to work on monster trucks and a good swath of land to practice driving. The executives of the company were all there, excited. Mike probably propped me up like I was this badass chick. It was like pro wrestling, except a girl coming into a Southern boy clique, with all these accolades behind her, and all this TV time. Some of them were wrestling fans.

But they'd given me no instructions, like what to wear. They found me a helmet but other than that, I was in the running shoes and firesuit I had for working in the NASCAR pits on the WCW car. I still had my massive boobs, so it was a hilarious challenge getting me strapped in — there were no HANS devices then, just a harness and neck brace to keep you in place. Dennis gave me a very basic lesson on the truck (an old ride, retired from competitions) and taught me some hand signals, so I could communicate with him. He explained how he could completely shut down the truck remotely if something went wrong.

Firing it up, the feeling was incredible, the roar of the motor, just the sheer power of 1,500 horsepower, the smell of the methanol. I was sweating bullets, but I didn't let them see the fear. Taking it out I inched along, *maybe* five miles an hour initially. What I didn't realize was how hard it would be to see, and it took some getting used to, as you had to look down, through the floor, which was Lexan (like a CD case), to see what was underneath you, rather than just looking ahead. And you couldn't turn around, either.

Dennis had me go all the way to the other end of the testing area and aim the truck towards a ramp. "Right before you hit that ramp, you gag that bitch." Huh? He had to explain that it meant to put the metal to the floor. I was supposed to "feather" it, another new term, which meant to keep the front end from nosing forward, leveling it in the air.

I got in position and gunned it — talk about a life-changing moment. When I came down from the small jump, Dennis waved me over. Something had come loose on the back of the truck, so while they fixed that, I got out of the cab and chatted with the execs. They wanted to see what I could do next — on Saturday.

After, I was the most sore I had ever been in my life. Every time you jump and do something, you bust hard. Your neck would be smashing forward, and your arms flailed out all over in the truck, hitting the roll bars.

I was in damn good shape back then, but it wasn't long until I started tightening up and really feeling it. I grabbed a little something to eat and went to my room for a hot-ass shower. I remember standing there for an hour, the water just beating on me. I got out of the shower and barely got some clothes on, since I was stiffening up quickly — I tried moving and stretching and all of that. I lay down and I did not wake up until the next morning. All I could move when I woke up was my eyelids. I could not get out of bed. It was triple any bad day I ever had in wrestling. I wanted to puke, but I couldn't move.

Somehow, I managed to look at the clock and realized the executives would be over to pick me up in half an hour. The bed was near the wall, and I braced my legs against it to push myself off the bed, onto the floor, and I crawled to my clothes. I don't know how I did it, but I got dressed. Walking down to the lobby to meet everyone, I was telling myself, *Suck it up bitch, you ain't going to show them your weakness. I've got this. Let's go.* I kept pumping myself up.

I was creating animosity in the mind: *They want me to quit. They put me through the worst tests because they didn't want me. Bullshit, I'm going to show them what I'm about.*

Grabbing some coffee, I walked out to where everyone was waiting. They said good morning, and I overdid it. "Good morning, guys. How are you?" When they asked how I was, I let them have it. "I'm fucking great. I love this shit. I'm so excited." The look on their faces is best described as, *Ah, shit.*

Saturday was incredible. Before they got me back into the makeshift gear and into the truck, Dennis and I walked the path. There was a course through some trees and a stack of cars after you came out. They wanted me to get through this maze like a bat out of hell and come out at the end for the big finish. I don't know if they just looked at me and said, "Yep, she can do it." Or, "Let's just give it to her and watch her fuck up."

Back in the cab, the first bump was oddly rejuvenating, and I could feel my body loosening up. The whole day felt looser, too, as Dennis's kids were now home from school and running around; they just became my kids, basically, as we grew up together in the business.

I was ready to go through the maze, but I didn't hit it hard like they thought I would. I drove slowly, because I wanted to get that first feel of what I'm doing by hitting cars, real cars. That freaked me out. I'm kind of a planner, and I knew what they were hoping for — but it's kind of like I was dick-teasing them, that I can play this fucking game, too.

Let me tell you, that second time, I hit that bitch, balls to the wall, just metal to the floor. I was screaming inside my helmet, "*Woo-hooo!*" I hit one pile of cars, and then another. On the second pile, near a pond, I jumped, landed on just two wheels, and almost went upside down into the water. My instincts just got my foot onto the throttle, and I feathered out of it, full speed. A comparison would be driving and slipping on the snow or black ice, and while you want to gun your car to straighten out, the opposite actually works: you feather the brakes, on and off, to regain control.

Pulling up to where everyone was waiting, I was high. My adrenaline was off the charts, and I was smiling from ear to ear. Later, I learned how close I'd come to dying. When I was coming down on two wheels beside the pond, they were shitting themselves, because if I'd gone in upside down, between the harness and the depth of the water there's no way they would have gotten me out. It was all luck.

Back in the moment, they asked again whether I'd driven before.

"Nope."

"You're hired. We'll get you suited up and ready."

Next thing I knew, I was in a monster truck entertaining 60,000 people without any further training. That's fucking stupid-insane.

Incidentally, they moved the test track at Kill Devil Hills away from the pond.

When my lawyer and I sat down with the Monster Jam people to talk contract, I surprised them with my insistence that I not be treated any differently than the rest of the drivers. It blew them away. They saw me as the first fly-in driver, coming in for the weekends. I was having none of that shit, as I wanted to work from the bottom up.

I said, "I want to learn the truck, work on the truck, to be in the semi going down the highway with the truck; I want to load and unload the truck."

It was my instincts taking over again. I'd dealt with men for so long in wrestling that I knew how they ate, slept, thought. By taking the harder road, I was commanding respect and wouldn't be seen as a prima donna.

I didn't understand the Southern mentality. It was good ol' boys, pickup trucks, Confederate flags, and drinking. What the hell is this? "*Whoo!* We're hard core!" Now, I'm not saying every single one of them, but it was pretty damn close.

Ah, but those boys loved their rasslin', too, so they knew who I was and what I'd accomplished. But they had their reputations to uphold. I can't say that I was accepted with open arms. Instead, they'd sneak up to chat with me, asking questions about the McMahons or Hogan. Initially, in a group setting, they would be cold.

Through the grapevine, I heard about the distrust from the wives, too. They thought just because I was an attractive blonde, I must be screwing all the other drivers while on the road. Nothing could be further from the truth. I preferred guys who were in shape and that, you know, had all their teeth, didn't smoke, and didn't have Confederate flag tattoos. Though, I did have my fun.

Monster Jam was the biggest of the companies promoting monster trucks. It would be like Major League Baseball, and there were all kinds of minor leagues out there. The drivers who were signed to Monster Jam were the big names, and I very quickly became one of them. Maybe I should rephrase that: the trucks were the big names, and fans knew about Grave Digger, Bigfoot, and Maximum Destruction, and not always the person behind the wheel. I was an exception since I had *my* name on *my* truck.

Since there were races around the United States and, later, the world, there was always a need for drivers to fill out the field. Those independent drivers, sometimes a husband-and-wife team working together, would be paid a set fee for their services for the Monster Jam show — but all the expenses were their own, including fixing damage to their trucks. A tire alone could cost $3,500. They would have their own sponsors, but not always be allowed to display them on their trucks. Monster Jam might be generous and allow them to race anyway, but with some of Monster Jam's sponsors slapped on *over* their current sponsors. Bigger-name independents were treated better.

The full-time drivers didn't have to worry about that, as Monster Jam owned our trucks, so we could crash and burn at will. It shifted a lot through the years, too; when I started with Monster Jam, it owned maybe a dozen trucks and used a lot more outsiders, independents. Later, Monster Jam owned probably 60-or-so trucks, could run multiple events on the same night, and didn't use as many non-company drivers and trucks.

At the shows, whether they were in big stadiums with 50,000 people, or smaller arenas, with 10,000 fans, the goal was the same — to entertain. But it wasn't like wrestling; it was real competition. We'd race, driver against driver, going around a circuit to see who could finish first. The other half of the show was freestyle, where you'd go out and perform tricks in your truck — wheelies, flips, donuts, jumps. Some of the trucks had extra gimmicks built into them, like lights or smoke. Later, Monster Jam added other elements to fill time, like motocross madmen racing around the track, or car-crushing metallic dinosaurs.

When I first started, Monster Jam primarily ran January to March — and we ran hard, the top dogs fighting it out until the World Finals. As the company grew, so did the demands on our time, with show after show filling out much more of the calendar.

Driving a monster truck is so different from a regular vehicle. For one, you get into the cab underneath the vehicle. The actual doors usually didn't work and were just painted on in some cases; Dennis's Grave

Digger was one of the only ones with proper doors. Since they weren't road-legal, none of the usual things were there, either, like headlights, wipers, or side mirrors, unless they were for show. There was a reinforced windshield, and the Lexan floor on the bottom of the truck was placed where the pedals were, so when your truck was up in the air, you could see where you were — remember, we were strapped in tight. That clear plastic could still shatter and cut you, or melt when the vehicle caught fire. But it gave you that ability to still drive and kind of peek out and look where you're going all at the same time you're ready to crash.

One of the first things I had to get used to, quickly, was that the back wheels turned separately. When you get in the monster truck, you have a regular steering wheel, and then you have a toggle to flip to steer the back end. So when you're racing, you have to steer through the front with the steering wheel, and then you have to steer in the back with the little toggle. It's called "dirt tracking," and it's the key to succeeding.

Lyle Hancock was the key to me learning how to drive a monster truck. After I was hired, I went back to Dennis's shop, and Lyle showed me how a truck operated. Everyone there wanted to dismiss me as a blonde bimbo, but I asked smart questions, showed an eagerness to get my hands dirty, and I listened and learned. When we got to driving that first season, Lyle — who was running in the Blue Thunder truck — showed tough love. (I made my debut on January 14, 2000, in Greensboro, North Carolina, if you are keeping track.) There was a point where he just fucking had at me and made me feel like shit. Yet we ended up being good friends. His schooling was everything from what to do while in the air to walking a track to see the dirt and the ramps.

The trucks run on methanol. I love the smell of it, though the gas burns your nose hairs. It gets me in a racing mood, my right foot twitching to hit the pedal the moment the tree turns green. It's a fuel that burns fast and hot, three gallons a minute, and it would overheat by minute five. But you never wanted a lot of it in your tank because methanol is extremely combustible, so trucks go *boom* if you crash. In a big stadium, you'd get at most two laps in before having to refuel. There'd be barrels of it at the venue, and it was one of those times when the various crews worked together — it was not a one-person job!

This is a good spot to salute the hardworking crews of all the trucks in the pits, and the teams that built the tracks and then removed them. Whereas I had plenty of trouble with Monster Jam management, the actual people on the floor doing the work were amazing. They were probably the greatest set of people I've known in my life; they were loving, caring, and helped out one another without question. Unlike in F1, where it's the Red Bull team against Ferrari, we were all being paid by Monster Jam, so there was a sense of camaraderie. Now, if your driver/truck was still in competition, you weren't going to offer your backup transmission. But if it was eliminated, that would happen.

In my first couple of years, I was one with my truck — I got what I asked for, but it came at a cost.

I rode in the semi with my Madusa truck, going town to town. After a show, you'd break apart much of the truck so it would fit into the trailer, hop in, and drive . . . and drive . . . and drive. The tires were key. We had to take off the 66-inch tires and replace them with regular tires so we could drive the truck into the semi. The big tires would be rolled in behind. The semi also held replacement parts.

We'd get to the next town eventually, and I helped get the truck out, and then to put it back together. At first, I stood around a lot, learning. I didn't know much about the mechanics of the truck, so I had to just absorb. They'd be 10-, 12-hour days, and I got to where I could hand them parts, and then I was allowed to start doing some of the work. It was hard, physical labor, and it made up for not always being able to hit a gym. The work itself wasn't all that different from the maintenance that happens to your car — tighten parts, check the tires, oil the motor — but on such a larger scale. At least repainting wasn't part of our jobs.

There was the learning curve in front of the audience, too. No one ever sat down and said, "Do this, don't do that" when it came to driving. Honestly, it was all trial and error, with thousands watching. Now, that didn't mean I didn't ask another driver how they did a trick, or why something I tried didn't work — of course I did! But, as I noted, it was a competition, and some things were akin to trade secrets.

I had to learn about the audiences, too, and dealing with fans. We'd have pit parties with the people who paid a little extra for the chance to meet the drivers before the show, for three or four hours. Then after the show, it was a quick signature with fans, and there were times we'd still be signing until four in the morning, and then I'd help finish breaking down the truck and would sleep in the cab as we rolled down the highway.

It wasn't always a peaceful sleep, as I knew how exhausted the driver was. After driving a monster truck during the weekend, they regularly drove well over the legally mandated amount of hours they were allowed to drive a long-haul truck, fudging the numbers in their books. It was dangerous. These guys could barely keep their eyes open, so I needed to stay awake and talk to them. There were times I feared for my life, but I reasoned it in my mind that they were seasoned drivers and knew what they were doing.

I raised my concerns with management, which empowered others to complain as well, until finally the company hired drivers for the semis whose only job was driving the semis. No more double-dipping, forcing drivers to drive and drive and drive.

Get this: at one point they wanted *me* to learn to drive a semi! I put the kibosh on that. I acted stupid real quick, "I can't get this," and purposefully fucked things up when they had me practice in a parking lot. I knew what they were doing — this ain't my first rodeo. I came from wrestling. You can't put one over me. I played stupid and purposely backed up and crashed the semi, just to put the end to it. I laughed to myself, "Here's your first rib!"

After a couple of years, when I was able to fly home after shows, I knew that I had both earned that reward and had earned the respect of the other drivers and the crews for the effort.

A week after I had my tryout at Kill Devil Hills, Chad Fortune had his tryout. He'd been a football player, playing professionally in Europe, and then ended up in pro wrestling, too. Chad was a six-foot-six beast, but for whatever reason, he never really got the *push* to be a star in wrestling like I'd had off and on. As he did with me, Mike Weber suggested to Chad to give monster trucks a try. His problems were different from mine, as he was huge, and they had to specifically build a truck to fit *his* chassis.

This is where our stories are particularly intertwined. While we knew each other from wrestling, we weren't pals or anything. But in Monster Jam, we had to have each other's backs, especially as we tried to bring showmanship to it all, which is what we had been hired to do!

There was so much resistance from the other drivers to two wrestlers coming into their world — even more than having the WCW-labeled monster trucks in Monster Jam, which preceded us. Plus, he was a fly-in driver, and I became one after I learned the ropes in the rigs, which meant we got hotel rooms and rental cars. The pattern was that you worked for years in the pits, a part of the crews, and eventually you'd graduate to driving a monster truck. We skipped the line, and that created animosity.

Because Chad's truck was being custom built, he used his mic skills from wrestling to create drama instead, trash-talking, cutting promos, and all that great stuff. So if Tom Meents was driving the Goldberg truck, Chad would be cutting down the others. I was no slouch on the mic, either, and I did what they wanted me to — play to the crowd, especially the moms and little girls.

This was all new in Monster Jam, and they didn't know what they wanted.

Once, early in my time there, I cut a promo on Tom Meents (pronounced "mints") and I said I'd make "mincemeat out of him" and that I'd "see him down at the green light." I was told that I'd better not talk like that ever again, or else I wouldn't have a job. I looked at the guys and I said, "What the fuck? You tell me to do a goddamn promo, what do you want?" "Not those kinds of promos." "I'm confused. Isn't that why I was hired?" So many times I said that — "What the fuck am I even doing here, then?"

Before a show, we would have a drivers' meeting. Usually it was routine stuff, noting anything unique about the setup, where to park, the order we were going out. This one time, Dennis Anderson began to rant about pro wrestlers and how we had no business being drivers. Chad and I just looked at each other. It was so out of the blue.

You know what it did, though? It lit a fire in me. When somebody tests me, pushes me, I want to fight back; know that I'm on your heels, on a mission, and I'm going to knock you down.

Eventually, I did. But to know how big a deal it was when I beat Dennis for the World Championship, you first need to know why he matters.

Dennis Anderson was the godfather of Monster Jam. He had started in 1982, putting school bus tires on his big ol' mud truck, and working his way up. He deserved everything he got in this business. He *is* this business and he *was* that damn good. If it weren't for him, I wouldn't have been able to do what I did.

There were dozens of versions of Grave Digger through the years, and they always stood out with their glowing red headlights — and the fact that they often won, especially when he was behind the wheel. The idea was that he was going to "dig a grave" for his opponents. Dennis deserves a lot of credit for innovations with the trucks themselves, much of it created at his Digger's Dungeon in North Carolina — the very place where I had my tryout. (He later sold the shop, and then sold the rights to Grave Digger itself for personal reasons; Monster Jam grew the Grave Digger brand even bigger.)

From 1999 to 2016, Dennis made 17 World Finals appearances, winning racing three times and freestyle once. He sold tons of Grave Digger merch, had videos made about him, and really was the top dog.

Just don't ask Tom Meents.

Like in wrestling, rivalries matter, and Dennis and Tom butted heads on the course and behind the scenes, a love-hate relationship; Dennis was Hulk Hogan, Tom was Randy Savage. Tom was also key to the growth of Monster Jam, driving Maximum Destruction for most of his time, but other trucks, too, like Bulldozer, Goldberg, and Max-D. When a Monster Jam University was established, it was on Meents's property, and he was the professor, actually giving lessons.

So here's little ol' me, wading into this minefield of good ol' boys with their big car-crushing toys.

I do want to clarify that these were not toys. Accidents have happened where drivers or fans have been killed, but it is very rare. Monster trucks have shut-off switches installed; they are operated by RRI radio, and the techs could remotely shut off your truck completely if you are out of hand, if you're causing damage to the building, or if you were going towards something or could hurt somebody. Of course, that could be maddening, too, and every driver has a story about the truck being silenced underneath you when you didn't think it was the right time. But the techs are seeing things that we can't from our seats.

Right from the start, I believed in myself, that I could be competitive, outshine them all, and be a memorable character. When I first got in, I loved the competitiveness and thought, *This is fucking* home, *this is for me, this is going to be great!*

I didn't count on the jealousy, the vindictiveness, and it wasn't just hazing the rookie — it was downright dangerous.

I can only call it sabotage. My tires were deflated just before a race, hindering performance, or they'd be set too high, even by a few inches, meaning I couldn't quite do the same things as everyone else. Worse, piles of baby powder were put on my seat, so when I went running to get into the truck and sit down — *poof!* You can't see to start the race, and the other trucks start off without you.

Today, if you got off the track and found a sign on your dressing room that read *Whore's Room*, there'd be an investigation, and people would be fired. That's the shit I had to live with. I kept that paper, by the way.

I can't say that I held my tongue, because that has never been my style, but all I could really do was prove that I belonged, and let my personality, my work ethic, do the talking.

What I needed was someone to believe in me, to truly see that I could compete.

That person was RL.

Monster Jam was not a work, like pro wrestling; nothing was predetermined.

But it was not an even playing field.

The best trucks got the best — whether it was publicity, parts, sponsors, mechanics, or crew chiefs. Everyone else was playing catch-up.

Naturally, that's not something anyone told me when I started. I had to see it for myself, how one truck would get a different muffler or spark plug than I'd get. Plus each truck had its own unique build. Different companies would make the chassis, and it would be adjusted to accommodate the weight of the horns of the bull or even made out of a different material than another truck; or the wheel wells would differ based on the design.

As for the tires themselves, I very rarely got great tires; in fact, many were used! Some would have slashes in them. Since the tires weren't high quality, when I'd go for big air, on the landing, I risked the chance of the tires popping off; when driving over cars, the broken metal could slice a thinner tire.

It's not like F1 or NASCAR, where each racing team has to make the car to certain specifications and there are marshals checking everything. As the driver, we had no say in any of this. Shut up and drive.

Now, if you happened to be in a sponsored truck, especially a big-name one, then doors started opening to you, more accurately, the keys to the good storage locker were handed over.

I started asking questions after a couple of years in: "Am I missing something? Why do the big-name trucks get that kind of transmission?" There was always an excuse. "Oh, you're not there yet, Deuce." The fuck I ain't!

It didn't help that I had a constant rotation of people working on my truck. The crew chief and driver need to vibe, to see things as one, and fight together to make it happen.

Then along came RL Arace, who was about as Southern a redneck as you could get. This tiny foul-mouthed character could lift many times his weight, slinging around 800-pound tires with ease. Honestly, until working on this book, I didn't know to spell his last name! Isn't that weird?

He basically told the company, in his drawl, to go fuck themselves. "I see something in this girl, she deserves it, let's give it a try," was his mantra as he took on a challenge. He'd heard the bullshit: "Oh, she's a prima donna, she's so hard to work with, she's going to be a pain in the ass." They were gaslighting me. It was horrible.

Instead, RL and I became a unit, a tag team. We got close, too, because when you travel together you become friends, and discover who you *can* trust. My life was in RL's hands. I could have died any time I got in that truck. That's the severity of a monster truck. It is powerful: it has more than 1,500 horsepower in a 10,000-pound machine.

We were in tune and didn't have to communicate verbally. We'd look at each other, and I would make a movement, he'd make a hand signal, and we were on cue. I'd suggest that maybe a screw was loose at the back, and he'd go hunting and fix it. Truly, being a team is a beautiful thing; I was only as good as my truck, and my truck was only as good as my crew chief and his team.

Until other women started driving, too, I had one requirement of my crew chief that no one else did. When I was in the truck, I never wore makeup, but did have on eyelashes and mascara. One of the prerequisites for my crew guy was to carry my lip gloss for me. Whenever I crashed, he'd always come running out, and as I was pulling myself out of the truck, he'd slip the lip gloss in my hand, so I could quickly put it on before the camera crews were on top of me.

The fact is that no one looks good after a fucking crash — or getting out of the truck even after a good run, for that matter! It's gross, since spit and snot would often come shooting out of you when you landed after a jump or bump, and if it was especially messy, it would get all over your visor, and you'd have to lift your visor while driving to see what you were doing. Being honest, there were times the piss was knocked out of me, quite literally.

We had no air conditioning in our trucks, and you'd be covered in sweat, hair gross and matted down, under the helmet. Getting out of the truck, you'd have trouble catching your breath and be achy. I'd unzip the firesuit to show off one of my T-shirts, but it was also to immediately cool off.

But, hey, lip gloss solves all!

My years in wrestling and traveling the world affected my time in Monster Jam in a couple of ways. For one, I had status with the major airlines, so I usually got bumped to a first-class seat. This created dissension in the ranks right from the start, and other drivers, back in coach on a flight from Tampa, Florida, to Dallas, Texas, would see me up there and believe I was being treated differently by management. Not the case at all, since management treated us all shitty.

The other aspect was that I had friends across the country, so I'd try to arrange to get into town a day or two early for visits on the company dime. Now, I was a good girl when it came to media and would offer to do any local appearances, but I was never their number one choice. Often, I'd get thrown the early slot on morning talk shows, meaning I'd be up before the sun, getting a workout in, and then my makeup to look good on camera. There would be a little media at the shows, too, usually at the meet and greet, and they'd wander around and talk to fans and a few drivers; those kinds of interviews I could do in my sleep. If it was a huge show, like in Dallas at AT&T Stadium, some of the trucks and drivers would be there days before doing promos.

A veteran traveler, I knew that we weren't being put up in the best places, but they weren't the worst, either. I knew to never get a room near the ice machine or the elevators, to avoid all the idiot drunks and the riffraff, and I tried to avoid the same floors as the rest of the drivers and crews.

I've always loved a good workout, so I'd scope out the gym at the hotel. If it was satisfactory, I'd always get a workout in; if it wasn't, I'd figure out something else, like a jog. The contrast was the peacefulness of being in my hotel room, curling up with a good book. I needed my Me Time knowing what was ahead.

When you got to the venue, whether it was an outdoor track, a massive stadium, or a small arena, the company expected you to stay there. I'd been used to WWE and WCW TV tapings, where the rule was the same — but there'd been catering. I lobbied for years for Monster Jam to finally provide us with some food. They'd do things like order 30 pizzas after a show, but the drivers were in the post-show meet and greets, so the slices would be gone before we ever got any. An enterprising crew guy might take orders for a McDonald's run, but I wasn't having any of that shit.

My food consisted of protein shakes and fruit that I had planned ahead and brought, bananas or apples, and granola. There were plenty of snickers from my greasy-food-loving colleagues, and I was looked at funny since I didn't eat red meat.

We'd spend so much time waiting, and I'd usually be either off on my own, or with my truck and my crew chief. When we got the okay, we were allowed out onto the track, to take a look at everything. This is also when we spent the most time together as drivers, a chance to see each other away from the roar of the motors.

Sometimes we drove on concrete, but usually it was dirt, and it was different in every location. You've got your black dirt, you've got your mixture, you got your dirt mixed with lime — yes, they put lime in our dirt, and we crashed on that and we breathed that, all of these years. Lime dust is a known irritant, and people working with it wear face masks. Dirt is the magic of the track, really. We're only as good as the construction workers, we're only as good as the techs, then as good as the truck, and then ourselves. The dirt is everything. I liked touching the dirt, walking on the track to see how well packed it was.

For an outdoor show, the weather determines even more. If it's a very hot day, they're going to have problems with dust. Loose dirt is hard to drive on, so they'd water it down; too much water and it's muddy. But then if it cooled down too much for an evening show, that water can turn to ice. We actually had tires with bigger treads, or cleats, that were better for gripping ice. If you go with bigger cleats, you run the risk of hitting a corner when you're dirt tracking at 50 miles an hour, tipping over them, because they catch.

And then there's a secret with a hot gun: you shave your tires. When you buy your tires, the rims alone are probably about two grand, and then the tires are probably another grand or so. You want to shave those tires as much as you can, making them as thin as you can, taking some of the knuckles off the side of the tire with a hot knife. It could take days. That lightens the tire by a couple hundred pounds so you could go faster and dirt track without flipping.

Closer to showtime, I had to have everything ready, and it had to be perfect, like a superstition. My seat belt had to be a certain way, the gloves in the current spot, and helmet nearby just right. If it wasn't done to my specs — which never changed — I'd have my crew guys straighten it out. Then everyone readied for their roles — the announcers, the show directors and assistants, the crews, executives.

After it was all done, there was no time to shower — unless you count a whore's bath in the sink with a washcloth. We were herded like cattle right out for the post-show meet and greet, everyone reeking of perfume or body spray or cologne just so we could stand to be around ourselves! George Balhan would race to the back, grab his can of hair spray, and transform as fast as he could into Mohawk Warrior. The post-shows were a slog, as everyone was tired and cranky, including the fans who had to wait to meet their favorite beaten and bruised drivers.

I started calling the freestyle portion of the show "90 seconds of pure pleasure." That was the amount of time you had to show what you could do, and, if you hit certain spots, you earned an extra 30 seconds of bonus time. The scoring system has always been a little nebulous.

People in the office controlled the voting, though fan voting was an element as well, and, more often than not, fans voted for the trucks they knew, like Grave Digger or Maximum Destruction. It took some time before I had my own following.

In freestyle, you did whatever you could do: a wheelie, donuts, a backflip. I did it all, though I didn't manage a full backflip until 2013. There was never any practice time in the trucks, and it was trial and error in front of the crowd every weekend. You'd pick up lessons here and there, watching someone do a trick. More often than not, they'd share if they crashed — "What went wrong?" — rather than explain to you how to do a trick. Remember, we were competing.

This advice won't make sense to you, but coming from another driver, I could translate and give it a whirl: "Just go out there and kind of pump the brakes, just go up to the brick wall, and just don't go too fast, go kind of slow. And then gag it as you go up in the air. Don't let your foot off the throttle."

The stunt I loved to do the most was one where I used to go up on two wheels up in the front. I would head over a hill and do a nosedive and I would hit my brake — and I'd be on the front two tires. Later, I was told to stop doing it, that I was going to break the truck. Now the young drivers are allowed to do it all the time. It was the same story when I used to drive on just two wheels on the one side of the truck, leaning over; that looked so crazy, but then I was told to stop that, too.

The crashes in freestyle were different from the ones in racing. When you were going full out, something could happen unexpectedly, but in freestyle, you knew at that moment you were pushing the envelope of what the truck could do and testing the laws of physics. So at some level, tipping over in freestyle wasn't a surprise.

But it hurt every single fucking time. Your bell gets rung, you're shaken around. If we were competing on concrete, the impact was worse than on the dirt fields. You had to have deep trust in your mechanic that the shocks had been set correctly.

There was a front-end loader to turn over the trucks if they weren't too badly damaged; others were pushed to the side with a bulldozer. But if it was in rough shape, or if it was an independent truck, it would be left out there, as it would have taken a long time to get it out of the main arena, so that meant it was another obstacle, but one that you weren't supposed to smash up, like you could with the junk cars. There were times we'd be trying to avoid four or five broken trucks.

At a race in Atlanta in 2013, I ran into trouble with the Ice Cream Man. During its run, a rear wheel broke off, and it stayed there on the track. I hit a wheelie off an obstacle, carried halfway across the stadium, and as the truck settled down, I crashed into Ice Cream Man — not fun. I severely damaged his right side, and the front end of my Madusa truck, and broke a breast implant. And while the comparison is logical, it's nothing like hitting a parked car in a parking lot!

This shouldn't surprise anyone, but fans love the crashes. I never purposely set out to crash my truck, as my thinking was, *Hey, if I can get through all of these great stunts and racing without crashing, and save my body, that would be just super*. But there were times, especially in freestyle, where it either wasn't going right, or I was so pumped up from everything working out right, that I just *knew* that a crash would leave a lasting impression with the fans — and my wrestling training had taught me how to play with their emotions, so . . . *smash!* Fuck, yeah! Go buy my T-shirts!

They called me "The Queen of Carnage" for a reason.

The medical staff on duty at each show could be dictated by local regulations, but in general, there was always an ambulance there with a pair of EMTs. That's it. There was no doctor. The EMTs sat there and watched the show and pulled us out if one of us crashed hard and broke something, or passed out, or had a heart attack. There was nothing else backstage, like a chiropractor or massage therapist, to make our lives easier.

There was no real education, either, with everyone fending for themselves. Here's a simple example: a lot of drivers popped aspirin to deal with the aches and pains. Well, aspirin thins the blood, and if you crash? You are in more trouble than you might have been. I avoided drugs, but that was me. I'd spent my entire life with fitness in mind.

In 2000, Monster Jam made a deal with Sam Boyd Stadium, in Las Vegas, to host its annual World Finals. This was part of the maturing of the company, to set up a focus on the season-end event. Media, sponsors, and fans descended for a crazy-busy, very long weekend. We'd have all kinds of commitments besides the shows themselves, and non-competing drivers would have meet and greets all weekend with fans. The independent drivers would set up shop and sell their merch. And, well, it's fuckin' Vegas, so next thing you know, you're tossing away money on the slots.

The drivers and the crews lived for this, because it meant something. If you were a driver employed by Monster Jam — not an independent — and you won a race or a freestyle competition at a stop in, say, Jacksonville, Florida, you got squat. Well, you could crow a bit to your buddies backstage, but that was it. There was no financial reward.

The successes you had week after bruising week did add up to an invitation to World Finals — but even that was never a given, as Monster Jam wanted the big-name trucks there. And you never knew what could happen, like in 2003, when Avenger, an independent truck driven by Jim Koehler, won the Freestyle World Finals. Now *that* was a magic moment for all of us company drivers. We loved Jim — and so did the media, since he was so charismatic and well-spoken — but we especially loved that he stuck it to Monster Jam. There were plenty of high fives, pumping of fists, and celebrating that Jim had won, against all odds.

Twice, I walked away as a champion, and I competed in the World Finals 12 times.

My old pal Mike Weber was tasked with getting Monster Jam on pay-per-view. He'd been involved with the wrestling scene and knew how it all worked. He was the right man for the job, but management wasn't very patient.

It coincided with Monster Jam on TNN, The Nashville Network, where we had a weekly show. Later, similar shows bounced around networks a bit. Unlike WWE, where TV mattered more than the live shows, Monster Jam never saw it that way, and television and pay-per-views were almost an afterthought.

The Monster Jam World Finals were available for people to order on pay-per-view in 2000, 2001, and 2002. We did good numbers, made some money, but it wasn't enough for the bigwigs. They wanted Mike Tyson buyrate numbers out of the gate, which was impossible. Not long after, Mike Weber left, and now he runs Fite TV, which does nothing but pay-per-views.

Going into the World Finals, held on March 20, 2004, I had confidence, and, more importantly, RL believed in me and had my Madusa truck ready to go.

The racing portion didn't go well. That's an understatement, actually. While racing against Little Tiger, I crashed, running headfirst into a concrete pile. The truck was fucked. If it weren't for RL working his magic, which included spurring others on to work alongside him, I wouldn't have gotten to even compete in freestyle.

As it was, I was lucky number 13 out there, meaning I'd seen what 12 others had done. Lupe Soza in El Toro Loco had gone just before me, and the fans loved what he had done, which factored in later. He got a 27, and I got a score of 31. Tom Meents in Maximum Destruction went after me and also got 31. The fans were roaring about Lupe getting hosed, so somehow his score was adjusted, giving him a 31.

A three-way tie; we were all co-champions.

At that moment, I was "The First Lady of Monster Jam," though I'd be lying to say that it wasn't diminished by having to share. There was always a question in my mind about why the numbers for Lupe were changed, and whether they scored Tom higher because I was leading. The $10,000 prize was nice, though.

For the next year, Monster Jam created a tie-breaking system to prevent it ever happening again.

There was always a banquet for the drivers in Vegas, after the World Finals. That was where the awards were given out, and the firesuits and helmets of the winners were up on the stage. But it was a rare chance for us all to be together, to let our hair down a bit, while dressing nice for once — it was part celebration, part roast.

Monster Jam, as a company, was on its best behavior, in the sense that media and sponsors were there, so it wanted to look good, unlike the rest of the year, when the drivers were an afterthought, at best.

The banquet after my co-freestyle win stands out, and not just because I was celebrated alongside Lupe and Tom.

Dennis Anderson had won the racing competition. Prior to his win, Monster Jam had arranged a special prize for Dennis ahead of time, and he got to choose any Ford model he wanted. He chose a Harley-Davidson Ford pickup.

Well, that was enough for me. I was a Harley girl and wanted one, too! Now I had a goal. It was fucking on.

The week-to-week competitions are, quite honestly, a blur for me, a mess of bumps and broken bumpers. The travel was constant, and it was like that scene in *This Is Spinal Tap* where the band tries to remember what town they are in. In many cities, someone would hit me up for a couple of tickets, family, friends, or old wrestling pals, and I'd try to carve out a few minutes for a visit, but often it was just that, a few minutes.

By this point, I was a well-known driver and had absolutely brought in a new fan base of female fans. It was evident by the lines I'd draw at the pit parties. The other drivers couldn't ignore it, and security had to adjust accordingly. In the bigger venues, fans who paid a little extra to meet the drivers had to choose one side of the stadium or the other and weren't allowed to switch lines. So if you were a fan of Grave Digger, you went one way to meet Dennis and other drivers; my line was often on the other side so we didn't have ridiculous lineups. (We still did.) Dennis was famed for taking his time with fans, chatting them up, thanking them for buying tickets so he could reroof his house — which slowed down the line for everyone. While I wasn't short with my fans by any means, I didn't ask them about what they had for dinner and who they liked in the weekend's football games. My post-show line moved even faster, so drivers would ask to sit near me and get out of there earlier.

In 2002, Monster Jam put on its first show in Europe, in Paris, France. Going to Europe, and then the rest of the world, would be a big part of our lives for years to come.

Europe had the craziest fans. Jesus criminy, in Finland, I had a young man pull down his pants and ask me to sign his balls. I had girls whip out their tits, and I signed a few until I realized how ridiculous it was. (I signed a couple of ass cheeks, too.) That was proof I'd grown the base of female fans! These hot chicks would come up to me at the signings, and the drivers realized it — "We're sticking with Deuce!" But nothing ever topped the balls-out request. I said, "Dude, pick up your fucking balls and keep moving, because I'm not signing those!"

The goal for 2005 was to get to the World Finals again, and I did.

I'd developed a ritual at the World Finals. Up early, work out, and then, with butterflies in my tummy, walk the track. I would have a moment to myself before the chaos of the day, to meditate, and it was very cool. In the quiet, I'd sit up in the stands, and I would picture myself coming down the chicane, going around the dirt track and hitting it over there, and crossing the finish line.

In 2005, I felt it. I'm winning. I didn't say that the year before, but this year I just knew. I'd think about that new Ford truck and bring myself back into focus on the race to come. Of course, I didn't say anything to anybody, as they would have thought I was nuts.

With a bye to the second round, I knocked off The Destroyer, then El Toro Loco, and King Krunch in the semis.

Pro wrestling's greatest scriptwriters couldn't have come up with a better finish, the King and Queen of Monster Jam going at it, having each made it through the bracket to face off in the final. Grave Digger was the best truck, with the best motor, the best mechanics. Everyone was on Dennis's side. I had RL and a few other guys.

I wasn't nervous. I blocked out everything. I got in the truck, did up my harness, and sat there. I reminded myself that my time was faster than Dennis's in qualifying, so I got to choose my lane. And I thought, *Well, that's odd. Why would they allow that? Why didn't they fudge the numbers?* I chose the right lane, because that's what I did the best in.

As we were getting close to the race, it started pouring rain, torrential, biblical. I'm like, *Oh, yeah, I'm a mud-bogger. I got this even more.* I didn't even flicker. And note that on monster trucks, you don't have windshield wipers.

Despite the conditions, the show's still a go, and as I pulled up to the start, I remember hearing the crowd going bonkers, and announcer Scott Douglass going: "Folks, you've been waiting for it all night. Can you believe it? Can you believe that she's in the finals, here she is up against a world champion. Here we are. Man against woman. Ford against Chevy. Student against teacher." I also knew that all the other drivers and crews would be clustered in the pop-up tent, around the tiny monitor, watching the action.

My foot was itching to press the pedal and start, and it was agony waiting. My mind briefly wandered to other women drivers, like Shirley Muldowney, Pamela Vaters, and Janet Guthrie. Finally as Scott kept talking with that famous monster voice that he has, I was screaming, "Shut the fuck up Scott! Let's get this party started!" Then a little voice said, "This is it, girl; you gotta beat his ass."

The light turned green. *Whoopa!* I'm out the gate, and it was like an out-of-body experience, as I could see myself, like I was in the bleachers, watching the truck swish and sway through the mud in the rain, which had lightened up. That bitch swung around the turn like a bat out of hell. From the start, I knew this was going to be risky, it was muddy as hell, the windshield was already covered with mud, so I automatically was watching with peripheral eyesight and I was good at that. It saved me from crashing in the chicane down thunder alley. When doing this the secret is to run your own race and have an idea where the hell your competitor is. I was focused but determined to kick his ass. I heard nothing but the roaring motor and the hot, high-pitched winding of the brakes as I came to the final turn before the big jump to the finish line.

And there it was — the perfect turn, the best one of the year, perfectly lined up in the center of the hill and *boooom!* I gagged that bitch and flattened all the way to the floor out the other fucking end, pushing so hard thinking it was going to make me faster or something, gripping that steering wheel so tight getting ready for the inevitable, and just like that, I cleared the jump beautifully. Then I saw Dennis right on my tail at the finish line.

Oh my God. Where's Dennis? What happened? At least I didn't crash. Okay, that's good. I don't care. I went to the finals. He probably won. That's all right. I got this. Oh, it's a good story.

Now that I was stopped, I could see through the muck on the windshield that Dennis was still sitting in his truck. He wasn't out waving. Why not?

The crowd is going nuuuutttss. I see everyone pointing at me, the techs coming out. *Oh my God, what happened? Is my truck on fire?*

Dennis fired up his truck and hauled ass out of there.

It was at that moment that I knew I had won.

I started crying in my helmet, and I did my little parade lap.

Before I got out of my truck completely, I tried to compose myself, catch my breath. Appropriately, RL was the first one to get to me. We were hugging and crying, and I thanked him, since I couldn't have done it without him. It was then that I truly heard the crowd, and it was deafening, like nothing I'd ever experienced before. Euphoric.

I looked around for Dennis, because I wanted to go offer my congratulations. He was off to the end of the course, in his truck, still staring through his windshield. I went over to Grave Digger, mouthed, "Thank you, good race," and shook his hand while he leaned down from the cab. (Here is something no one knows: I snuck into Dennis's dressing area later and stole a Grave Digger crew shirt as a memento.)

A few girlfriends were up in a suite with the executives from Monster Jam, and the bigwigs didn't know who they were. Later, they told me that when I won, the one exec said to the other, "A woman just won. Now what the fuck are we going to do?"

One friend told me, "Debrah, I didn't know what to do. I didn't know who they were, but I kept quiet, so I could hear more."

Later, I competed in freestyle, too, and wanted so desperately to win both, but it was not to be. I was spent, the truck, too, I suppose. Madusa in Madusa finished 18th in freestyle.

At that year's World Finals banquet, I got a plaque and a cash award. No truck. My visualization only came half true.

But I nearly got into a fight!

Jimmy and Dawn Creten were a husband-and-wife independent team. At the banquet, Jimmy came up to me and said, "You were supposed to win freestyle, and I was supposed to win racing. I just don't understand how this happened." And I'll never forget saying, "Well, maybe because I was good."

To use a wrestling term, I had had heat for a year, since at the 2004 World Finals, I had nicked Jimmy's truck during freestyle, as he had crashed, and it had been left out there by a jump. When I went to do my jump, my tires slipped, and I ended up crawling up the ramp, touched his truck, and it flipped my truck over backwards to do a backflip.

Dawn had seen Jimmy talking to me and stormed over. She got up in my face, though she only came up to my chest, and, three sheets to the wind as she was, Dawn challenged me. "I'm gonna kick your ass right now." And I was like, *What is happening?* "You ever fuckin' hit my truck again, I'll get you. We spend that money. We're not like you and can just fly in and drive a company truck and crash it and not pay for things."

I looked at her and said, "It's best that you back up, Dawn, back up right now." That's all I said. Others who were there saw it and interceded, holding her as she started trying to kick me. Someone talked her down, "Dawn, you don't want to mess with her." Kudos to her, but I was giggling inside because the first thing that came to my mind was, *God, this would be a great wrestling promo*. Then, after that, we became best friends.

As far as I know, Monster Jam sent out one press release about my racing win. Then they sent my ass home.

I should have been on talk shows. I should have been pushed everywhere — it's a publicist's dream! Nothing.

The Monster Jam people were scared of me.

Instead of going for a third title, Monster Jam took RL away from me, and I was never told why. Once again, the rotation of crew chiefs started up. Now, they knew the basics — oil change, taking off the monster truck tire — but when I would say, "Hey, this is making a noise," I was told, "You don't know what you are talking about." I'd go back to RL, and he'd say, "My hands are tied. I can't do anything." I'm like, "What the hell's going on?"

Another new crew chief wanted to impress me, and the first day he came to work on the Madusa truck, he'd shaved his head into a Mohawk and dyed his hair pink. Awesome. From that day forward, Mike Osborne was "Pink Ozzy." We worked together for a few years.

Excuse the pun, but I rode out of the difficulties and lasted until 2018. For all the headaches, the concussions, the injuries, the fights with management, the trials and tribulations of travel, it was just fucking *fun* to drive a monster truck.

I do have the *best* story about a mechanic to share, though.

At one point, around 2006, I was walking through the back with all the trucks, when a woman stopped me.

"Excuse me."

And I went, "Oh, hi. What's your name? When did you start working here?"

"My name is Becky. Becky McDonough." I think she thought I'd know her name.

"You're a mechanic?"

"Yes, ma'am."

"Well, that is badass. It's about time we get a woman mechanic here."

"Yes, ma'am. You told me to."

It turns out that she'd seen me at a couple of Minneapolis shows and pictured herself driving a monster truck down the road, too, whipping off her helmet and shaking out her hair, just like I did. When she was in college, she dropped me an email. I used to get a lot of email, and now direct messages, and can't possibly respond to them all, but I did with Becky. In the note, I encouraged her to stay in school, but that if she was serious about driving, to call a number and learn about becoming a mechanic. When Becky finished college, she called, and two weeks later, she was on a plane to North Carolina to learn the ins and outs of monster trucks at Digger's Dungeon.

She told me the story that night, and I just started crying.

It wasn't until 2010, including time as a crew chief for my buddy Cam McQueen, that they let her drive a monster truck — Donkey Kong in Costa Rica, but she became better known later for driving El Toro Loco. I was her biggest supporter and fan, and still am. Becky still races, along with her husband, and she used her marketing skills to start a company, which creates killer clothes, based around a slogan I suggested to her: "Rough, tough, pretty stuff."

I'm one proud Mama Deuce.

While I was the first woman in Monster Jam, I'm happy to say I was not the last. The door wasn't just opened, it was destroyed. They've come from all kinds of places, too, all walks of life.

For every Kim Crosby, who'd driven on the various NASCAR levels, there were people like Candice Jolly, who had raced go-karts and swamp buggies. I already mentioned Dawn Cretin, and I developed mad respect for the independent drivers, carving out an existence among so much uncertainty.

There is a very, very strong bond with women in motorsports, because we just *know* instinctively the challenges they've faced, from misogynistic assholes to fitting your boobs into a firesuit. We fought similar fights. If anything, I think the women can be more competitive than the men, especially with one another out on the track. But backstage, there is definitely a kinship.

I went to bat for Brianna Mahon, because I saw a lot of potential in her racing. She had that "it factor," and I could see her being the champion. She started getting a lot of publicity, and her popularity skyrocketed. Monster Jam started seeing that, and you could tell that they were like, "Oh, shit." It's a powerful, powerful movement.

To her credit, Brianna, and her parents, asked me lots of questions, "How do I do this? How do I get that?" She's hardly the only driver I helped educate, male or female.

But here's an example of subtle sexism that existed in Monster Jam. The women almost always got assigned a truck designed like a dog — Scooby-Doo, Monster Mutt, or the Dalmatian. Pretty soon it was a running joke: just put the woman in the fucking dog truck because that's where they belong, in the doghouse. "Well, they're driving a truck," was the comeback.

Dennis Anderson's kids were around all the time I was in Monster Jam. I'd send them birthday and Christmas presents. The apples didn't fall far from the tree, with both Adam and Ryan winning World Finals, and their sister, Krysten, a kick-ass driver in her own right, setting the world record for the highest leap in a Monster Truck at 33 feet, 9.6 inches. Their youngest brother, Weston, who we called "Teeny," recently started driving Grave Digger, too.

Whether it was speaking to friends, media, or fans, questions were similar, so let's tackle a few.

Do you need a special driver's license?

Nope. Most of the mechanics weren't even certified car mechanics; there was no Monster Jam mechanic license, either.

What is it like to drive? What's the difference between a normal car and a monster truck?

I'd talk about the technical aspects, the giant wheels, the cage around the driver, the sheer power of the motor and the awesomeness of the transmission. The interviewers loved it when I talked about wrecking — it was someone else's vehicle and someone else's money, which is the opposite of your personal vehicle.

How loud are the monster trucks when you are inside?

Back in the day, the guys put cotton in their ears or earplugs, since the trucks are loud, very loud. I did not put anything in my ears, as I needed to hear the sound of the truck, the clatter, the motor, the vibration, the transmission, to hear if a tire popped. The sound alone helped me drive. If I had a dick, I probably would have had a hard-on from the sound of the engine, it was that amazing.

Years later, we finally had a two-way radio system, where they'd mold an earpiece with the wires attached, just like in NASCAR. It took some adjustment on my part, but I figured it out, listening to the truck with one ear and my crew in the other. I'd hear warnings like, "Deuce, you've got an axle broken in the back. Be careful when you take your right turn," or, "Hold off, you got a popped tire. Do a donut the opposite way, so you can pop your tire back on." They had strict instructions to only talk if it was important, and even then, no yelling.

What was it like to be on fire?

It happened to me twice, once while driving for Bigfoot and once with Monster Jam. But before I get to that, a note that no one *ever* told me what to do if it happened; there was never a safety video to watch or anyone coaching me. Even my firesuit and boots were a learn-it-yourself experience. You might think I'm full of shit, but I'm not.

Both times, the truck just went up in flames after a crash, and I reacted on instinct and panic. I quickly released my five-point harness, and as soon as I did that, I reached over and pulled the pin in the fire extinguisher that was in the cab. Then you try to get the fuck out of there as fast as you can. I remember closing my eyes and holding my breath as I shimmied out of the truck, which was on its side. It helped that I was a veteran by then and knew every inch of my truck, even as the flames raged, and the smoke was everywhere. It was only when I was out of the truck that I sensed that I was on fire, too, with this warmth coming over me, feet on up. I dropped and rolled, like we were taught in grade school — and sometimes it was on fucking concrete! — as fire crews raced out to help with fire extinguishers.

What is it like driving a regular car after being in a monster truck?

I miss driving a truck a lot, because it really helped me control my road rage — I can't stand idiot drivers! For 19 years, I got to drive a monster truck. It was always the same, whether we were done on a Sunday or a Monday: I was sore and banged up. That meant my movements were slow and methodical afterwards.

The goal was always to be on one of the earliest flights possible to go home. There were plenty of nights where I didn't actually sleep, just hung out in my room waiting for that early morning wake-up call. It's a policy that remains today when I'm at bookings.

But I have *never* traveled light, never been a minimalist when it came to packing. Yeah, I know there's all kinds of shit that I didn't need to bring, but that's me, with seemingly enough stuff for a month when I'm gone for an extended weekend. I learned the hard way that you couldn't leave your helmet with the truck early in my run, as it disappeared, stolen, I guess. So I had to bring my firesuit, boots, helmet — everything — with me.

When I got out of the airport with all my luggage, I'd go looking for my car, which could be a real challenge, as my mind was always fried, and no doubt concussed many times. Improvements in technology like key fobs and taking a photo of where I parked (and then searching through hundreds of photos) has helped.

In the car, driving home, I'd relish the silence after the constant roar of engines for days. And I'd happily cruise along in the slow lane. People would get stuck behind me in the slow lane, and they'd come around me and would flip me off; I'd be like, "Right on. You go, bro." I was the nicest driver after a weekend of racing.

After settling in for a while, relishing that whole peaceful, easy feeling, reality would kick in, and I'd hit the gas and roarrrrr down the highway. "Here I am bitches! Get out of my way!"

It was cool to have the two different realities, but I will say that I never got any speeding tickets in a monster truck.

What was it like crushing cars?

Once I got over the initial thought of me *being crushed in an accident on the highway*, it became second nature. You don't hear the car being crushed, but there is a sensation of it folding up underneath the weight of the truck, and your adrenaline is pumping like crazy. It never got old. The cars themselves would be from the local junkyard, and they'd work out a deal to promote the junkyard in exchange for getting the old cars for less money. Over the years, car manufacturing changed, and they just weren't as good to crush, so we went to mostly dirt hills. Visually, fans missed the crushing, but the truck tires didn't take nearly as much damage.

What did the wrestlers think of you going into monster trucks?

One time at World Finals, Bill Goldberg saw me and said, "Damn, Deuce, you're insane! I wouldn't get in that fucking truck." Others, like Terri Runnels, Lisa Varon, and CM Punk, would hit me up for tickets to come see the show; it was nice getting to know a different generation of wrestlers, and we all share that bond.

Did anyone else ever drive the Madusa truck?

Yes. Brianna Mahon drove it a few times, including in the World Finals in 2015 in the Young Guns Shootout, and then in 2016. Kim Crosby drove it in South America, and BJ Johnson is the only man to ever drive her, and that was in Adelaide, Australia, in 2014 when I got hurt.

The efforts to push Monster Jam worked, and we were soon in demand internationally. Europe was first, then Australia, Japan, South America. The sight of a monster truck demolishing cars and creating chaos was a universal language.

Of course, there were all kinds of challenges with events around the world — like getting the trucks there! Fortunately, that wasn't my job, but they went by ship, so the schedules had to allow for it, and not everyone wanted to go, either. Dennis Anderson only brought Grave Digger overseas once or twice. It could take months for a truck to get somewhere by container ship.

Europe was usually in the early summer, and then Australia since the seasons are reversed there.

Those first few trips overseas were insane. Most of my colleagues had never even been out of the United States and associated the trips with stardom. "We're traveling, we're going places, we're superstars!" Yet, I'm looking at these guys with greasy hair, old jeans, their nails black with grease, thinking, *Yeah, you're a superstar, baby.*

When we got to the new city, there was culture shock. They looked to me, a veteran world traveler, for guidance.

Here's a specific example. We had a great show in Arnhem, Holland, and were scheduled to go to Zurich, Switzerland. Problem: the tickets for our roaming band of vagabonds had been bought for the wrong day. I'm at my best in the worst moments, like my mind can quickly calculate outcomes and put together a plan (I would have been great in combat). With some extra money from a corporate handler, the train let us on, though it was chaotic, with some people in baggage cars, sleeping in bunks that weren't ours, or even on the floor. Then in Zurich, I had to collect everyone, zombie-like from lack of sleep and scared of the unknown, and get us on a bus and in cabs to our hotel, like the teacher chaperoning a class to the Capitol for a tour.

Those situations were actually the norm for the first few years, and it pissed me off. I'd already been through this with wrestling — and so had Chad, and he deserves a mention for helping in the worst of times — and that was 20 years ago, so why wasn't this company better? I put it down to a lack of respect for those who made them money. They forced people to share rooms, techs or crew three or four to a room; since I was the only woman much of the time, that wasn't an issue for me, and then I had my own room written into my contract. On the long flights, everyone got economy seats (thank God for my status again, leftover from wrestling). They'd expect us to fly 13 hours to Australia and then jump into a truck the next day. It was insane. They wouldn't even let you change your ticket to come back a few days later so you had time to be a tourist and enjoy seeing the world. I made my opinion known, and wasn't the only one, and they came around to slightly more humane treatment of their livestock.

The animal analogy works in another way, because the international tours were where we could really let our hair down. We only had one another, no spouses or kids to worry about, so everyone let loose.

I'm pretty sure this was Finland, and we were up in our rooms, dumped out our suitcases, and hopped in them to slide all the way down the damn stairs. At the bottom, I stole the fire extinguisher and I started spraying everybody. We'd play all kinds of ribs on each other, locking people in their rooms, stealing furniture. Oh my God, it was fun, and definitely a way to pass the time: strangers in a strange land.

The international fans were quite different and didn't know what to expect from the monster trucks. They'd only seen the action on TV, so we had to educate them on what it all was. There was an initial awe factor that is hard to describe, like this massive part of American culture invading their city with all the noise and smoke. In turn, they cheered differently, too, less interested in a favorite driver and more about the spectacle. And their cheering was deafening!

Though I was often a loner during all the downtime on the domestic shows, on the longer tours I bonded with four awesome guys. I consider ourselves the "Fab Five of Monster Jam," but if you ask any of them — Damon Bradshaw, George Balhan, Cam McQueen, and Lee O'Donnell — it was the "Fab Four+1."

Damon came from the world of motocross, George had raced ATVs and motocross, and Cam and Lee had driven all kinds of vehicles. They all just lived to compete, more than even I did. When that light turned green, look out! It was on! They challenged me to be a better racer, while I taught them a lot about showmanship, whether it was their characters or freestyle stunts.

Since we were all outsiders and hadn't done the traditional route of working your way up from grease monkey to driver, we saw the way things operated differently than everyone else. Damon had been a star, a champion, in motocross, and brought in his own sponsor, Monster Energy, and his own fan base. He knew his worth and was stubborn, outspoken, and brave in the face of management — sound like anyone else you know?!

Monster Jam, especially when Feld Entertainment was in control, was maddening, and we fought and fought, and led by example. Feld discouraged drivers from having a lawyer look at the contracts. Not shady at all. I was the one handing out my lawyer's number to everyone else. But you know what pissed off management more than anything? That we were damn good at our jobs.

We had both the guts and the standing to be able to change the rules, to do things our way; there was power in numbers. Instead of having to fly from one end of Australia to another for a show the next weekend, we got a minivan and drove, with adventure after adventure on the way. On another trip, we booked a house on the beach instead of the hotel and all stayed together. An established goal of the Fab Four+1 was to find a Harley-Davidson dealership in every city, so, time permitting, we'd find a way to get there. We were the ones leading the wacky pranks, trying to get everyone else involved, so we weren't exclusionary by any means.

In October 2014, the Fab Four had my back when the company didn't.

Every driver has stories about crashing, broken bones, dislocated joints, bruising, concussions; every driver still has aches and pains to this day. For me, my wrists and forearms are a constant source of pain, from all those years gripping tight to the steering wheel. My neck is a mess, my back, and I could go on.

And every driver has that one story that tops them all. For me, it was on October 4, 2014, in Melbourne, Australia, when I was competing in racing. It wasn't anything particularly gruesome to look at, the truck just took a wicked hit as I almost did a backflip off a small hill. The bitch knocked me silly.

After the accident, I still did an interview, and it hurt when I tried to wave to the crowd. I didn't say anything, but accepted a ride back to the dressing room. That was not the norm, because I'm usually walking around talking to people, coming down off the performance high.

For me to just exit and go in my room was out of the ordinary, and people noticed. They asked if I was okay, and I brushed them off. Knowing that if I just sat there, I was going to be stiff as hell the next day, I got up to walk around. As I was walking, I smelled something funny, and I tasted some weird shit, like metal. Blood started coming out of my mouth. Did I bite my tongue? Son of a bitch. My mouth is not even sore. I kept spitting blood, so I knew something was up. My medical background came back. *Okay, this is severe. This ain't good.*

When one of the female techs in the dressing room asked me, "Deuce, you all right?" I said no and asked for the paramedic. She went running for help, and the EMTs wasted no time and said I needed to go to the hospital. They took my vitals, and my heart rate was okay. "Do you feel faint yet?" I went, "No, noooo, noooo . . ." and could feel myself fading. But I can remember someone from management asked the paramedics whether I'd be able to go for the freestyle portion!

They filled me up with drugs, and I started hallucinating. I saw psychedelic fucking monkeys, running elephants, and I was like, "*Whoa*, you need to pull back on the drugs. I don't do drugs. Get this shit off me" — and I ripped out the IV. My body was reacting to morphine and shit that had never been in it before. I was so pissed that I was cussing people. My pain threshold is high.

My ribs were X-rayed, and even while doped up, I started screaming because it felt like the rib was puncturing something inside. So they shot me up with some more shit, which finally knocked me out.

When I came to and said, "You just can't do that anymore, please, no more drugs," everyone started laughing in the room.

The diagnosis was a bilateral contusion of the lungs, which meant that I almost ripped my lungs out, and everything was bleeding inside my lungs. I also broke all my ribs on the left side. There was probably a concussion, too, but that was the least of my worries. I settled in and was immobilized from Sunday through to Thursday.

When I was aware enough, naturally I had to tell the world:

> Hello all my #pinkwarriors just want to give you an update I have had hundreds of questions asking if I'm okay so I want to set the record straight. Yes. #timewillheal Had an awesome night in Melbourne the pit party was phenomenal and I did take a bad spill during freestyle . . . however I am on my way to recovery and I will be in Adelaide and Sydney. I was at one of the best hospitals in Melbourne. I want to say thanks to all the doctors and nurses and staff you guys were great, all of my fans who are such great supporters I thank you. The biggest of big shout out to my colleagues of monster jam.

My Fab Four pals checked in on me, but we were scheduled for two more weeks in Australia. I was released on Friday, but not allowed to fly home, because of the threat of blood clots while in the air. So the boys drove me to the next town, rather than having me crammed on a bus or with someone who didn't know me very well.

In Adelaide, Monster Jam insisted that I go to the event and sign autographs for six fucking hours — with broken ribs. I made a scene, a big one, and there were plenty of people around when I ranted. "Listen, you son of a bitch. I'm going to go get my crew shirts. I'm going to put that on. And I'm going to stand here. And every single one of these fans, they know what happened in Melbourne, that I'm hurt, and they're going to see exactly what I'm going through, what you're putting me through," I threatened.

I tried, I really tried, and I think I lasted about two hours, nearly fainting. My female crew chief stood up for me, bless her heart, and offered to sign Madusa team autographs instead. I went back to the hotel, and not long after, I got on a plane and went home.

It was the beginning of the end of my relationship with Monster Jam, even if I drove for them for another few years.

The accident in Australia woke me up, and I think it terrified the people at Feld Entertainment running Monster Jam. The next two contracts that I signed, two years apiece, 2015 and 2017, were the best of my career. It's like they *knew* they'd wronged me, and that was a small concession to acknowledging that. In both cases, during negotiating periods, I missed races as we fought over terms. If you heard I was "injured" during those years, chances are I was just butting heads.

Looking back on it, my driving changed. I was going through the motions. Don't get me wrong, I still loved to drive, especially to race, but I just wasn't enthralled with the idea of crashing in freestyle for the sake of a company that barely gave a shit about my existence.

With monster trucks, it was such an uphill battle, and being the only woman for so long, it was very tiresome. And it was such a fight, often for things that would have been obvious to a child: proper harnesses and safety features in the truck; catering for everyone stuck at the venue all day; merchandise to promote the trucks and drivers.

There was so much change there, towards the last five years of my career, it was just ugly. It was like my last days in WCW, where I knew, "I'm fucking out." When you know your love isn't in something and you're just there to collect a paycheck, get the fuck out, because you're going to be miserable. That means you're going to be miserable to yourself, you're going to be miserable to the people you work with, and you're going to bring that shit home.

For 2019, I was supposed to have a farewell tour. The truck was repainted chrome, but it was pulled out from underneath me. After a few appearances signing autographs — without my truck — they just paid me for a year to sit home.

At the end, I got a call from Keith Speller saying, "We're going in another direction. We don't need you. Thank you." That was it.

I did get to drive two more times before the world shut down.

My gal-pal Kim Crosby had a hookup with an independent monster truck show in Australia. I was medically cleared and itching to drive again — and keep my name and brand out there — so I got in touch with the promoter. We struck a deal, and the Madusa truck raced in March and April 2020 Down Under. Then came the global pandemic, and I got home to Florida just before everything closed down.

The COVID-19 pandemic affected the whole world, and Monster Jam was no different. Its parent, Feld Entertainment, slashed staff since there could be no events. Many friends lost their jobs, as did some who I felt got what was coming to them.

You know how some companies get praise for their appreciation for employees, knowing that a happy worker puts in a better day's job, with pride in their work? Feld was the opposite. Lee O'Donnell, one of their top drivers and the first to ever complete a four-wheel front flip (at the 2017 Monster Jam World Finals, go find the video!), sent emails, texts, and made calls to find out what was happening. Lee ended up getting the company president on the line to determine he was out of a job. Cowards.

It's frustrating because I left one of the biggest legacies in monster trucks, period. Yet I'm never mentioned with the trailblazers. It's like my story has been conveniently cut out of their narrative. There's both a Monster Truck Hall of Fame and a newly started Monster Jam Hall of Fame. I've said, if you don't expect something, you won't be let down.

The obvious proof is out there with the women drivers who have made their own noise after I busted down the door. The more subtle story has been shared here, the things I helped fight for behind the scenes.

When you are in the midst of a battle, you don't have the privilege of seeing the big picture. Looking back now, Madusa, driving the Madusa truck, made a difference.

14.

FANS, MARKS, SMARKS, AND STALKERS

THERE IS NO FEELING in the world like having thousands and thousands of people cheering for you. It was always magical and never got old. The reasons for the cheers were different in my two professions. In wrestling, the goal is to take the fans along on a roller-coaster ride, the ups and downs of the match causing them to react by booing the villain and cheering the hero — and I was usually the hero! Driving, you couldn't

Keiko, Kisska, and me alongside the All Japan Women's bus.

hear the fans when you were in the truck, but when you got out, it was like a wave washed over you, whether it was joy at your success or relief that you were okay after flipping upside down.

It's a cliché, but the fans are the reason you keep going back.

Since I got into both pro wrestling and monster trucks without any experience in either field, I was a clean slate, and early on, I studied both the action in the ring or arena and the fans.

I'd find a hoodie or a baseball hat, tuck in my hair, and sneak out into the crowd and be a part of the experience — and it is a whole different view from a seat. It got tougher to do that, though, as my fame increased.

I've been asked through the years about the two fan bases. There is definitely some overlap — which is what WCW was trying to capitalize on by sponsoring monster trucks in the likenesses of their wrestlers — but I'd say that's primarily on the male side.

When I was in wrestling, people referred to it as a male soap opera. There would be some women in the crowds, but not a lot. Early in my career, it seemed my main fan base was teenage boys! When the *Monday Night War* was on, a lot of those boys were now young men in college, and *Nitro*-watching parties in dorms at school was a thing, and again, WCW jumped at the opportunity, sending camera crews to film fandom.

But monster trucks were all about families. Of course, the kids loved the size and power and noise of the trucks, but ticket prices were always meant to be reasonable so everyone could go and still have some money left over for parking, hot dogs, and a Madusa T-shirt.

And those fans were so loyal, always there to support me, cheer me on, bring me a handmade card at a pit party. This is despite the fact that I was never pushed as the face of Monster Jam; if anything, I was pushed away — yet the fans kept coming. After a while, my colleagues would just laugh, "No matter how they try, Deuce, your fans are always dedicated."

My heart swells just thinking about those moments.

Along the way, I learned some sign language, as I encountered many hearing-impaired kids. Some of them came to the monster truck shows, and when they finally got through the long line to meet me, I'd be able to sign to them, and they would lose their mind. They'd sign back how I was their idol.

Today, I've forgotten a lot of the main signs, but I still know key words — like "thank you" — and can run through the alphabet. When I see somebody signing, it will catch my eye. I'll just kind of smile, and they'll look at me and ask if I understand. I'll sign back "hello" and my name. They get so excited because it's very rare that people know sign language. We take it for granted that we can hear and talk. But with a deaf person, it's not a common thing to get on an elevator and someone just starts talking back to you.

Of course, not all fan interactions are positive.

When I was living with Greg Valentine in Florida, I had this stalker who'd call at weird hours and leave strange messages. Or faxes, if you remember what they were; imagine the shriek of the fax machine going off when you're sleeping. It was a trying time.

I'd been in Los Angeles, with Brandon Pender, trying to break into acting. Since Greg and I were on the road all the time, we had an answering machine where you could call in to hear the messages from anywhere, and with the press of a button, you could listen to the house as well. While in L.A., I called home, knowing Greg was on a tour. I listened and I heard noises in the house and freaked, thinking it was my stalker.

Brandon had connections, and he called his friend in the local marshal's office, who got in touch with the Florida cops. The cops arrived, opened up the door, and found Greg there. They laid into him: "Who are you? Who lives here? Show us proof . . ." It got sorted out.

The police actually did find my stalker, and he never bothered me again. The whole idea of celebrity stalkers had been in the news, with laws being passed to protect stars.

It was tougher to protect actors and actresses from sleazy movie types, though. One guy pretended to be a Hollywood producer and sent me scripts, promising me roles. He wouldn't stop. There was no "ignore" button on your phone then.

The shit that I fell for. I mean, I could have been slaughtered and dead 10 times over on the side of Hollywood Boulevard. I got lucky. Damn. I just knew shit wasn't right. My intuition — which I call my money maker — was on point.

And then you'd have some creepy men who would mail you pearl necklaces and jewelry. That shit would go right back to them or be trashed if there was no return address — I never accepted anything.

Now, there were in-person gifts that I would accept. In some interview, I mentioned my love of Butterfinger candy bars, so fans would bring those to the pit parties, and on occasion, I'd have so many I'd hand them out to the other drivers and our crews.

Through the years, fans have compiled videotapes and then DVDs of my matches, many that are rare. Fan letters can go from sweet to scary, but it's part of being a celebrity.

Every gift was a wonderful gesture, and here's a universal "Thank you!"

You had to learn to accept the oddities, too. Some fans knew my blood type and wore necklaces with a vial of it. Creepy. *It must be food coloring*, I kept telling myself. I would find myself questioning what I did to earn such undying loyalty.

As a rule, I shake everyone's hand, and little kids get high fives. Promoters who bring me to signings get annoyed since I like to talk to everyone, too, a little one-on-one time. Hugs are reserved mainly for kids, with few exceptions, and anytime a guy moves in, I step away gracefully.

Autographs weren't a business when I started in pro wrestling, and I just signed here and there when fans asked or if there was a personal appearance. With Monster Jam, they whored us out with the pit parties, and then post-racing events, too, autograph after autograph. It got to the point where I started signing a stylized *M* instead of *Madusa*, just to protect my brand. I tried to convince other drivers of the worth of their autograph, and a few bought into it, but most did not. Now, with sports collectibles shows and specialized wrestling ones as a big business, I pick and choose which I want to appear at, knowing that if it is more than a couple a year, it devalues me.

My Madusa truck became an extension of me, and the *MADe in USA* idea went over great with the fan base in monster trucks. It changed through the years, too, with different designs and colors, but the one constant was pink.

Sure, pink is usually associated with women, but I initially played to a very masculine audience and tried to change their minds. I would say "Real men wear pink" in my interviews, and soon enough, men were coming to the pit parties in pink shirts, pink hair, tutus, and tiaras, just like the little girls. It was so funny.

The LGBTQ+ family found me and loved me. It was great. I had every walk of life supporting me, and I loved them for it.

Worst fan interaction? Hands down, it came in Angels Stadium in Anaheim, California. After the freestyle part of the Monster Jam shows, drivers would usually come out to wave and salute the fans, a way to say thank you for coming out. There was a cool rush from doing it, as the motors were silent so you could hear the cheering . . . a bit, since your own ears would still be ringing. This time, I was one of the last to compete, so still had the adrenaline coursing through me. As was the norm, there was carnage, with broken trucks all over the stadium, so you couldn't necessarily see down to the other end.

Drivers have to have good peripheral vision, to the point where you should be able to see behind yourself if you're looking forward! In this case, out of the corner of my eye, I sensed someone coming. A fan was streaking towards me — he'd hopped the barrier and was coming at me.

All I thought in those five seconds or so was wrestling, and how we destroyed any fan who ever jumped into the ring. Rather than run away from this madman, I went towards him, tripped him down to the ground. I put my weight on his back, grabbed his hair, and started wiping his face in the dirt, with all the oils and transmission fluid contaminating it. I took both of his hands and almost tied them in a knot behind his back.

The fans went nuts, and the rest of the drivers and crews came racing over — remember, some of them couldn't see what had happened and probably figured I was getting knifed or something — and they pulled me off the idiot. I briefly thought I'd killed him, since he wasn't moving. I got up and said, "Get rid of this piece of shit." Of course, the police had to ask what happened, and I told them the truth: "I thought he was going to kill me and I saw something shiny in his hand." That was fine with them, and it was the last I heard of it . . . except for my tough-girl reputation backstage!

I do want to highlight a few fans who have meant a lot to me through the years.

My first and longest-lasting fan is Keiko: more than 30 years. When I went to a Stardom event in Japan a few years back, she was amazed that I remembered her. Well, of course I did — in 1988, she bought me a dog! Kisska was a Pomeranian, the cutest little thing. Whenever possible, Kisska stayed with me, and the rest of the time, Keiko looked after her. Keiko lived in Osaka and would drive to Sendai with Kisska, and we'd have a little picnic down by the river, watching Kisska play in the water. When I went back to America, Kisska lived out her life with Keiko (the paperwork would have been nuts to bring her over). While working on the book, I reached out again to Keiko and asked what it was that connected us. "When I saw you coming to Japan alone, I wanted you to have a good time in Japan," she explained. "I wanted to cheer for Madusa, I wanted to make you more exciting than anyone else, so I hung a pink flag at ringside." Keiko confessed that I helped her with her personal confidence, too — female empowerment!

The idea of sharing strength appealed to Ashley, who was in college around 2015 when she started following me on my socials — she'd only heard of me through wrestling, and the WWE Hall of Fame put me back in the spotlight. When I began my Twitch channel, Ashley really connected with my tone; naturally, I had to ask what she meant by that. "Your personality on Twitch is very strong, very out there, funny, but also kind and sweet. And very sarcastic, which is like my kind of sense of humor and I love it," she recounted, adding that my competitiveness makes her laugh. Through the occasional personal message, Ashley has shared some of her own mental health issues, and I have done my best to help her out. Some people are more comfortable online. "It's a very safe environment for me. It's just like hanging out with a friend, supportive, but also connecting with one of my favorite people, one of my biggest inspirations," Ashley said. "You see your strong, sarcastic smart-ass side, but you are also super sweet, wise and helpful."

There's an old carnival term that is used in wrestling, where fans are called "marks" because, as a performer, you are trying to put one over on them, to make them believe (and "smarks" are fans who think they know everything). So when I deal with my friend, Mark, I can't help but chuckle at his name, but he has helped me here and there with graphic designs. He saw me in the early 1990s in WCW and followed along through WWE, WCW, and into monster trucks. Terri Runnels, who was Marlena in WWE, was a friend, and she'd worked with Mark on some graphic stuff and recommended him to me. We met at a monster truck show in Baltimore, Maryland, and he started helping me. And Mark ran a little NFL football pool for my husband, Alan, and me, and some of our friends in wrestling, too. When I was asking Mark about why he liked working with me, he hemmed and hawed a bit, and then let loose: "I've had a lot of friends in the wrestling industry over the years. You are definitely on the top as far as the most humble and real and true person. You check up on me when you don't have to, randomly. Honestly, you are one of the nicest people I've ever known."

Then comes Jaker, who is in a class all his own. Jaker and his mom, Suzi, live in Nashville, where I first met them at a monster truck show. Since then, they have been to see me drive or appear at fan fests from St. Louis, Missouri, to Florida to North Carolina. Through our interactions, I have become a fan of Jaker himself; he's autistic and just powers through, in good times and bad. We should all be as strong-willed. Jaker runs an Instagram account (@jaker4449) dedicated to me, and he constantly finds photos I have never seen. Since he only started following me when I was a driver, Jaker then went back and has watched a ton of my matches. When he was still in high school, Suzi dropped me a note saying that classmates were giving him a hard time, since he claimed to know me and they didn't believe him. Well, that was easy to solve, and I gave him a major shout-out on Instagram. When I talked to Jaker recently about it, he said that not only did it solve the bullying at school, but "I also had many monster truck fans who were jealous of me."

The online world changed. When it was just my website, interaction was on my time and selective and I could ignore any nasty messages. But now with social media, it is instantaneous and, way too often, vile. Codi Smith sure makes my life easier, managing my socials and arranging some appearances.

While I don't watch all the wrestling that is available — who can? — I do like to catch some of it. Like any other fan, I will comment on something I enjoyed, trying to be positive and encouraging. Then I'll get blowback: some troll will call me an old hag who is out of touch with today's product. When the younger talent doesn't come to the defense, it's mind boggling, an unacknowledged assent. But then, do they even know who I am, what I accomplished? Wrestling does such a shitty job talking about its past.

Through bad experiences — shitstorms — I have learned to think once, twice, three times, before I even post anything. If I put something out there that half the universe doesn't like, it's gonna go viral, and then everyone jumps on for a group attack. It's horrible to experience.

And weird. One time, I went live on my Instagram page, getting ready for a gig, and fans kept asking me, "Are you barefoot?" You folks are weird. Enough! Why are you asking about my feet?

In person, people are far more polite, and you can see whether they are shy, nervous, handicapped, or whatever, and you adjust accordingly. That is what being a human being is all about.

"How are you doing, Madusa?" or "Hello, Ms. Blayze" are common opening lines. A lot of them say, "It's so good to see you out. So glad to see that you're still healthy and you take care of yourself." It took me a bit to wrap my head around that, but it makes sense. From my era, you don't see many of the women go out and sign, or at least not at the high-profile shows, like WWE Fan Axxess. And then a lot of them are like, "We lose so many. We're just glad you take care of yourself." I'm not kidding, that's a popular one.

I have stayed fit and I've got a rocking bod for 60 — but fans don't see me like that. They still see me as a young woman. It's odd. And just I guess a lot of it has to do with how I handle myself, how I interact with my fans.

The other questions I get often are, "Who was your favorite opponent?" and "Are you coming back? Do you want to have a retirement match?"

The answers? I say my best years, where I honed my craft, were in Japan and that I had many good opponents, but that I didn't have enough. Then they'll mention Bull Nakano or Sherri Martel.

As for a comeback, never say never.

15.

AN EXECUTIVE AND A BIGFOOT

PEOPLE THROW AROUND the term "circus-like" referring to some sort of disorganized chaos. Well, working for Feld Entertainment was *the* circus.

Two brothers, from Hagerstown, Maryland, Irvin and Izzy Feld, were honest to God snake oil salesmen during the Depression, peddling wild concoctions to rubes. They went legit when they bought a variety store in a Black neighborhood in Washington, DC, in 1939, and that was the start of the Super Cut-Rate Drugs chain of pharmacies. When they added records to the stores, Irvin Feld ended up as the manager of

My Bigfoot truck.

musical star Paul Anka, and he started packaging tours of rock 'n' roll acts; this gave him an intimate knowledge of all the arenas across the continent. Following this so far? Here come the elephants . . .

In 1957, the Felds began teaming with the Ringling Brothers Circus, as the old style of setting up the three-ring acts in a town for a week or more no longer made sense. By bringing the circus up to date, hitting the arenas that the Felds already had their hands in, streamlining the delivery by train — and now truck — and creating multiple touring acts, the circus business exploded. Then the Felds bought the circus outright from John Ringling North in 1967 for $7.5 million, cash, and a lion cub, with the deal consummated in the Colosseum in Rome, Italy. Really, I'm not making up this shit.

Mattel saw all the money the circus was making and bought it from the Feld family in 1971 for $47 million . . . and ended up selling it back to the Felds in 1982 for about half of that.

What's this got to do with monster trucks? Feld Entertainment has owned Monster Jam since 2009 and were the owners for the longest swath of time while I drove. (The circus was closed as a touring entity in 2017, but, hey, they still own Supercross and Disney on Ice.)

Here's the key, though — Monster Jam was always majority controlled by the United States Hot Rod Association (USHRA). The USHRA (also known as SRO Motorsports or SRO/Pace) would find partners for the other 49 percent: Clear Channel from 2002 to 2006; Live Nation, 2006 to 2009; Feld, 2009 to the present. So the people controlling Monster Jam never really changed, just where the money was coming from and the accompanying TV deals.

Therefore, I was butting heads with the same ol' boys in power, continually.

Chomping at the bit to do much more — I could see it wasn't going to happen with Monster Jam — and coming from my wrestling background, where competition between promotions was healthy and beneficial to everyone, I helped spearhead a massive attempt at revamping the industry.

If only it had worked.

First, we need to talk about Bigfoot. Or, more correctly, Bigfeet? Bigfoots? Out of humble beginnings came an empire.

Bigfoot was the first monster truck, essentially a 1974 Ford F-250 with big-ass tires that could drive over cars. Bob Chandler was so ahead of his time, more genius than driver, and kept tinkering, eventually building a frame for this new creation, trying all kinds of different metals and setups — think Dr. Frankenstein creating his monster! And he was studying the impact on the driver as much as the truck, worrying about how the body would cope with the pounding.

His wife, Marilyn Chandler, was the first woman to drive a monster truck, paving the way for me and so many others. I met her a couple of times, and she is as awesome as you would expect.

I drove for the Bigfoot team for almost three years, starting in the fall of 2006, making me the first woman to compete in that truck. There were always multiple Bigfoot trucks out on the independent circuit, since the Chandlers and Monster Jam had a huge falling out — and the full reasons have never been disclosed.

So, here comes my own embarrassing money talk.

Negotiating with whoever ran Monster Jam was always a pain in the ass. They never saw value in the drivers, ever. We were replaceable, and Feld's circus elephants got treated better than we did, with pedicures every day, their baths, rubdowns to scrub downs, and lots of fresh food.

For the first two years I drove, I got paid $500. Per show. Sometimes there were two shows a weekend. Then I got up to $1,000 per show . . . the concussions were a bonus! Those were the early days before all the (so-called) safety gear got put in. Remember, I rode in the cab of the tractor-trailers with my truck from town to town, too. My lodging would be paid for at the destination, but there were plenty of times I slept in the truck. Food was always on our dime, though.

People think because you're on TV that you're a millionaire. It couldn't have been further from the truth — in either career.

"Ah," people ask, "how about those championships?" That must have been a good payday. Well, sorta. I got a $10,000 bonus the first year that

I won at World Finals — which is better than nothing. I only got $5,000 after winning the racing title, though. If we won at a regular show? Nada.

Are there perks? A little, and it often depended on the local host or promoter, who made a deal with a small company in town. Free pizza? *Whoopee!* We couldn't leave the arena on race day to go get something different, so the crew guys, being the creative geniuses they were, began bringing their barbecues, and we had our own little tailgate parties — just with really, really big trucks! I saw that it was like wrestling in the 1980s, all bare bones, but both Chad Fortune and I had come out of WCW, where the company had really upped its game and provided catering on TV days. Chad and I lobbied for years until they finally relented and offered food for everyone.

At World Finals, the drivers received a $1,000 bonus, in cash, and a party bag. But, really, the bag was all bartered stuff from sponsors, like gift certificates, power tools, T-shirts, or jackets. I'd give it to my crew or friends. It was important to me to reward the people who worked on my truck, and as my pay went up, so did what I slipped them on the side.

Since I mentioned sponsors, let's talk about that. The independent monster truck owners could make their own deals with companies to provide cash to run their trucks in exchange for signage. Those of us under contract could not make any deals of our own. Still, I was a company gal and continually gave suggestions for new sponsors that would appeal to women — you know, the demographic I was hired to help increase! I get that putting *Tampax* on the side of a truck might upset some people, but how about a makeup company? Nope.

Can you imagine, we could have done a commercial, me walking out of the house, kissing the husband, squeezing the baby, and I've got a business suit, looking smart. I get in my car, drive to the airport, and then coming out of the airport, I've got my firesuit on. The transition there would have been freaking amazing. "Before I get ready for a race, I color my hair with Clairol. I can wear it with my helmet and it doesn't come off." I pitched that idea for years.

In one of my contracts, we put in a clause where I could bring in a sponsor, for a 60-40 split in Monster Jam's favor. I found one, a new healthy energy drink, and it was immediately vetoed. They said, "Sorry, it can't compete against Monster Energy." What a crock of shit, as it was a health drink. It wasn't worth my while.

Sponsorship is a key part of the racing business, because it's expensive. Through my years at Monster Jam, some major industry leaders, such as Ford, Cadillac, Advance Auto Parts, Marvel, DC Comics, Nintendo, T-Mobile, Safe Auto, U.S. Air Force, and Del Taco pumped money into the company, which didn't trickle down to the drivers. And I'm leaving out the media partners, like Clear Channel, Live Nation, Fox Sports, and ViacomCBS.

But they'd ask us to shake hands and kiss babies, and Chad Fortune and I got called upon a lot, because we weren't good ol' boys, with grease embedded under their nails (respect for their hard work, though). They knew that we could schmooze, chat 'em up, and then they would reap all the rewards. Later, since the industry had moved away from the redneck stereotypes, younger talent was used. Progress.

Our firesuits would have a number of company logos on there, but we didn't make any of the money, we didn't get any product — we didn't get jack shit. I started asking questions about those sponsors and asked point blank why I had to wear the logos for no reward. "Because you work for us. You're getting paid. And those are our sponsors." I said, "Wait a minute, I'm promoting it on my body and you want me to talk about it?" And they said, "Yes. That's your job." I said, "Where's all the money from this?" They went, "Well, we barter, we barter for products."

Hot Wheels was selling small versions of monster trucks in a deal with Monster Jam. I had to fight so hard just to get a goddamn Hot Wheels truck. Remember, they'd hired me to bring in female fans, and little girls buy toys, too! Plus, I was a two-time fucking World champion!

Near the end of my run with Monster Jam — where I knew I was leaving, and they didn't — I had a huge argument with a Hot Wheels rep at a World Finals in Vegas.

"Why can't I have a pink Hot Wheels Monster Truck?"

"Because it won't sell."

"Are you fucking kidding me?" I whipped out my phone and searched for other pink Hot Wheels cars that already existed.

"Well, that's more of a purple. And it's a classic car."

I just let Hot Wheels have it. "I think you guys are no better than fucking Feld" — and the Feld people were standing there, too, so I turned to them: "What is wrong with you guys? I want your support in this."

I got my pink truck. Hot Wheels dropped its sponsorship with Monster Jam not long after.

When I couldn't get $1,500 an appearance out of Monster Jam, I said I was done and walked away.

While I was not privy to the actual financials, let's consider some things about the money-making machine known as Monster Jam. We would sell out big hockey arenas with 16,000 fans to large stadiums with maybe 60,000, and usually three or six shows a weekend at the same arena. At its peak, there might be a dozen shows in North America on a weekend, in different-sized venues, plus an international event. Do the math, and at $20 a head, average, plus all the T-shirt sales, the video game, the TV show, the videotapes and DVDs, the replica monster trucks put out by Hot Wheels and other companies, the extra paid tickets for meet and greets, and sponsorships, and it doesn't take an MIT grad to realize there was plenty of money out there that wasn't getting down to the drivers.

How cheap were they? Most of us weren't allocated money for a new firesuit every year. Now, these things got so gross, the armpits alone could knock you out from across a room. But the thing is, when you wash them, the firesuits become progressively less effective, as the retardant erodes, so if you are using it a second season, it's worth dick-all. There are also different qualities of firesuits, from single-ply to multi-ply; one guess which they bought for us! It was a big deal when they finally provided drivers with Nomex fire retardant socks. I did my due diligence and realized there was more out there, so I bought my own Nomex underwear and a shirt to wear underneath the fire suit. People would ask, "Why is your suit so dirty?" I'd be honest and say that Feld wouldn't buy me a new one.

Damon Bradshaw had a kick-ass Kevlar helmet when he drove, and I wanted one, too, but, hey, it wasn't in my contract.

Bigfoot got word of my split from Monster Jam, and within 24 hours, I got an offer — "Hey, do you want to drive a truck?" — for $2,000 an appearance. I met with Bob and Marilyn Chandler's daughter, Ann Trent, and her husband, Bob, at their condo in Florida. They ran the Bigfoot empire, and we hit it off right away, not just because they rode Harleys, too!

What a great feeling it is to be wanted. In the press release, I heaped on the praise: "These people care about you and your well-being and for me that is a once in a lifetime feeling in this business. I am so thrilled to be in a truck again . . . Bigfoot hired me because of my style and they are ready to take it to the next level . . . a woman in a Bigfoot . . . way cool . . . what opportunities for both!!"

I remember telling myself that I could never ever tell anybody in the world how much I made because I was embarrassed. In wrestling, I was paid shit in comparison to my peers, and then I went to Monster Jam, became a bigger name, and made even less.

When I did return to Monster Jam, they made some concessions, and I started back at $2,500 per weekend. After that, I had a guaranteed contract for $100,000 for two years, then $125,000, and when I left, I was on a $225,000-per-year deal. While it might sound like a lot, it really wasn't for someone who was one of their biggest draws, a two-time champion. Remember, taxes and road expenses came out of that money, and I received very little merchandise money!

I won't lie, I got some blowback from the office and other drivers when news of my contract leaked. "Who the fuck is she?" "Well, I'm the one who helped pave the way. Sit down and eat popcorn!"

The flip side, though, is that I was the one encouraging the other drivers to get better deals for themselves. I'd give them my lawyer's number and tell them that they had to have someone else read the small print, not just let the company dictate everything. The drivers were always told they didn't need a lawyer — Monster Jam wanted to be able to control these good ol' boys (and later, girls) who just wanted to get into these amazing trucks and crush cars.

Riding in Bigfoot was both an honor and a privilege. I got to drive a truck labeled *Bigfoot*, and another that they did up as a *Madusa* Bigfoot truck, which was the first time they ever did that — was I smart to trademark my name, or what? Plus the schedule was a lot less strenuous, and the actual events a lot more easygoing, without all the whoring, signing for hours in the pit parties. We'd do county fairs, or a dealership would hire us for an appearance to draw people to the venue.

But it wasn't the same. Bigfoot had different axles, chassis, and transmissions, and overall, the truck was heavier by hundreds of pounds. And it was a loaner, and I couldn't tell you how many times I heard variations of, "Don't crash it. Don't drive hard. Take it easy." Stifled, I couldn't go all out.

My smile was always genuine, though. I was driving fucking Bigfoot!

During my time behind the wheel on Bigfoot, I got to meet all kinds of independent promoters — it was like pro wrestling all over again. One, in California, stood out. Joe Froome and his wife, Kellie, had grander ambitions than one-off shows, so we started talking.

Out of those discussions in late 2006 came the dream to compete with Monster Jam. At the core, I'd been driving long enough that I wanted change. I wanted equality, fairness, people getting paid correctly, legitimacy with prize money, and wins. I wanted monster trucks to be looked at in a different way, with more respect.

The Froomes called it the Major League of Monster Trucks (MLMT), and the logo was a jumping truck in red, white, and blue — think Major League Baseball's logo, but with a truck!

I was named vice president, and boardrooms became my new home. Joe was the president and owner.

Through our research, we determined that the nation's NASCAR tracks were hugely underutilized, with maybe a couple of races a year, and that was our plan. NASCAR wasn't as hot as it had been a few years earlier, but still massively popular, particularly with men. Our thinking targeted the family. Dad already went to NASCAR, but he'd bring the family for the bigger monster truck show, and, in turn, the kids would learn more about NASCAR and want to come back for those races. We priced it reasonably, too, around $20 an adult, $10 a kid, plus a little extra for any meet and greets.

Plus, on the wider infields at these superspeedways, we had the potential to set up some really kick-ass tracks for the drivers to show their stuff, way bigger than the cramped arenas we often had to be in with Monster Jam.

The real challenge, though, was that, while NASCAR was the parent body, each track was individually owned. If we wanted to run at Charlotte Speedway, we had to negotiate with that owner, and then fly to Texas to figure out that one next.

We had investors backing us, so we had a nice chunk of change to start, get everything rolling. Pretty quickly, we signed up a few NASCAR speedways. You could feel the momentum starting.

Needless to say, Joe and I didn't do it all on our own. Rich Shaefer was a key figure, who knew the trucks and business. As loyalty matters to me, I called my old pal Mike Weber and brought him in as VP of marketing; he looked after booking stadiums, marketing the events, and some of the TV production. I tried to poach a few more people who I'd known from wrestling to help in the office or with security, but that didn't pan out.

Corporate Debrah was something to see. I always had the innate knowledge to play to the room, be showy if I had to be, or just a good ol' girl hangin' out.

We talked about sponsorships and thought about Coca-Cola, but as someone who never had cola in their life, I didn't get it. Joe convinced me we had to pitch to them.

When Coca-Cola agreed to meet with us — quicker than expected, which meant we were on to something — we had a little celebration in the office. But then the real work began. Instead of just your typical proposal booklet in a clear binder, which would be easy to get lost in the shuffle, I suggested something else. I wanted a "holy shit" moment when they got it.

We made up 20 proposals in diamond plated metal, with metal rings to hold it all together. The idea was that it represented racing, haulers, and ruggedness. I had a friend that we call "Tattoo Al," whom I knew through the Harley world and did my first tattoo; he did die-cutting and etching, and he cut out 20 nameplates that said *Coca-Cola* in its stylized font, and we put a piece of red velvet behind it. They looked freaking phenomenal.

We walked in there with a box of these heavy booklets, handed them out, and they signed on.

In all, there were seven MLMT events in 2007: Nashville; Charlotte, North Carolina; Dallas; Las Vegas; Red Bluff, California; Sparta, Kentucky; and Memphis. Chuck Plumlee and Chad Nicholson were our hosts, hyping the crowd and introducing the rotation of drivers and their vehicles. Some of the monster trucks included Bigfoot, Avenger, Brutus, Equalizer, Gunslinger, Hot Tamale, Nitemare, Raminator, Samson, Bounty Hunter, Scarlet Bandit, Sudden Impact, T Maxx, Tailgator, and War Wizard.

We built the best courses and the drivers loved it — there was space to really get going, and they all loved being at the NASCAR tracks to boot. We had a tree light beginning, an up-and-over start, tunnels, and a school bus to jump over. There were races, long-jump challenges, freestyle competitions for the monster trucks, and we didn't stop there: we let the motocross guys race around, too. We wanted a show, and there were bands (usually country music) playing in the concourse.

I got to drive, too, of course! We had so much more freedom than in Monster Jam. Impromptu, I could get on the mic and challenge another truck to a donut contest — and monster trucks do great donuts! I would challenge myself to get up on two wheels, but not tip over.

Dan Runte, driving Bigfoot 16, was our one-and-only champion in 2007.

In the end, the money just wasn't there.

I may have been a VP, but I wasn't privy to all the numbers — that was Joe's responsibility. Sponsorships didn't come about for the planned second season especially, and without any promotional deals, we were dead. There were 18 shows on the books for 2008 that didn't happen.

Poor Joe lost a ton on Major League of Monster Trucks. I regret that we didn't stay in touch.

Man, Major League of Monster Trucks was a fucking great idea. How do I know?

When I returned to Monster Jam, one of the top names at the company and I were chatting after a show one night.

He went, "You know, Deuce, I have to tell you something: we were a little bit worried there for a while."

"What are you talking about?"

"Well, MLMT was a good thing. Your product was excellent, and we felt the competition."

That was all I needed to hear, and I laughed. "Well, good. You should be scared. You never know, it might happen again!"

Just before I stopped driving with Monster Jam, I made a pitch to the company that could have changed things for the better for the drivers after they retired. I'd just been honored by WWE, put in the WWE Hall of Fame, and was signed to a *WWE Legends* deal. Essentially, that meant that they had a vested interest in promoting me as one of the veterans of the company, letting me rub shoulders with younger talent. Others on similar deals got DVD packages or action figures or whatever, but there wasn't much for me.

My pitch was a combination of retirement plan and *Legends* deal for veteran drivers. I knew my time was limited in the truck.

I put my proposal together, flew up to Chicago, and handed out the packages to all the executives. I was myself, honest, blunt, impassioned, with a touch of business. They said, "Well, this looks good. It's interesting; we'll see what we can do to implement it." Nothing ever happened; they probably laughed at it, to tell you the truth. I worked really hard at it, just fighting for all the drivers.

While I had their attention, I also suggested licensing the Madusa name, so there could be a few trucks under that name racing at different venues, all driven by women. Just like Dennis's Grave Digger had with his kids driving. I broke down all the logistics, legal stuff. That scared the shit out of them. They didn't want anything to do with it, they never did. They sugar coated everything just to get me the fuck out of there. Why did they hire me to build a brand and not capitalize on it? So dumb.

As much as I had been hired to be a strong woman at the forefront of the company, bringing in a different audience, they never, ever used me to the extent they could have. They seemed scared of moving forward with women.

16.

BABIES AND FUR BABIES

AS AWFUL AS IT HAS been revisiting the pains of failed pregnancies, it's a part of me, who I am, and who I was not allowed to be. Much of this is unknown to even my closest friends, and if they do know something, they don't know all.

To deal with the pain, I've learned to be matter of fact about it. You won't find me dwelling on the past. That's the way I've been my whole life, not just when it came to having a baby.

Snuggling with my wolves, Glacier and Stroker.

The other constant has been my pets — dogs, cats, birds, men, wolves. They all need the same things — food, water, love — and you have to clean up after them.

Though I can't be certain, my biological troubles may have indeed begun at the beginning. Mature beyond my years, in mind and body, I was sexually active from my early teens. When I was working at a Perkins restaurant, at about 19, I got pregnant. Or so I thought. Worried, I went to a Planned Parenthood clinic that dealt with unwanted pregnancies. This wasn't a back-alley situation, but a real doctor, who told me that I wasn't pregnant, and then proceeded to do a clean-up procedure anyway. It was horrible.

We always had cats growing up. The last one I remember was named Buffy. So Betty could be loving towards a cat, but not me. Even now, she'll sit on the back patio and will have squirrels and chipmunks race up to her for a treat — instead of a crazy cat lady, she's a crazy fucking squirrel lady. It's cute, though.

I'll often say that I'm like a cat, always landing on my feet and I've got nine lives.

I love animals and had cats on a regular basis until about a decade ago. Two of them stand out — Phantom and Ewok, when I was living in Florida. I'd gone to the store to buy Ewok, a Himalayan blue point, for $500 or so. But there was this cat in the next window, just staring at me with his face pushed up against the window, *Meow, meow*. I couldn't resist, like she had a sign on, *I'm only $40. Buy me, too!* Phantom lived to be 22, and Ewok, 20.

As a young woman, with a rockin' bod and work ethic to match, I looked great on the outside. But on the inside, something was amiss.

Deeply entrenched with my first real love, and in love with his parents, too, we planned to get married, and, before you knew it, I was pregnant. It didn't last. I suffered what is called an ectopic or tubal pregnancy, which is when a fertilized egg implants and grows inside the main cavity of the Fallopian tube. A long needle came out — it was about a foot long, and as thick as your pinkie, and it went up inside my vagina. They were trying to see how much blood was filling up inside. It looked like a horror movie with blood everywhere. A priest came in to deliver my last rites.

The relationship didn't last long beyond that, for a number of reasons, but no doubt that was a factor. It was scary and unexpected, as we were both so young. No doctor was ever able to explain the *why* of it, either, which made it worse.

When I moved in with Greg Valentine, the house was like a zoo, with the two cats, Ewok and Phantom, a young Keeshond named Kisska (see how much I like the name!), and then I got a bird, Parador. That green-winged macaw was absolutely freaking beautiful and smarter than hell. He was only probably two years old when I got him, just a baby, and they can live to be 90.

When Greg and I went our separate ways, I had a roommate who took care of my house on the golf course. I came home after being on the road, and we were relaxing, when I heard crying. "What the fuck is that?" And she started laughing, "That's Parador." I'm like, "Why?" She said, "It's because you leave the soap operas on TV for Parador, and all they do is cry."

Parrots are basically one-person birds, and he was my bird. I taught him shapes. I taught him to identify fruits, so I'd lay out a grape, and I'd say, "Get the grape," and he'd do it. I would lay out blocks like squares, rounds, triangles, and I'd say, "Get the square," and he'd get the square. This bird was more intelligent than half the humans I knew.

I'd teach him a vocabulary, very studious words, and it would just blow people away. When I was gone, though, my roommate had a run-in with Parador. She was so scared to feed him and would throw food on one side, and he'd run over there, and then she would quickly fill up his water dish on the other side. I was very lucky that she would do any of that, and I was appreciative.

He bit her one day, and she yelled, "Fucking bird!" One day, I'm sitting there and all of a sudden I hear, "Fucking bird!" And she started laughing. "I got really mad at him one day; I say one word, and he picks it up."

I would bring him outside, let him sit on the perch out in the pool area with all the golfers. The players would come around, and we taught him to say "Fore!" so he would yell "Fore!" and then screech "Fuck!" It actually got to be a problem, and I sought out a bird-whisperer. "You've got to help me. Why is he so adamant on this one word?" It was because of the emotions with which it's said. Whenever he said "Fuck," we'd try to ignore it and that helped.

Against the advice of my (former) accountant, I bought some property in Florida, north of Tampa near Crystal River, and that land has probably been my best investment, period. On a five-acre lot, I put up a house — and, soon enough, an enclosure for my wolves.

Not long after, I met Ken, and we opened the motorcycle repair shop, which was on a busy highway. Our dog, Kisska, chased Ken on his Harley out onto the road and was killed by a car. We debated getting another dog. I always wanted a Mastiff, they're amazing and huge, and he was into it.

And then we ran across a friend who had wolf pups. Ken asked about getting our own wolf pup. I told him that he was crazy . . . but I did my research and read up on the rules. The more I dug, the more I got pissed off that people were actually getting wolves and breeding them for hybrids. That is insane. But I still loved wolves and their intelligence. There was a need for people to take in wolves and wolf hybrids, because the state was taking them away from people because wolves are wolves, and they're not meant to be pets.

We got two rescued wolf hybrid pups — Stroker and Spooky. (She was Spooky because she could disappear in a room like a ghost.) To acclimatize them to humans, we started to raise them in the house. Stroker would lay like a mink stole above the pillow with Ken. It was amazing.

Ken and I built a sanctuary in the back of the property for wolves, spanning almost two acres.

Then we started getting others. Our first mistake was we didn't get them fixed right away, so two of them had babies. After they screwed, so were we.

We brought the mother inside the house to have her babies. Next thing we knew, she had torn apart the couch, and puppy birth was all over the cushions. Essentially, she had burrowed into the couch to give birth. We kept the pups in the house for a while, and then we couldn't keep them in there anymore, not even to feed them. She'd be howling to the other wolves, and then they would howl back. She wanted to be with the pack. We didn't keep all the cubs, and people we knew took them. Wrestling fans will recognize two of the people who got cubs — Shannon Moore and "The Demon" Dale Torborg, who drove up with his wife, Christi "Aysa" Wolf, in a tiny Mercedes SLK and managed to get two of the wolf puppies in there.

The fencing was a huge issue, too. According to the law, I had to get a nine-gauge fence, six feet tall, so the wolves couldn't chew through it or jump it. Wolves can dig and they love dens, so I got another four feet of fencing and laid it on the bottom and had it all linked together on the bottom. I had it dragged inward four feet, so when they stepped up to it, they felt the chain link and they didn't dig; they couldn't dig under and get out.

Or so I thought. One time, the wolves climbed up the fence in the corner. They put one paw on each side of the corner and jumped over — they're that smart. I was getting citations left and right, for prized geese that were killed, or they'd drag back carcasses of some animal and cats. Remember, they are pack animals, so they would bring back the kill to share.

After I figured out how they were climbing out of the corner, I had to get another fence company come out and build a 45-degree inlay on top, bending in, to keep them in the pen. In the end, the fencing ran about $35,000.

Since I was still traveling a lot, I had it all fixed and rigged for food and water to be automatically dished out. However, before this amazing feeding idea I was blessed to have one of the best neighbors to care for and look out for my wolves when I went on the road. She was never able to go in the pen, but they knew her and trusted her to feed them.

They were my babies, my life. I was the only one who could get in there with them, because I was the alpha. I camped out there, so they could get used to me. They'd come in and out of the tent, smell me. It was amazing. I had them for almost 18 years, and the last one died here a few years ago. I'm not going to do it again. It's a lot of work.

Ken and I ended up with a huge property in Virginia on 200 acres. It was heavenly, with my two toy poodles, Shyanne and Freddie, horses, and a goat, named Billy, who was such an asshole he should have been a pro wrestler. I forgot to clip his damn horns, and he almost speared me through my gut when I was against the barn.

We brought the whole fucking zoo up to Virginia. And again, we had to build the fencing for the wolves, but we built it a little bit smaller, and it was probably around $20,000.

When Ken was playing for the Bengals in Cincinnati, I packed up for a drive from Florida to our place near there. The two wolf-dogs were in the back seat, the cats were in their cases, and Parador was in the cage. Everyone was singing and howling, and it was a great ride all the way up there. Looking back, par for the course in most of my relationships, I'd be fully employed, driving from my home to wherever my current man lived.

In Georgia, I stopped at a hotel and went to meet my old WCW friend Janie for dinner, but first I did my ritual, where the wolves got to run around, the cats got a little air, and then I left them in the hotel room, the cats locked in the bathroom, and the bird sat up on the pole where you hung up your clothes. We'd done the trip a few times by that point, so they knew the drill.

After dinner this time, I opened the hotel room door, and there's the two wolves sitting there, guilty as fuck. And there's feathers everywhere. My mouth dropped, and I started screaming. But they didn't eat Parador; the bird loved to tease the dogs, imitating their barking noise. It drove them crazy. I found Parador on the floor. He was dead. They didn't chew him, they didn't puncture him. They chased him, exhausted him, and he couldn't get back up.

I put Parador in a Ziploc bag, got him on ice. I should have kept him and stuffed him, but I didn't.

The real trauma of my pregnancies happened while married to Ken. It wasn't too long into the marriage that I got pregnant. Months into it, though, I was still getting my period, which was weird — and a sign we missed. Driving home on Highway 19 in Florida after a WCW show, I was exhausted and felt like I was going to pass out. Instead of going home, I drove myself to the hospital. That was the right call. It was another tubal pregnancy, and the bleeding was because the baby was stuck in my Fallopian tube and my stomach had filled up with blood. Ken was with the Tampa Bay Buccaneers at that point, and he was told to get to the emergency room immediately.

That time, a doctor told me I would be unlikely to ever carry a baby full term — or at all. But I'm stubborn.

Ken and I tried again, and I miscarried. Our marriage died, too.

I still wanted to have a baby so bad, and after my monster truck wins, living on my own, I decided to try again.

In vitro fertilization (IVF) seemed the way to go, though expensive. It took three tries, and $70,000 or so, but I got pregnant with twins. Everything was going great, but around six months, both heartbeats stopped — and I had to live with little babies inside me who were dead. Then I had a D&C to clean them out.

No one knows that story.

While gathering material for the book, I came across all of my baby stuff. My twins would have been over 20 years old. Their names are on my tattoo sleeve, close to my shoulder, *Whiskey and Freedom*. Rereading details with the sonograms, I found a reference to cystic fibrosis in the blood work. What the fuck? How am I just learning this now? Is that the reason for infertility? And the doctors just took my money for IVF, knowing it wouldn't work? The hits keep coming.

Well before anyone had heard of the "Tiger King" Joe Exotic or his adversary, Carole Baskin, I had my own dalliance with big cats. Through a friend named Kyle, I met Wild Bill, who had a cat sanctuary near my Florida home. With so much time off between monster truck racing, I wanted to fill my days. My end goal was to get a state license, so I could take some of the cats from him. I even had the name of my sanctuary picked out! Cat Scratch Fever would have rocked.

You needed so many hours for your license, and I'd head there to go in the cages and learn how to feed the big cats. We'd cut up the raw meat and we'd serve them. With the baby cats, we'd train them. The most amazing animal he had was this majestic white tiger.

Then I just stopped doing it, never got my license or the tigers. I probably just smartened up and realized I didn't want to do it, even though I loved the animals.

Given all my trauma, I made myself scarce when people invited me to baby showers. Those were impossible to be at. When the baby was born, I could handle it a little better and tried to be a good friend, sending gifts or attending birthday parties when I was able, or even babysitting.

I get really emotional watching a baby commercial. It's not anger. I feel like a failure. For someone who fought so hard to control everything in my life, I couldn't control nature.

On some level, I feel that because of everything I went through as a child, from the rape to the emotionally distant parents, that it was a higher power just saying that the genetic line needed to be severed.

Early in my days in Virginia, I decided to go back to school, to learn to be a master groomer for pets — after all, I had my test subjects at home! Not long after finishing the class, I opened up a bricks-and-mortar store in Lebanon, Virginia. It was called Paws and Claws, and it kicked ass. It was so cute. After Ken and I split, I kept it running for a little while, but I realized I needed to be back in Florida, so I closed it.

KoolKats and HotDogs was my pet grooming business in Beverly Hills, Florida, which included organic bakery treats for your dogs. The slogan was, "Where the Koolest Kats and the hottest dogs are groomed!" and "Where hugs and kisses are free." I kept it open for a long time. Two things forced me to close: one, I couldn't find anyone who was as good as I was at customer service to keep the people coming back and who wouldn't rip me off; and two, I met Alan, who was in the military, and was about to be deployed to Germany. (I'll tell you more about him later.)

The life of a military wife is not an easy one, and loneliness can be really tough. I looked around at all the American families that were stationed at the massive Ramstein Air Base in Germany and saw opportunity. They had their pets, but were getting fleeced by the German groomers, who raised their rates when they saw an easy target of a foreigner come in.

Technically, as an American, you can't open up a business there, but I wanted to buck the system and groom, and I did in our house. I made up business cards:

KoolKats and Hotdogs

20 years' experience — Grooming for the military for free

Business took off. The appreciative Americans would throw me $50 in the tip jar, which was still cheaper than what the Germans had been charging at the off-base clinics. It was a win-win. Then Alan came home one day and said, "I don't know what you did, but you pissed off Germany." I kept operating but had to open it up to Germans in the military who wanted their dogs groomed, too. In the end, the "free" business worked better than either of the physical stores I operated.

With my mother being who she is, there was never the badgering about wanting a grandchild, like a lot of women get, for which I was thankful.

My current dog, Daisy, another toy poodle, is a service dog, so she is allowed to travel with me everywhere, including on the plane. Daisy has her own backpack and goes crazy when I get it out, as she knows she's headed for an adventure — and there are patches sewn on it for every state she has been to. On trips back home to Minnesota, I'll present her to Betty: "Here. This is your granddaughter, this is all that you're getting."

Daisy rides on the Harley with us, too, in a special attachment, and has doggy goggles.

My last attempt at being a parent was to try adopting. On my own, I started the process, attending the classes required by the state, having my house inspected, my finances pored over, and background checks. I did it all, expecting a happy ending, and even mentioned it in some monster truck interviews.

Much of the story has to be left vague, but I was connected with a 17-year-old girl, ready to be aged out of the system, who had a young son, who was a year and a half old. She had no means to take care of him, and even when she aged out, she could still stay in the system under assistance. The understanding was that I'd take them both and adopt the baby. They'd spend weekends with me, and I bought all the baby things that were needed.

You can't change a stubborn teenage mother, especially one who had seen so much nastiness already. I believed by showing love and how I had overcome my tough life, that she would be inspired, and I could guide her. Then she said that she was just going to age out of the system and rely on government handouts to raise her son.

I was crushed. The next one was harder.

A nine-year-old boy was returned into the adoption system by foster parents who didn't want him any longer. *Damn*, I thought, *this shouldn't be a rental service*!

The social worker knew this could work for me. "He's a great kid. And he's smart. And they just didn't want him anymore."

It could have been any kid, but it happened to be the brother of the girl who had already been to my house. So I asked the obvious, whether they kept in contact. Apparently, they hadn't been in touch in years. I figured he couldn't have been poisoned by her ways.

I did the same thing for him, changed up the room, making it for a boy. I bought some clothes. Through it all, I knew not to go overboard. We got to know each other on weekends over the period of a couple of months. We went camping, or little day trips, or as simple as getting his help in the yard. I started laying down normal things of life, working with family, and preparing for school.

After about six months, we were getting ready for adoption.

It just didn't dawn on me that he was not developing. My case worker said, "Do you notice anything different about the child?" "What are you talking about?" "Do you notice that he isn't fully developed for his age?" She meant everything from his height to his intelligence level. I was surprised she hadn't mentioned anything until now. There was nothing about the issues in the book they gave me on him.

I took him to a psychologist, through the state. We were halfway through, and the doctor came out and said that the child had a low IQ and would never develop beyond a certain level. The doctor was surprised I didn't know any of it.

I did some soul searching and realized it didn't matter to me. He was just slow, probably on the autistic spectrum. The testing opened up my eyes and I started seeing the signs, but I wasn't alarmed or scared off by it.

At one point, the boy asked, "Are you okay that I'm not smart?" Talk about a heartache. I said, "I think you're the most brilliant, smartest boy I have ever met. And you're going to be great at whatever you decide you want to do." He broke down crying, sobbing that no adult had ever said anything that nice to him. I was holding back tears.

Again, I looked back to my mother, and how she never told me she loved me.

I was in elbows deep, and I never quit, so I was getting ready for the court date to make it all official.

One day, two cars came up the driveway, and women from the state came in and took him. His family had requested him back. His sister turned 18 and asked for her brother — because she got even more money from the state.

I said, "Fuck it." And then that was done.

Alan was in my life at the tail end of the adoption saga and even attended a few adoption classes with me. He had kids from his first marriage, and I love them, but they are adults. After I told him some of my story, he volunteered to undo his vasectomy for us to try together. It was the sweetest thing he ever said to me.

It's important to me that I share my stories, since I am hardly alone with infertility issues; God just didn't grant me the beauty of what women are gifted to do. As much as I would like to blame someone or something specific, there is nothing to pin it on. It just is.

I chose two careers where I got physically beaten up, with plenty of mental stress to boot. Maybe if I didn't take so many kicks to the stomach in Japan . . . maybe if I didn't take so many bumps . . . maybe if proper harnesses existed when I started driving the monster trucks . . .

But I did all that and have the scars, externally and internally, to prove it. Without all the scar tissue, would I have been able to hold my twins for more than six months?

And now I see pregnancies, like wrestling stars Brie and Nikki Bella or Becky Lynch, get celebrated — glamorized even — and it fucking kills me. You can't be angry at the people, what's happening, and their success. It's almost post-traumatic stress disorder, and I have to shut down to cope.

As crazy as it sounds, I took strength from visiting sick kids in the hospital; I don't know how else to describe it.

I begged for assignments, whether it was in wrestling or while driving. I'd get thrown an occasional charity gig, but these were few and far between. They made me feel like a goddamn pimple on their ass just for asking.

Eventually, I learned I could just do it myself. While I was a nurse, I worked often with handicapped children, so I had no issue heading to children's hospitals, pediatric wards, where all they wanted was someone, something, to distract the sick kids and their families from life's harsh reality for a short while.

It was tough, knowing that the child didn't have long to live. My own pain, my fertility issues, took a back seat in those moments.

I tried so hard to have kids my whole life, and then I realized that my kids are in the crowd, the thousands and thousands whom I entertained every weekend.

They might have watched me fight Bull Nakano and wanted to follow in my footsteps, or they saw a kick-ass woman behind the wheel of an even more kick-ass monster truck and realized that their life held possibilities, too.

I got more girls and women to the monster truck rallies than anyone. I did my job, and I did it well.

But I am not immune to the pain. At the rallies, the little girls would come screaming and crying into my arms. My heart melted. Often, I had to turn around like I dropped something, to excuse myself to pop into my truck, just so they didn't see my tears.

17.

THE SONG REMAINS THE SAME

"WHO'S MADUSA?" WAS A HIT, but to me, it was shit. That was the single I recorded while I was wrestling for All Japan, and if I had my way, every copy that ever existed would be drop-kicked into the Pacific Ocean. My singing is bad enough, but I actually sang the majority of the song in Japanese, so there's off-key warbling combined with butchered phrasing.

That time that the band Kingdom Come came to my match; it's guitarist Angi Schilir on the left and bassist Johnny B. Frank.

Looking back now, I recognize that it was a great opportunity provided by the promotion to record the song, make the accompanying video, and expand my brand. But I wasn't cut out for it, and I was expected to sing it before matches, too!

The video itself was perhaps more suitable for the *Playboy* Channel. I wasn't ever completely naked, but pretty damn close, whether I was in a helicopter, pool, or on the beach. I was a bit uncomfortable, but what an experience.

Here's the backstory: On one of my trips back to Minnesota, to re-establish my U.S. residency, it was arranged for me to record at Paisley Park — yes, at Prince's recording studio in Chanhassen, a Minneapolis suburb.

Oddly, I'd been there before. An old boyfriend was a drummer in town and ended up in a band for a time called Maserati with Prince's regular bassist, Brownmark. When Paisley Park Studios opened in September 1987, I ended up at the gala. All the pretty people were there, but for whatever reason, singer Taylor Dayne got on my nerves and I called her out for being loud and rude, resulting in a death stare.

Back to the actual recording, which was produced by Rik Stirling. We spent hours on it, and it was released by Rivstar. I just thought, *What a great full-circle moment. Here I am at Paisley Park, Prince's studio, and I'm "singing," and Prince listens to everything.* He was probably upstairs cringing, going, "Someone needs to shut off this girl's mic."

I never did actually *meet* Prince, but I did talk to him. He dated a roommate of mine for a time. He'd call our landline from the phone in his limo. In his soft, sexy voice, he'd coo, "Hey, could you tell her that Big Daddy's outside?"

The Prince tie-in runs throughout my early career. So much of my look was based upon him and Madonna — it's like we were all becoming stars at the same time! I'd present ideas to the designers in Japan, and they'd come back with these super-cool clothes that I'd sing in before my match, and one was a tear-away, so I'd give a tug and be ready to fight.

For hard-core record collectors, there's a single, "Rough, Tough, Pretty Stuff," written about me from that era, but the people behind it wanted to milk me for cash to use it, so I only ever used it once heading to the ring.

A love of music runs through my life, too.

There are early memories I associate with music.

It was a rare visit to a restaurant with Betty and Mike, and the jukebox started playing Elvis Presley. I knew Elvis because Betty was in love with him, so I jumped up on the table and started dancing. She grabbed me and dragged me outside. Fast-forward to 1977, and I came home to a locked door. When Betty finally opened it, she was in tears, "Don't you know who died?" No. She slapped me and said that Elvis was dead.

At home, I had a small record player, a Close and Play, which only played when it was closed. There was no money for extra 45s, but I would beg Mike to buy cereal boxes that had 45s on them, like The Monkees and Bobby Sherman.

There's one song I can't listen to without bad memories overpowering me. I would play "The Lion Sleeps Tonight" by the Tokens over and over until Betty hit a breaking point. She came barging in my room, "Enough with the song!" Grabbing me by the wrist, she dragged me into the kitchen, turned on the gas stove, melted my records — and then burned my hands over the flame.

Once I was out on my own, music came to dominate my life. Led Zeppelin was my favorite, and I would have married Robert Plant in an instant. I had tickets to see them play November 9, 1980, in St. Paul, Minnesota . . . and then John Bonham died, and I was crushed. Though I never met Plant, I did see him reteam with guitarist Jimmy Page in 1995 for an amazing concert, with Bonham's son, Jason, on drums. I still have a T-shirt from the show and plenty of other shirts from shows I went to through the years.

Minneapolis had a pretty good music scene, with many of the big bands of the 1970s coming through town. Thin Lizzy was my first rock concert, in October 1977, at the St. Paul Civic Center. The pot we had that night had been laced with angel dust, which we didn't know. No wonder I freaked and wanted to jump off the balcony. The plus was that the guitarist, Scott Gorham, seemed like he was playing right to me.

I would go to a lot of rock concerts, usually with a pal from work. We would always end up getting backstage passes. We were underage, but, of course, we didn't let them know. She would always leave me, and I never understood it: "Where do you go? What do you do?"

"You've got to mingle more, you've got to talk to these guys."

"I thought we did, but what else am I supposed to do?"

She just smiled. "Have fun."

Then I got asked to come back where the bands were, and there's my friend blowing somebody. And I'm like, "What the fuck?"

It was exciting meeting all these rock stars, getting the best seats, access to the food in the dressing room, the booze, the drugs. The men had longer hair than the women, and I soon had a rule/obsession that I wouldn't date any man who wasn't in a band or didn't have long hair. The first who fit that bill was Kevin, and he educated me in so many ways, including about groupies. There were some groupies who were almost road wives, for that 300- to 500-mile radius; others were labeled as one-night stands and nothing more. No matter, the locomotives (band members) were always ready to start their engines, and there were always trains and conductors . . .

I'm going to plead the Fifth on any more details. *Banger Sisters* until we die (now go watch that movie with Goldie Hawn and Susan Sarandon!).

One time, we were in a hotel bar with Bad Company. It was cool. But then a murmur started, and someone said, "The Stones are coming!" All the girls got up and left. By the time I got outside, there was a limo pulling out, towards another hotel. So my pal left me with Bad Company.

That wasn't the breaking point in our friendship, though. She dated my uncle for a bit, and all my warnings were ignored. I couldn't stand being around them. Not only were they into drugs, but also I clearly saw how he was manipulating her, and she bought into his bullshit.

The early 1980s were a glorious time for big-haired rock bands, and I loved it. Still do. I am so glad I was born and raised when I was, what I experienced, how I experienced it. And the things I went through — it was my best time of life. You weren't judged, you were free. Life was good.

Drummers were my jam. Influenced by Ted Nugent's "Cat Scratch Fever," I bought a pair of drumsticks and I would carry them around with me, drumming on everything.

When the COVID-19 pandemic happened in early 2020, and I realized I'd be stuck at home, I treated myself to a drum set and banged away. There's life in this ol' gal yet! After watching Alicia Warrington perform on her drums, who later joined WWE's NXT brand and is known as the announcer Alicia Taylor, I reached out to ask for drum lessons. She pointed me to online classes from Sheila E. — there's another Prince tie-in!

When I was in Japan, I met all kinds of bands, as they all seemed to head to the Tokyo Hard Rock Cafe. It was *so* refreshing having real conversations in English. I wasn't starstruck. I mean, I'd already met half of them when they came through Minnesota. Off the top of my head, I remember Cinderella, KISS, Mötley Crüe.

The security guards would know who I was from wrestling. Like royalty walking in, they'd exclaim "Madusa-san!" and talk into their radio, then I'd be whisked backstage, or into the pit. Actress Heather Locklear was dating Tommy Lee, and we met off to the side of the stage and had a little chat.

Kingdom Come are one of my favorite rock bands because Lenny Wolf, the lead singer, reminded me of Robert Plant. At the Hard Rock, I was telling them about my wrestling life, and they were all in. The next night, they took me up on my offer for tickets, and the whole fucking band came, sitting ringside. The bass player was just smitten with me. I'm like, "No, this is gonna be arm's length, bro. Been down this road, not happening."

When on the road wrestling or driving monster trucks, there wasn't always time for concerts. Your body was beaten up and needed to recover. But there were moments.

Dale Torborg was a pro baseball player, following in the footsteps of his father, Jeff. Dale also loved pro wrestling. His biggest role was as The Demon in WCW — a KISS-inspired gimmick — which worked great, because Dale was a massive music fan. He arranged for a few of us (including his future wife, Christi, who was known as Asya) to go see Metallica at Atlanta's Georgia Dome in July 2000. Kid Rock was on the bill, and his late hype man Joe C was a huge wrestling fan, who kept peppering us with questions backstage. The show was memorable because singer James Hetfield hurt his back and couldn't perform, so all the other bands offered to sing the Metallica songs. It was wild seeing that all come together behind the scenes.

After the show, we were just hanging out, chatting with the guys from Metallica and Kid Rock. Dale never lets me forget this one, as I asked Lars Ulrich, Metallica's drummer, where he is from, which is Denmark. "Oh, you're my little Danish popsicle. I could just lick you," I instantly said.

The most important musical connection, though, comes through Command Sergeant Major Alan Jonason, my husband of the last dozen years. KISS is his band, the music getting him through high school and into combat missions. Our house is a virtual shrine to the band. He loves other bands, of course, and is decidedly a rocker (but maybe not into as much death metal as I am).

The story of us meeting, though, doesn't really have music involved, but vomit. After one monster truck race, the crew were on a flight home, and one of the tech guys got so drunk he puked, and Mama

Deuce had to step in. A handsome gentleman helped me out by offering a clean shirt, and we later started talking. He was in the military and . . . nope, that wasn't Alan! But after we dated a short time, it opened my mind to the possibility of finding a soulmate who was in the military. They're deployed, live a structured life, and I am on the road. We understand each other.

Did you know there's a website just for that? I didn't. It's called MilitaryCupid.com, and, though I didn't know it until later, I hit up Alan on his first day on the site! His mention of loving Harleys was a good start . . . actually, loving Harleys was a prerequisite. We started chatting, and he got to know Deb, a dog-groomer in Florida, and I got to know this lifetime soldier, whose expertise was in Patriot missiles and who was living in El Paso, Texas. Late one night, before we said good night, I said, "Google *M-A-D-U-S-A*, and tell me what you think in the morning."

When we spoke the next night, he asked "Why didn't you tell me?" I told him that I wanted to make sure he was interested in me for the right reasons. He understood my thinking. Next, I was upfront: "Do you think you can handle being with somebody like me?" His reply? "Well, do you think you can handle being with a soldier who's going to be deployed and away from home a lot?" We both agreed that we could, and the rest is history.

There were hiccups, from nearly driving off a cliff on a mountain road, sliding on ice, on our first date, to a divorce that we called off at the last minute. Maybe I'll do a book on relationships one day and go further in depth! We've both had people tell us that we are well suited for each other, that we had finally found that person who completes the other. Now, there are plenty of times that he pisses me off, but that's normal, right?

He's been there through some of the toughest times of my life and brought so much light and laughter into my life, too.

I was a "Hard-Luck Woman" until I found my man.

One year, I wanted to do something amazing for my husband, and I called in a favor — a rarity for me. I hit up Dale and said, "Dale, I never fucking do this, but I want to surprise Alan on our anniversary. KISS is coming. I'll pay for the tickets, but is there any way that you can get me a connection so Alan can meet Gene Simmons?" He goes, "Oh, yeah, consider it done."

Dale came through, and I didn't tell Alan ahead of time. When he met Gene Simmons, his long-time hero from the band he listened to all through his military life, making it through everything, I thought he was going to have a heart attack. It was one of the happiest moments of my life — and his.

It didn't stop after that. It was never enough. Then we had to go see every goddamn concert and go on the KISS Kruise.

Hanging out at a pre-show event before a KISS concert, with Dale, Christi, Alan and me, Dale kept needling me about "Who's Madusa?" He wanted me to get up and sing. Finally I told him, "Will you shut up. I'm not singing that song!"

18.

MY BODY, MY CHOICE

"911. WHAT'S YOUR EMERGENCY?"

"I think I am having a heart attack!"

It was May 17, 2018, in the afternoon, a gloomy Florida day. Five months after my second total knee replacement, I'd spent the day on the couch, reflecting on way too much. My stress level was through the roof, my marriage a crumbling wreck, and I didn't know where my career was going, whether I'd ever climb into a monster truck again.

Recovering from my first nose — and boob — job.

Throughout the week, it felt like the middle of my back was collapsing and tightening at the same time; I thought I had pulled a muscle from being sedentary since February. This time, though, I got up, took a few steps, and everything went dark gray and foggy, and everything started spinning. Instinctually, I reached for my phone and called for help.

"Ma'am, stay with me. Can you tell me what happened?"

I mumbled what I could. "Miss, I have an aortic aneurysm and I think it may have bursted. I know I am going to die."

"Okay, ma'am, the ambulance is on the way."

A whirlwind of thoughts went through my head: *so much for the divorce . . . who will take care of my dog?* Flashes of memories hit me.

I started to tear up, looked around the house, and said to myself, "Oh my God, is my house clean?"

How wacked-out is that? Who thinks of *that* at Death's door?

While waiting for the ambulance, I managed to throw a couple of things into a bag to take with me and left out some water for the dog.

The EMTs arrived and started asking me questions. I demanded to go to my doctor's office in Tampa rather than the closest hospital, and while they got that okayed, I called my neighbor, Sylvia, to let her know what was happening, and she told me I had to call Alan.

While riding in the ambulance, I wondered, *Why aren't I dead yet?*

Then I called Alan. While I didn't want him to come out, he started crying and insisted that he be there and started making arrangements to get back to Florida from Texas.

The doctor did countless tests and couldn't find anything wrong. Sylvia came and got me — where would I be without her? I love her so much. She is everything a neighbor should be: loving, trustworthy, and there to help.

Alan was at the house when we got back, and the health scare was perhaps the key turning point in our relationship. Just knowing that someone would be there for me, no questions asked, was a revelation.

In October 2018, I was back in a wrestling ring.

I've always tried to be in tune with my body, whether it was working out, teaching aerobics, wrestling, driving a monster truck, doing yoga. "Health conscious" is another way to put it, and it's certainly not anything I learned from my family. As a kid, I'd always been a milk drinker, and whenever I was thirsty, I'd run in the house and grab some milk. Betty would whack me across the head because a gallon of milk was 50 cents and even that was a financial challenge. No one connected my stomach ulcers or hives to the milk, but I figured it out that I was lactose intolerant. That was a real turning point in my health. When I got really crazy into athletics, everything changed — in myriad ways.

For one, I had my first orgasm as a teen running an 880 race. I never knew what it was. I was overexerting myself, and when you're running, you get hot and heavy, your skin loosens, and, well, the right parts rubbed. I was like, *What just happened?* And I got scared, as I was still a virgin. I have spoken to other women, and it is a common thing, so don't go thinking I'm a weirdo.

Somehow I knew, without researching or reading, to eliminate red meat, though the dissecting of a cow in class didn't help. From there, it was partly experimentation, listening to my body; nursing school gave me a good foundation to build upon.

It got tougher once I started living on the road. At a fast-food restaurant, I'd order the chicken sandwich and not eat the bun. I avoided soda, ketchup, and potato chips. My body just adapted, and I grew solid in bones and muscles — and have kept it up, which hasn't been easy.

The science of working out changed through the years. When I was in the WWF, Heidi Lee Morgan and I lived on protein mixes, IcoPro, MetaRex, whatever. It was horrible-tasting shit, but it worked. The nasty side effect was that it made you fart, and the hard-core gyms we sought out often just reeked. Inspiration came from reading the workout magazines and trying to emulate the badass women in them, like Cory Everson and Melissa Coates.

My interest in nutrition sent me to school in my fifties, and I became a certified natural health practitioner. It was amazing learning about how to read the eyes, tongue, fingernails, how what we take in changes our bodies. I freaking loved it and took it twice, because it was so much to take in. A couple years later, I started down the path to becoming a naturopath, but have not finished my studies as of yet.

Somewhere between 7 and 10, I was getting a regular checkup. The doctor found something on my lungs, which was very unusual for someone my age. I had to drink those awful drinks and then get X-rays done. The Minneapolis Government Health Center was for people without health insurance — welfare cases, like us — and we sat in a room full of people with little to no agenda in life, which made me realize how bad we had it. I was scared to death.

The doctor said I had been exposed to tuberculosis. I had to take three pills a day for a year to save my life as well as not spread it. I had been exposed to someone else who had it. I had a strong immune system, which is why we didn't learn about it earlier. Later in life, doctors would always note scarring on my lungs and be concerned, so I would have to explain. When COVID-19 came along, the way it attacked immunocompromised people, I was concerned. I had COVID twice and it kicked my ass, though in different ways. I'm thankful to still be here.

My lifetime bestie from the world of bodybuilding was Mike Muzik. We met at the Chicago health clubs that I was managing — without any training, I just knew the right people — where I hired him. He was a workout fiend, and I took inspiration from him.

For as much time as we spent together, there was never anything between us, though, he tried a couple of times, and I shot that down. "Quit looking at my ass," I'd scold him, and he'd tell me to stop wearing skintight spandex.

When I was traveling for wrestling, I'd stay at Mike's parents' house in Chicago, and he'd come to the shows, where I'd parade him around backstage, and the wrestlers would feel threatened by how *big* he was (but he never got into wrestling).

Over the years, Mike has battled alcoholism — he is more than 30 years sober now — and on one of his times through the Alcoholics Anonymous programs, he needed someone there to come clean to, someone you trust implicitly. I drove seven hours to help him, listening as he bared his soul over the wrongs he committed through the years.

I can hear the naysayers, slamming me for being two-faced. Here I am preaching good health, and I've had four boob jobs, a couple of other cosmetic treatments, like Botox, and tattoos — lots and lots of tattoos. The tanning booth was key to looking good in the ring, too.

And there was one round of steroids, just before I ended up in the AWA. It was Anovar, but I did it under my doctor's watch. After six weeks, I started peeing blood, dropping to my knees in pain. My doctor ordered me to stop immediately. The results were obvious: I could lift more, had great definition, the fat disappearing, but I also looked a lot less feminine. I never did steroids again.

No one is going to deny that pro wrestlers have used performance enhancing drugs, like 'roids, but it was always a personal choice from what I saw with my own eyes. When I was in the WWF, there was a doctor who came by my room one time, knocked on the door, and had a red toolbox. He opened it up and asked, "What do you need?" I'm like, "What?" Once I got my bearings, I took a B12 shot, which gives you energy. I never saw him again; I guess he figured out pretty fast that I wasn't going to be a good client.

You're not going to hear stories about partying, booze, and drugs from me much, either. I did that when I was younger and just came to the conclusion that it wasn't the lifestyle that I wanted any longer, that it certainly wasn't sustainable. I've always been high on life, setting goals, achieving — that was what brought me pleasure. Or going to see a movie on my own. Pretty exciting, I know.

But boobs? I'm happy to talk about them.

The initial reason I wanted breast implants is that I was very flat. I had an *A* cup when I was very athletic, and what depletes when you're in great shape? Fat, and there is fat in your breasts. My boobs, as small as they were already, were even smaller — like almonds — when I was in great shape.

I went a little bigger, somewhere between a *B* and a *C* cup, depending on the bra.

One broke while I was in Japan, and it stayed broken for almost a year. I got it fixed back in the United States, and the doctor specifically said he tried to get all the silicone out, but some of it was stuck to my insides. Foreshadowing.

On my second enhancement surgery, I went bigger yet again, but these were saline implants since there was all the concern about silicone, women suing doctors about issues with their boob jobs. I did *not* like saline boobs. When you're doing the wild thing, and your chest is moving and you hear water, it kind of breaks the moment.

One of the saline implants broke very early in my monster truck days, so I went back to silicone.

Those were the big ones that I had in WCW, that everyone talked about. They were big, yeah, but I was also wearing the most risqué clothes of my career, so everything was out there to see.

It's odd, all the issues were always with my left breast, and my right boob was always beautiful.

In monster trucks, I went back to a more normal size, and then, when I stopped driving, had them completely removed.

My boobs did not define me. When it was time to get them out, it was not a hard decision. I said to myself, *I just need to be healthy. I don't need them to feel beautiful; I don't need them to be accepted.*

I've had them through my whole life just because of my career and it was what I thought I needed to do — no one ever ordered me to change. Boob size shouldn't define anyone as a person.

Now, for all those tattoos. That first one? Oh, what a story. We were somewhere near Washington, DC, with the WWF, and I mentioned to Luna Vachon that I knew a local tattoo artist named Tattoo Al. He and I had ridden Harleys together, including one epic trip from Florida to Corpus Christi, Texas, where we left our bikes, crossed by foot into Mexico, and came back shit-faced, trying to smuggle in more booze than we could carry.

Luna had already been inked plenty of times and wanted more, and the next thing you know, he was in our hotel room. My first tattoo was a sun with flames around my ankle; I did my best not to show pain around Luna, who also got another tattoo. Then she learned that he did body piercing, too, and we arranged to meet him again after our match before we went on to the next town. So, in the back seat of our rental car, Luna had her belly pierced . . . and then so did I. It always bonded us, and I can still hear Al laughing, "I've never done it this way before!" It wasn't the greatest idea for a wrestler, though; I usually wore outfits that covered it, but I had to tape up the belly ring.

Was that my last tattoo? Hell no!

My second one was a tramp stamp, because, at one point in the 1990s, every woman in America seemingly got one; mine was done in Los Angeles in a trailer, and it has Japanese emblems in it. The third was done in Florida, on the right side of my lower ankle, an angel with a crown, but it's a little racier than you think; the front of her growler is showing, and I made sure that that was magenta, and down below was a flying flag with a dude's name on that will not be disclosed . . . and it's been erased anyway. What a mistake, lesson learned. The fourth one is on the back of my neck, and it was inked in Minnesota when I was driving monster trucks; it's actually beautiful, but people can't always make out what it is (it's an image of a pierced vulva, for the record). Somewhere in Texas, I got the baddest tattoo on my ass of my Madusa truck, with the words, "I am that damn good."

Then I started getting into piercings, but never had my lip pierced or my nose pierced. I always said that my face is not that wonderful to begin with, and jewelry will not change that. I'll leave it to your imagination what's pierced.

Then came my left arm sleeve, which took 15 years to finish. Clowns are scary to some people, but I love 'em. I also knew that I worked in some messed-up businesses, and the art is representative of that — a clown pulling open his jaw, ripping apart his face, with another face coming out of the clouds, which represents being pulled in so many different directions. The two flags represent my championship wins with monster trucks, and there's also *Queen of Carnage*. There are two angels, but one has devil horns, and there's a pink gerbera daisy because it is my absolutely favorite flower. In Germany, I got a fish that's just bones, and it looks like it's coming through my skin, making it so badass; it represents the fact that I got the last fish in the sea when I married Alan — and he's on there, too, as there's a chain with dog tags on it with his military info.

But the one that most people notice and comment on is an American flag blowing in the wind, with letters of the alphabet floating through the air around it, representing the lost lives of my twins. That may be what they see first, but then they'll ask to see the whole sleeve and thrill to the story of each one.

It's a small regret, but on my right arm, there are lightning bolts. I've always said that my right arm is my business arm, for shaking hands. Right arm to be serious, left is a fucking party. And, for the record, the tattoos have nothing to do with the biker lifestyle; that's a false narrative.

And every tattoo has been done by a different artist.

Before getting into the big, heavy shit, here are some little scars and scares. Okay, maybe not so little.

When Al Noga surprised me out of the blue in Japan, he wasn't alone; he had a big boil on his arm and had tried everything to get rid of it. The close quarters in Japan didn't help, and he ended up infecting me. A boil on my back, by my shoulder blade, only got worse through wrestling, and there's still a scar there today from it. If someone asks about it, I blame wrestling, battle wounds, or making something up, like I was hung from the metal hooks that attach the ring to the ropes — that always gets a great reaction!

About a month after Al left Japan, the gland under my armpit swelled up huge — it was almost as big as my head — and the All Japan office swept me off to a hospital, where they drained it with a massive needle.

Decades later, living in El Paso, with Alan, I went out to jog on a cool morning. The next day, when I got up, the left side of my face was paralyzed. I went into the bathroom, where my husband was shaving. He thought it was a stroke: "Don't look in the mirror." Of course, I looked in the mirror and started freaking out. All I can tell you is, thank God to the military and the health insurance we had because I got top-notch treatment for Bell's Palsy. We did electric shocks to the face, right away, and it saved my ass. Every so often since, when I am super-tired, I'll notice a droop, but I do heavy massages.

To keep my job driving monster trucks, I never told Monster Jam that I had had discs in my spine (L4 to L7) fused together — my husband, Alan, didn't know until a few years into our marriage. Even the surgeon told me that I would need to quit driving because one wrong hit and I could be paralyzed.

In short, my spine is a mess. The pain in my neck has been a constant. When you look at me now, carefully, you'll see that my head automatically tilts to one side. My neck is just worn from all the shit I went through in the truck and in wrestling. When I realize my head is leaning to the right, I stretch to the left. My neck, with cervical nerves C1 through C4 fused, doesn't move, so I have to turn my whole body.

This is why I'm so adamant with my yoga and working out and setting goals and just keeping fit going forward. My husband thinks I'm crazy, that I go overboard buying organic food or whatever. The extra vitamins are there that I need — because I hurt. I want to do this instead of having surgery on my neck and surgery on my back and taking fucking drugs.

I don't complain. My problem is my pain threshold is through the roof. I'm probably in 10 times more pain than I even realized; I've built a tolerance that my doctor says is dangerous. My last race in the monster truck was in Australia, and I took a hit in that truck going over just a little hill, and there was shooting pain down my neck and my spine. I knew that was it.

There are so many times I hear people complain about whiplash from a car accident, where they were belted in, and the airbag deployed.

For my first go-round in monster trucks, there was really nothing other than the seat belt; if you watch any of those old videos, I'm like a crash-test dummy bouncing around, and my hands, arms, and neck took so much of the brunt. My ability to handle pain is definitely higher than most people's.

If it hadn't been for the lessons learned in Japan, about keeping my neck strong, I'd never have lasted as long as I did.

How about I mention a path that I *didn't* take that avoided some different punishment?

When I was living in St. Petersburg, Florida, I was approached about seriously training to become a boxer. In the early 1990s, Christy Martin was putting women's boxing onto the map — and onto pay-per-view. Based out of this old, smoky gym, which was really not much more than a garage, I learned how to train. It was like *Rocky*, and we'd punch telephone poles, run on the beach for miles in the sugar sand, skip rope. It got me into incredible shape, and truly I had the confidence. *Christy Martin?* I remember thinking. *I can beat that bitch. I want a piece of that.* There was even talk about me moving into Don King's camp to take it up a notch, but it never happened, and women's boxing sorta petered out and didn't come back until Laila Ali.

I've always wondered how I could have done at mixed martial arts, too. Lord knows I had the discipline to train, and had the opportunity been there when I was younger, who knows.

Ask Jeff Tankersley whether I could have kicked ass! A wrestler and promoter, he owned a bar in Kingsport, Tennessee, and at the back of the bar was a punching-bag machine that gave you a score based on how hard you hit it. Guys would get a few drinks in them and show off for their girlfriends. One time when I was there, probably around 2004, I overheard some dude talking about how tough he was. I couldn't help myself, "You ain't tough. Hang on." I put my quarter in the machine, set it up to the right height, and I spin-kicked it — and kicked it so hard that I broke the machine. Sorry, Jeff!

With an eye on a post-driving career, I started thinking of combining all my interests and realized that throughout my whole life, I've been helping people. They'd come to me for guidance, like I have some sort of gravitational pull. Mental or physical questions, I was there for them, with my positive outlook and my innate ability to roll through chaos and focus on the good.

Before matches, I'd always stretch, but never really did get into yoga until much later in my life, though I have always carved out some time for meditation. During a break in the monster truck season, I signed up to study to become a yoga instructor. After some research, I chose Sivananda Ashram Yoga Retreat Bahamas, and not because it was in the Bahamas. What it offered was a complete experience. I lived in a tent, rising at 5 a.m., meditating, listening to scripture, chanting, studying yoga, reading up on yoga, and then participating in the communal experience — making meals one week (completely vegan), doing the dishes the next, laundry another, and toiling in the garden another. We all dressed the same, in these white baggy pants and oversized shirts. You were back in bed, exhausted, by 10 p.m. It was six weeks of personal growth, and I was wonderfully disconnected from the "real" world, walking barefoot everywhere, grounding myself in Mother Earth.

I came back a whole different person, I really did. Now I'm just caught up in the world again, but I really would like to go back. Once you're a member, you always get the opportunity to go back and take more classes.

The other piece of the puzzle came through online courses while Alan and I were stationed in Germany, and I had some downtime. All told, it was about nine months of studying a couple of days a week to get my diploma in life coaching and get certified by the International Federation of Coaching.

I came up with F.I.T. — Feminine Intelligent and Tough — my brand for life coaching. I was always skilled in personal fitness and was a certified personal trainer, so there's one aspect. I'd studied nutrition, so there was another element.

In another life, I likely stayed with nursing; in this one, it took 40 years to get to the point where I'm focusing on helping people again.

Pre-pandemic, I had started to do seminars, which I called KWR: Kick, Wrestle, and Roll. The goal is to educate others about the entertainment business, from what goes on behind the scenes, the logistics, how to apply for trademarks, and the needed medical and financial details. In short, I share all the stuff they don't teach you.

For all the scars and scares, nothing compares to that 911 call, but it was also a turning point on so many levels that I have to look on it as a blessing, as strange as that sounds. It was an element in fixing a marriage and put me on a better path, so bear with me as I try to explain.

It starts with boobs and a knee. Knowing that monster trucks were behind me, but that I was still under contract with money coming in, I scheduled two surgeries. The first, in March 2017, was having my breast implants taken out. It was time. They'd served me well during my career but had popped a few times, too.

This was during a rough patch between Alan and me. He had some serious trust issues and had invaded my privacy, going through my computer, emails, texts, thinking I was having an affair. I won't deny that I have a flirty personality, not so much sexual but very loving and quick to compliment, "You have a nice ass," or, "Damn, that girl is absolutely gorgeous and has some nice tits." He tried to change me, saying, "I don't like the way you speak to people." Here I was thinking that I had been nothing but accommodating to his life, flying to meet him somewhere, making time for us to see his two sons.

Alan's behavior had changed; he was mean, aggressive, and thought I had disrespected him. That stems from him going through my computer and making wild assumptions. Who the fuck does that? I have never cheated on my husband, though the opportunities were there. I was on the road a lot, as was he.

It's tough in the military, I get that. He came home from deployment in a third-world country, applying what he'd seen there to life in America. "I'm a man, dammit, and I will do what I want!" Hurt and confused, I found myself making excuses for him and his actions — until I couldn't any longer. One Friday night, our traditional pizza, beer, and movie night, I snapped and told him the bullshit had to stop. It was not a good scene.

While Alan was deployed, I arranged for a friend to help out at the house in El Paso while I recovered from that surgery; she was also supposed to help me pack up the house a bit, as Alan and I were thinking about selling that place and setting up life together in Florida, but said she couldn't lift things. (It was partially my fight-or-flight instinct kicking in, and I was claiming things that I didn't want to leave behind if the marriage continued to go down the toilet.) Three days later, having done most of the lifting of shit myself, my left breast turned black, and I was scared shitless! I immediately got a hold of my doctor, and she told me to head to the clinic even though it was after hours. An implant had become lodged under my armpit, and it took her two hours to get it out. That wasn't the end of it, though.

I'd had my implants for more than 30 years, and she said that some of the nerves and blood vessels in my breasts were severely damaged, dating back to my time in Japan, and there was a risk of losing them. She applied some liquid nitrogen to get the blood flowing around the nipple area and warned of major headaches. Within seconds, I was on the floor, screaming and holding my head. It got slightly better, but then she told me I'd have to do it myself three times a day for a few days. Talk about torture, but, in the end, my breasts, deformed, were okay, and no more implants — and hopefully this is a lesson to anyone thinking about getting their boobs done.

As my friend and I packed up a lot of stuff in El Paso — and it was just after my breast surgery, so my stitches came out — I weighed my options. As I made that drive with a trailer full of our shit from El Paso to Florida, I wasn't sure I was coming back.

But I did. It was another ugly scene when Alan and I met again. He was upset I'd moved so much stuff while he was gone and he was not in a good headspace for us to coexist. My total knee replacement was next. My first night home was a nightmare. Two nights later, Alan left me in the living room, drugged up, so he could go to a baseball game that he had to attend as a unit function. Somehow we managed to keep it together until he left again.

When he was at work, I packed, grabbed the dogs (one of whom had cancer, so I had to go back for the medicine), and hauled ass out of town. I found a divorce lawyer on my phone while driving, stopped at a hotel, and convinced them to print the papers and send them back for me. Filing for divorce would either wake up his ass or end our relationship.

We got down to the nitty-gritty, were in mediation and preparing to sign the papers. I was sitting in a room in the courthouse, alone, as my lawyer and his lawyer were talking in another room. An old-school phone rang, and, with no one else there, I answered. It was Alan, calling from a Kinko's parking lot in El Paso, to check in with his lawyer. It was the universe setting things right.

We started talking, I made him laugh while bitching about lawyers, and then he said, "Do you want to do this? Deb, I don't want a divorce." I didn't, either. Thousands and thousands of dollars later, we didn't get divorced — we call it our "trial-and-error" period. He stayed in a hotel for a bit, and we worked on ourselves. The way I see it, we had a bad year and a half in the long marriage we've had. Now, our marriage is better than it was. Being married to Alan is very good for me in so many ways. He lived a structured, military life, where respect is both earned and demanded, which was very different from my vagabond career choices. His first instincts are common sense and empathy, not fighting back or fleeing. What I thought were efforts to control me were him trying to help me see another perspective.

I'm not glad we went through that dark period, because I wouldn't want anyone going through anything that hurtful. But I am just so blessed to have him in my life.

Oh right, my life. That seemed gone a couple of times, too.

Not long after I filed for divorce, separate doctors delivered bad news. One said that I had an aortic aneurysm, meaning my heart wasn't working quite right; I was freaking out. How long did I have? I never got a straight answer and lived in fear. It wasn't until that 911 call, where I was checked out again. That time, the doctor was puzzled. "We did all these scans; who told you that you had an aortic aneurysm?" I replied, "The cardiologist across the street that you recommended!" "Ma'am, we can't find anything. We don't see anything at all."

One scare survived, one more to come.

About a month later, I went for a breast cancer checkup, and they were very, very concerned with the nodules in my breasts. They were going to study the results and said I should schedule another appointment and get things in order. That was a long wait between doctor visits, thinking I had cancer. I began to wonder how long I had, whether this was it. I didn't tell anyone, either.

At the follow-up, I sat there feeling overwhelming dread. When the doctor came in, she said, "All right, you're good." "What do you mean?" "What we're seeing is just the saline and silicone that leaked out, hardened inside your breast. No cancer."

I got myself together, and in the dressing room putting my clothes back on, I just fell to the floor and started bawling. Your life changes when your doctor tells you that you have cancer, and your life changes when they tell you that you have an aortic aneurysm. Here I thought I had both within the space of a month.

Both those experiences were awful, made worse by the fact that Alan and I were separated. I relied on pals Judy, Merry Beth, Sheila, Rosie, and Shannon.

And if you thought I was done, I had *another* total knee replacement. The surgery I'd just had in El Paso didn't work right, so they had to chisel out and get rid of the first knee replacement and redo it in Florida. Knowing I was on my own, I arranged for everything, except the bathroom, to be close by. After the surgery, I took pain meds for a couple of days and stopped cold turkey. It was tough filling time between the visits from the therapists every couple of days for someone as outgoing as I am.

To be clear, I don't want anybody's sympathy at all. It's a reminder that we all have an inner strength, something untapped, that is there for us when needed. It's called survival.

19.

TRUTHS

EVER SINCE MY MOTHER told me that Mike Miceli was not my real father, I have sought out the truth.

The truth of who my real father is. The truth about why our family was the way it was. The truth about myself, which has included a lot of "come to Jesus" talks, where I look deep into who I am and who I want to be.

My father, Clyde, in uniform, and me at his gravesite.

Not all the answers have been revealed, but a couple of key ones have been.

Growing up, I continually wondered about my real father. I asked Betty, Granny, my aunts and uncles. There was a cone of silence, or worse: "He worked in a circus," "He was a pilot and died." It fucked me up as a child.

One time, I was home from monster trucks and somehow got talked into going to visit my uncle Jim Lewandowski, who was in prison for child molestation. He never tried anything with me. Long story short, he raised prize-winning thoroughbreds, and at one point, he even had the biggest horse in the world, which made the *Guinness World Book of Records*. He opened an equestrian academy and was caught molesting some of the young girls who were there.

But, trapped in the car on the way home, I started badgering. I was in the back seat with my Aunt Judy, and Granny was driving with Betty in the passenger seat. Honestly, I had a wild hair up my ass, because I had had it with Betty. As much as she might have wanted to jump out of the moving car, that wasn't going to happen.

"Hey, does anybody in the car here know who my father is?" I began. Betty turned around and shot me a look. And I said, "What the fuck are you looking at? I know y'all are sisters and mothers. There's a daughter sitting right here. Somebody needs to fucking tell me who my real father is." Granny's eyes met mine in the rearview mirror.

"Oh, shut up. Your father's dead. He was just a two-week excitement; that's all that was, and that's all you were," Betty spat out.

Aunt Judy, shaken, said, "Ma, isn't he buried up in the Mille Lacs Lake area?" I looked at Judy. My eyes got big, Betty sank down in the seat, and Granny said, "Maybe."

I exploded. "You've known this whole damn time that I've been trying to find out who my real father is. What's wrong with everybody in this family? Fucking someone grow a pair and just tell me so I can move on!"

The car stayed silent, and I turned my head to look out the window and just started bawling. I couldn't look at any of them.

Aunt Judy kept going. "What was his name? Wasn't it Clyde or something?" It's like she wanted her conscience clear, on this at least; her brother was in prison for abusing kids.

We got to Granny's house, and I wouldn't let up. "Betty, who's my dad? Who the fuck is he? What's his name?"

She finally told me. Clyde Bergman.

"Awesome. Thank you!"

"They call him David because he couldn't stand Clyde."

"Okay, keep talking, bitch."

"He was a fucking drunk. He was brutal."

I'm like, "Okay, so you knew all of this in just a two-week affair?"

They all shut up after that. It would be up to me to dig up more.

The Don CeSar Hotel in St. Petersburg, Florida, has a rich history and is said to be haunted. One year, for my Chica's Forever reunion of girlfriends, I had us all stay there and arranged for all the normal stuff — massages, a nutritionist, an acupuncturist — and a medium.

Now, I'm not a complete believer in all that stuff, but my mind isn't closed, either. I went into my session somewhat ambivalent. We sat up straight, eyes closed, and she placed her hands on mine. "I can feel a strong presence." It took all I had not to scoff out loud. "I see a man. He's very tall, about six foot six, blond hair, blue eyes. He's been trying to get a hold of you, trying to connect."

"What?"

"He's dead. I see shiny shoes. And there's something about yellow, he liked yellow. Yellow is his color. Is there something yellow with you?"

"Yeah, I can't stand yellow. I don't even have one yellow shirt."

She opened her eyes, and said, "It's military. There's a military man trying to reach you."

That was weird. After the Chica's event, I was home and noticed that there was a single yellow rose in the vase in my bathroom. Why would I have bought that since I hated yellow? Why did I even have a yellow flower in one vase in my bathroom? It was just weird.

Minnesota's Mille Lacs Lake was about three hours from where Granny lived. Whenever I was able to get up there, I made it my mission to dig. First, I went to every funeral home, asking people about burying a Bergman. Then I hit the cemeteries. Finally, at one cemetery, someone said there was a Clyde Bergman buried there.

When the guy at the desk said it was a military grave, I nearly shit myself. The medium was right.

My father was six foot six, had blond hair, and blue eyes. His name was Clyde David Bergman. He died at age 48.

Now that I had the information I needed, I was able to find an obituary, and I called up his brother's wife, Mabel. The conversation is still etched in my memory.

"Hello, I'm Debrah. You don't know me, but just give me a minute. I don't want to alarm you. I don't want anything. I'm just calling because I believe that we are related. I'm looking for information on my father."

"Wait a minute, what's your name?"

"Debrah."

"Debrah what?"

"Debrah Miceli."

"Ahh, yeah." Just like that. "I think that he may have known about you."

"What?"

"If you are who you say you are, can you give me a date you were born?"

I was quick with it: "February 9, 1963."

"Can you give me a minute?" A few minutes later, she came back, and did the math. "Hi, Debrah. Let's see, 2/9/63, your father was home from the military for his father's funeral, he was home for a month. Your conceivable point would be about this. Yeah, pretty much, you could be his daughter."

"What? How did you get that?" It's like she had a box or a file waiting for me or something. I'll never know.

We chatted a little more, and I talked about Granny, her family, and Mabel had no problem putting two and two together — the world was a lot smaller then, so David and Betty sure could have met.

"I'm pretty sure you're his daughter. You have a brother and sister."

"What?"

Quite honestly, I hadn't even considered the possibility of siblings. My dad and their mom had split when they were living in Kalamazoo, Michigan. Mabel said she wanted to call her niece and nephew, as it had been a while since they had talked. I was the reason for a call.

But I insisted to Mabel that all I wanted was a photo of my real father. She took down my address and phone number.

Before we hung up, out of the blue, she said, "His favorite color was yellow." I thought I was going to faint. The medium *knew*.

I received this really cool picture of David Bergman in his military uniform — he was a U.S. Marine — wearing shiny black shoes.

It got me thinking more about my upbringing. There's a vague memory of me sitting on my grandmother's front doorstep as a kid, and a semi was parked, and in my mind's-eye, it said *Bergman* on the side. Whoever was driving didn't get out. Was Betty getting money from my real dad? They were a very well-to-do trucking company. And if she did get money, I don't know what she did with it, because we lived poorly. The speculation will continue, because Betty won't come clean.

The call was from a Miami number, and I just assumed it was a promoter wanting to book me for something. Instead, my life changed.

"This is your brother."

I fucking just about dropped dead. "What? My brother?"

"David Bergman."

"Holy shit. Mabel did get a hold of you."

"I hope you don't mind. I'm so glad. I want to tell you this right off the bat — I knew I had an older sister."

"What?"

"I just felt it. Do you ever feel like you just know something?"

Inside, I was freaking out. "Yeah, yeah, I guess I do."

We spoke on the phone for two hours. It was so cool. We talked about the things we'd done in our lives, about school, music — he even played guitar for me over the phone.

Our father, who was of Swedish descent, died on March 11, 1986, when he was 48. David filled me in on a lot of things, and Dad just drank himself to death. Yet he'd been MENSA-level brilliant, and David went and got his own MENSA card. Did I have one? "No, I don't need a card to tell me how smart I am, David!" He laughed so hard. "I'm gonna bug you forever now to take the test."

And we talked about our sister, Inger, who was pregnant. Of course, I wanted to talk to her, too, and I did, not long after, and I soon had a niece, Gemma, to spoil.

When we finally met, some similarities were obvious, including our common brilliance. But they'd inherited Dad's height, as David is six foot five, and Inger is six foot, while I'm five foot ten, but then my mother is barely five foot.

Less obvious, but also inherited, are some traits. David and I both have minds that go a mile a minute, ADHD-like, having to really focus on what's on hand; often people don't know what to make of our intensity. Whereas Inger and I have the same sense of wry humor — and we call each other "Sissy." Nicknames are apparently another Bergman signature. I still can't believe I've got a sister; it just seems so healthy.

Even weirder, there are similarities between our *mothers*. Inger uses the term "distracted" to describe their mom's parenting style, and that would be one of the nicer things I'd say about Betty. While they both did the best they could as single mothers — Clyde left Nancy, too — neither was especially cut out to be a parent.

In September 2022, David died. I regret that we never met that often, considering we all ended up in Florida. He once told me, "I don't want to die young like Dad." David was 56.

During the process of working on this book, we've been able to dig up some things from the past of Clyde David Bergman. We found an old yearbook photo and his military records. It's a continual process of learning about him and, in turn, about myself.

In a short amount of time, I felt more in common with someone I'd never met than the man listed as my father on my birth certificate. I'm so sick of being Debrah Miceli, as it's a constant reminder of all that Mike Miceli did to me.

If I can handle all the paperwork, the plan is to legally change my name to Debrah Ann Bergman.

That is, after all, who I really am.

20.

A HALL OF A CAREER

THE MOST HANDSOME MAN in the room was pinched by Ricky Steamboat and tripped Rowdy Roddy Piper — but no one saw either. What they did see was the massive Mark Henry stand up and salute my husband, Command Sergeant Major Alan Jonason, at the WWE Hall of Fame ceremony in 2015, in San Jose, California, at the SAP Center. I'd just mentioned Alan in my induction speech, with appreciation to the U.S. military for allowing him to come home from Turkey, where he'd been deployed, for my moment.

I inducted the Fabulous Moolah into the WWE Hall of Fame in 1995.

Instead, he got his.

The Hall of Fame crowd, always lovingly appreciative and maddeningly unpredictable, spontaneously started a "USA! USA!" chant for Alan. He gave a little wave, and Steamboat, sitting beside him, leaned over, and ordered, "Don't ruin her pop!" Not one to seek any glory, Alan continued to wave until "The Dragon" pinched him — hard — and told him to get up. Finally, Alan did, as the crowd erupted further.

To me, *that* was the highlight of my induction. Unscripted and 100 percent real, it was magical. The rest of the evening was pretty damn cool, too, except if you had asked Piper; Alan stretched out his legs just as Roddy was jumping into a skit with the Bushwhackers, and Roddy fell on his face.

But I'd better back up and mention The Call first.

I was in a Monster Jam drivers' meeting when I got a text apparently from WWE, but I figured it was a fan. The next text asked me to call, and I figured they wanted my updated address for tax reasons, or something equally trivial. There was a follow-up text, from Mark Carrano, who worked in talent relations at WWE. Not wanting to be rude, I didn't answer, listening to our marching orders for the show later that evening. In my dressing room, I started getting ready to drive and called Mark back. At no point did I think the call would alter everyone's perception of my career.

Standing there in my underwear, my firesuit at my feet, Mark asked if I was interested in being in the WWE Hall of Fame. I scoffed, "What? Are you kidding me? Is Vince good with this?" It had to be a joke call, right? Mark started giggling, "Well, yeah, we're past all of that. Everything is so good. We want to induct you." I said thank you, but that I had to check my racing dates.

After I hung up, I just started to scream. "Oh my God! Oh my God! Oh my God! I just got asked to be in the Hall of Fame!" Then someone knocked on the door, "You all right?" "I'm good. I'm really good!"

Checking the calendar, there was a conflict with a Monster Jam show. *Arrgh!* It took some politicking, since the people who ran the monster truck show saw my wrestling days well in the past; some of them didn't even know much about it, since I'd been driving for 15 years by then. As it was my name on the truck, I could dictate who would drive it — if they let me go to the WWE Hall of Fame. Well, you know already that I went, and I chose Brianna Mahon to drive Madusa, an early step in her great career.

The fear set in later. I had been away from pro wrestling for so long — on purpose. I didn't go to fan fests or shows and only kept in touch with a select few people from that part of my past. The women wrestlers of today are all beautiful, in incredible shape, and can do moves I never dreamed of; would they even know who I was? And, more importantly, *what would I wear*?

There were about two months until the ceremony, and I started working on the speech. I wrote out key points by hand, highlighting what I thought was important and hitting the key players in my career with shout-outs. To prepare, I watched some of the induction speeches by other women, like my old foes Sensational Sherri (who was hilarious and sparred with the crowd) and Wendi Richter (who was regal and so well spoken).

It made me think back to the WWE Hall of Fame ceremony in 1995, where "The Fabulous Moolah" Lillian Ellison became the first female inductee, and, as the WWF Women's champion, I got to introduce her. I can remember them asking me to do it: "You're our champion. It would be a great honor if you would consider inducting the first woman ever, and, who knows, maybe someday you will be in one." I'll never forget that.

Here's part of what I said about Moolah: "As the current World Wrestling Federation Women's champion, and the leader of the feminine movement of the New Generation, I realize that neither I, nor the entire state of women's wrestling, would be here today had it not been for Moolah and her courageous fight to survive in a predominantly male-oriented business."

The ceremony itself was just a dinner with insiders, and I got to sit with Lillian. It wasn't for a few years until the WWE Hall of Fame became one of the highlights of *WrestleMania* weekend, a ticketed event with fans.

Getting Alan to San Jose for the event was complicated, too. He was deployed in Turkey, and, fortunately, his superiors saw the value in his leave. The military guys love wrestling, and he said that it was around 3 a.m. when *Monday Night Raw* aired on the Armed Forces Network, but plenty of his colleagues got up to see the announcement of my induction anyway. A WWE documentary crew filmed some of the frenzy around induction weekend, including him coming home — it's called *TrailBlayzer: The Alundra Blayze Story*. Before they filmed him, I gave him a crash course on pro wrestling, since he'd never been around it. We both had to get used to cameras everywhere, and he was awed at my ability to "turn it on" when the shooting was happening.

They didn't film everything, like me practicing my speech in our beautiful suite (I had to tell him that this was not the norm in pro wrestling). Alan was one of the top speechmakers in the U.S. Army, so he knew his shit and urged me to be more, well, me after I did a run-through in the room, as it was very dull and lacking any pizzazz. He insisted on recording it and making me watch my trial run. I brushed him off: "Believe me, when I walk out on the stage, and with this fucking audience, I've got it. I'm going to control it." He just shook his head, anticipating doom, more nervous than I was.

He did agree with me having my speech available on my iPad, rather than relying on the teleprompter, though he didn't understand my reasoning. I was scared that someone was going to rib me and turn off the teleprompter, and then I would be standing there clueless.

Before the Hall of Fame ceremony, on Saturday, I got to do a signing at WWE Fan Axxess and was welcomed there with open arms by the fans and everyone I met from WWE. There were a few holdovers from my days there, whom I was eager to see, like Sue Aitchison, who helped organize so much of the company's charity work, while also acting as a den mother to the wrestlers.

Now, as any girl knows, it's all about the dress, and holy fuck do I have a surprise for you!

To start, I looked at previous ceremonies and the dresses that the women wore. I thought, *They must be making some jack because I can't afford that shit.* I never could.

In my mind, I wanted to make a statement, that I might be a woman of age, but that I was also confident in mind and body, and classy. It had to be sparkly and elegant, gray, silver, or black, so that my hair would pop when I went out on stage. I didn't want to be trashy, my tits hanging out or revealing down to my back. I wanted to be the conversation piece, not the dress.

I looked and looked, hitting the usual suspects, like Neiman Marcus to smaller stores, and just couldn't find anything for less than $3,000 (and up, way up!), which was way too much for something I'd probably wear once.

Then I changed my tactic. A place in Tampa rented prom dresses; did they have anything for someone way past prom age? It turned out that they would, on occasion, buy a dress that they knew they could rent out again if you found something that would work.

And that's what I did. At the store, they brought out the dress, and I stood on this pedestal in front of this huge three-way mirror, from ceiling to bottom of your feet, trying it on. I knew it was the one, and all the salespeople agreed.

The final product was a two-piece dress. It's all black, with countless stones and sparkles — silver, red, purple, yellow; it looks heavy, but it isn't. The top has a normal neckline and descends to my midriff; the arm covering switches from the dress material to a black sheer fabric near the biceps, and the shine returns on the wrists. The bottom picks up at my waist and carries down to the floor, with a short train. I accented with diamond stud earrings I owned.

Until now, only Alan knew that I rented my WWE Hall of Fame dress . . . for $179, plus tax!

Now, the shoes. I was similarly frustrated and wouldn't spend a couple of thousand on shoes that would barely be seen. Then, with the dress in my possession, I reassessed the shoes I already had and was perfectly fine with a silver-and-black pair. Of course, they had cost more than $179 when I bought them, but this time millions of people would briefly see them! And really, I only wore them to go across the stage; the rest of the time, I was wearing custom Adidas running shoes, and there's a good story there, too!

Today, Dan "Mache" Gamache is a famous shoe guy, someone whom football players, rappers, celebrities all call to get custom-painted shoes. I found him before he was a superstar, just poking around on the internet, and we had a common love of the Minnesota Vikings. We chatted, and he was thrilled to make some Alundra Blayze kicks.

Now another story no one knows. When Mache shipped me the shoes, in Florida, I just packed them without trying them on. When I got to San Jose and went to test them, I was shocked to see that one shoe was a size 10 and the other a size 8. *What the fuck? Is this a rib?* I quickly called him and did a little video to show him the issue. He was devastated but reacted right away and overnighted a new pair. Now that's customer service!

And though the guys reading this won't understand, the ladies will: I had one more pair of custom-made pumps with me and switched partway through the event. They were designed by a woman in Europe, and my image was painted on the bottom of each shoe, and the date for the 2015 WWE Hall of Fame induction was painted at the back of the shoe. There are rhinestones all over them. They are stunningly beautiful and remain under lock and key in a glass curio at my house.

In the end, I have never gotten so many compliments on my shoes, on my dress, and it just made me think, *Who in the hell have I been dressing for all these years? Everyone else or myself?* I was trying to keep up with the Joneses. So the moral of the story is, if you look hard enough, you can find it.

The way the WWE Hall of Fame is set up, someone important from your past is asked to introduce you, like a tag team partner or manager. Immediately, I asked to have Paul Heyman do the honors. It didn't happen. WWE had chosen Natalya Neidhart to introduce me. While I didn't really know her, of course I'd known her family — her father, Jim "The Anvil" and uncles, Bret and Owen Hart — through the years. She was a fan of mine, and I quickly became a superfan of Nattie.

We got our makeup done together, and I felt like a princess. I'd never had that treatment through my years of wrestling. The most nerve-wracking part, though, was knowing I'd see Vince McMahon, almost 20 years after dropping his women's title belt in the garbage. My fears were foolish. We were rehearsing on stage, my hair still in curlers, and I heard Vince's booming voice, "Alundra!" He gave me the biggest hug. He was so thrilled that I was there and also explained the reasoning for Nattie to introduce me, which helped ease the hurt of not getting my way. In short, he wanted today's women wrestlers to be like I had been. Wow!

A walk-through was next, and there I got to see Vince's son-in-law, Paul Levesque, better known to wrestling fans as Triple H, again. Together, they showed me my induction ring prior to the show, and all I could think was, *That's really huge.* At the time, they didn't make smaller rings for the women, and it's big and gaudy. Let's just say you wouldn't wear it to the supermarket.

Alan was swept along backstage through all this, a whirlwind for him, meeting people he'd only heard about, taking some personal photos, and trying to keep me grounded. I even had a personal handler to make sure all my needs were met, that I was on the bus at the right time, whatever.

The WWE writers wanted to read my speech, okayed it without any changes, and asked if I had any other ideas. Funny that you should ask!

The WWF Women's title that I'd trashed was still mine, and WWE had borrowed it for a display at Fan Axxess. My idea was simple — to pull it out of the trash, along with some of Jim Ross's barbecue sauce, and an Eric Bischoff book. They were game, and the runners were sent out at the last moment to fulfil my wish list.

Showtime.

In wrestling, the spot just before you walked out into the spotlight is called the Gorilla Position, in honor of Gorilla Monsoon, a monster of a man who was a wrestler-turned-commentator-turned-backstage-producer; I got to know him a little in my WWF run, and he was a sweetheart. At the Hall of Fame, Vince McMahon, Triple H, and The Undertaker were sitting in Gorilla Position. I was listening to Nattie, waiting for my cue, and she told the story of me tossing the belt in the trash in WCW. The boos started big time, and my heart dropped. Oh, no. Behind me, Vince went, "Good luck with that, Blayze," and he started laughing. I just gave him a look like, "What the fuck?"

Finally, it was my time. Deep breath. "Fuck yeah, I got this," I whispered.

Then I kicked ass. Now, he's obviously biased, but Alan raved later that it was the best speech of the night, and that he couldn't believe that I could turn it on like that — he'd seen how much I sucked in practice. I said, "Alan, that's the beauty of being an entertainer. Once you walk on stage, it's on."

Now, as for going to see the WWE Hall of Fame? Good luck with that. As of this writing, there is no physical building. I see the online comments, "That ain't no fucking Hall of Fame. There's no building." And my comeback is that it's a traveling Hall of Fame, they use it during *WrestleMania*. I am still a Hall of Fame inductee, even if there is no building.

There is, however, a physical place for monster truck stars, the International Monster Truck Hall of Fame, which is a part of the Kruse Automotive and Carriage Museum, in Indiana. Monster Jam just launched its own Hall of Fame, too, and in January 2020, Grave Digger creator and driver Dennis Anderson and announcer Scott Douglass were the first two inductees.

Over the subsequent years, I got to go to a few more WWE Hall of Fame ceremonies. I struggled with how to explain this, but essentially the interest in you dwindled each year. The first year, everyone was doting on me. The second year was still a little like that. By the fourth year, it was like a shrug and off to the side. I never got asked back on my fifth year of my *Legends* contract, my final year.

In 2019, Torrie Wilson was inducted, and Stacey Keibler introduced her. Here we were, Mama Deuce with two of her WCW Power Plant trainees, all together in a dressing room. I realized I screwed up: "Oh, shit. I forgot my damn T-back underwear." Stacey went, "Deuce, I've got you." Out of the blue she gave me a new pair of underwear. The kid grew up nice.

That's a positive Hall of Fame story. Here comes the rants.

WWE needs to do a better job acknowledging the women of the past — while they are still here. Leilani Kai. Joyce Grable. Susan Green. Bambi. Peggy Lee Leather. Toni Rose. It's like the 1970s didn't exist in their world. As for the 1980s and '90s, it's not much better. What about Bull Nakano? Velvet McIntyre? Heidi Lee Morgan? Aja Kong? Every woman from the Attitude Era is praised like they changed the world. Respectfully, they didn't, and the women I just mentioned and so many others created a landscape whereby they could succeed.

The other rant is a lot more personal. By this point, you are familiar with some of the, *hmm*, complicated relationships from my years in wrestling. I was hardly the only woman to go through this. At one point, "The Kliq" was a powerful backstage unit, able to influence WWE in myriad ways, from storylines to who should be hired or fired. They'll deny it, of course, but it's the truth. The Kliq was Kevin Nash, Scott Hall, Triple H, Shawn Michaels, and Sean Waltman. It's like a Mafia thing — they'll always stick together. Nash told me as much once, calling just before Triple H married Stephanie McMahon. "We're in, we're gonna have everything in our life. We're always going to be a part of WWE," is the gist of what he said. Doesn't it sound like something Don Corleone would say?

Now, the women. Triple H and "Chyna" Joanie Lauer trained together, dated, and came into WWF as a unit. Then he dumped her — literally leaving her waiting for him to pick her up while he flew off with Stephanie. She spiraled in the years after, doing drugs, porn — even a sex tape with Waltman, finally dying in 2016.

"Sunny" Tammy Sytch dated Shawn Michaels, but she does not talk about that much.

All three of us, Sunny, Chyna, and I, were on the outs with WWE for the longest time. That's not a coincidence. When the doors started opening again, with a Hall of Fame induction for Sunny in 2011, who was in the same class? Shawn Michaels.

When they inducted Chyna, it was as a part of the D-Generation X faction, with her, Shawn Michaels, Road Dogg, X-Pac (Waltman again), Billy Gunn, and . . . Triple H. And as for me, not everyone had my best interests at heart.

You can call it a conspiracy, but they all have a long track record of doing shit to the women they wanted on the road.

I'd become close to Joanie in her final years, and Sunny and I had always been friendly, though, she had her own demons, too. On one call, she was so whacked out of her fucking mind that I contacted WWE on another line and had them send over the police to check on her while I had Tammy on the phone; she was pissed that I narked on her, but understood why. She has been in and out of prison since.

The three of us talked about doing a book together, focusing on the men's mistreatment of women, and how they got to rise above all and become millionaires. They got to keep their families, they got to keep their jobs, and they got all the glory — and we got shoved to the side. There was even talk of a reality show as we took a bus across the country to promote it. We were getting ready to pitch it, and then Joanie died. How many people in power do you think said, "Phew, she's dead"?

I am tired of not speaking out. A turning point was a revolting moment at one of the Hall of Fame ceremonies. Waltman walked up to me, started laughing, "Deuce, we're so happy for you, and we're glad you're here." Or whatever the fuck he said. I just smiled, tried to be cordial. He's like, "We knew you were one of us. The reason why you're so cool, Deuce, and the reason why you got on well with the boys is because you were one of the boys and you kept your mouth shut."

No more.

In early 2021, I signed a new *WWE Legends* deal, though my deal might not last much past the publication of this book, but not by my choice! It's an honor to be an ambassador for the company.

My first *Legends* deal kept me involved in WWE, when I could fit it into my schedule. I was still driving my truck, but things had slowed down and I knew I'd be done soon. What would be next for me? I got a chance to try different things with WWE.

They had me as a backstage interviewer at NXT for a bit, on the Mae Young Classic women's tournament, until they realized I sucked at it — it was definitely not the role for me. On a couple of occasions, I got to be a guest on a WWE talk show, which I was much better suited for, as I wanted to talk! On one of them, I dug out a vintage red leather outfit, designed by Michael Hoban of North Beach Leather. I've never gotten so many compliments in my life. "Holy shit, who made that?" I was smiling from ear to ear. "I paid $1,500 for this 30 years ago." I found an old picture of me in the outfit to prove it.

Since it's not that far from my home, I was invited to come in as a guest instructor at the WWE Performance Center in Orlando. It was fun, but I wasn't interested in a full-time commitment, and the other trainers probably could see that. It wasn't my thing. But what an unbelievable facility.

You're going to think I'm full of shit, but this is the truth. Randy Savage and I had talked about opening a school, and I still have the mock-up for our "Wrestle Warehouse Academy of Professional Training" as we awkwardly called it. Randy and I were looking for a place on about 10 acres, where the trainees could live, eat, train. There would be three rings, weights, aerobics, cardio machines, and even a store to buy merch. The basement was going to have hanging bags for boxing and kickboxing, the dressing rooms, and a first aid room. Ideally, we wanted a balcony where we could have our offices, to overlook everything that was going on, and both a classroom and a place to practice interviews.

Sure sounds like the Performance Center. Great minds think alike. I still have those rough drafts.

You can't compare the WWF of my day to WWE of today, as the scale is just too different now. In 1994, it was still a family-run business, and you knew most of the people. Now, when you get to the arena, they have to put out a huge easel at the backstage entrance with arrows pointing to everything from food to Vince McMahon's office, with maybe 50 things on the list. It was military-structured shit, so organized, and I dug it.

The sewing room boggled my mind, and I thought of Granny, toiling away in her basement. They had the top-of-the-line machines, men and women sewing away, creating, fixing, improvising. Compared to some of the places I had to get dressed in for WCW, the makeup rooms made me tear up — huge mirrors, artists working on the girls (and guys). Everyone had an appointment time, and they were allowed to pop back in just before going out to the ring.

And the food? It was like a grocery store, the spread of food out there for you all day, and the coffee area had every flavor of coffee and latte and espresso imaginable, with every creamer flavor, too. But every time I was there, I would think, *Too bad I can't enjoy this.* Still nervous about being seen in high-definition — another new development — I didn't want to look or feel goddamn bloated. It got me thinking, *Do these kids really eat this much before they go? Because half of them are paper thin! Of course, they do what we've always done: you pack up that shit and you take it to go!*

When I got back into WWE, I really fell for the Bella Twins, who were inducted into the WWE Hall of Fame in 2021. Quietly, I attached myself to them in my head, because I looked at them as my twins, even though my twins would have been about 10 years younger than them. I just envisioned my twins getting in the business, and then being like the Bellas. Just as you live vicariously through your kids, I find myself getting excited by what they are doing. For example, I've always wanted my own wine, and they went and did that. Given my life, I know I could have been a reality show, too. The Bellas were living the dream that I wanted, that I fought so hard for, but I was so ahead of my time everyone told me, "What are you talking about? You can't do it." I was just in awe of all of the opportunities that they had right there in front of them, given the WWE machine.

I had a small part in the E! reality show *Total Divas.* At one point backstage, off-camera, one of the E! producers asked me what I thought about one of the Bellas having a baby, how that would do on TV. Of course, I was all for it. Then they had their own reality show, *Total Bellas*, and Brie had her baby, Birdie. I took such a loving to Birdie and watched her grow up through the show and social media. Are you considered friends if you comment on each other's tweets and posts?

I would speak to their mom, Kathy, on the back end through a direct message. I told her, "I bet you are so proud of the girls." We opened up to each other a bit, and I told her that the Bellas remind me of the twins that I would have had.

Then watching Nikki have her baby, and then Brie have her second, I just live vicariously through them. It makes me wonder what my life could have been like. What I was unable to do, they and so many others have been able to do, like Maria Kanellis, Becky Lynch, or Renee Paquette, who get to celebrate being moms. How lucky they are to be in a world where it is accepted.

In October 2018, WWE ran an all-women's event called *Evolution*. The call went out to many names from the past to be a part of it, myself included. But I had a secret that I hadn't shared. The years of mistrust and the mentality of work-at-all-costs is hard to shake, and though I'd just had a total knee replacement, I was determined to still compete in the battle royal.

Post-surgery, I wore long dresses that covered my legs and walked slowly, trying not to show a limp. After a while my knee started blowing up and it ached. This started when WWE asked me to do some interviews backstage with all the Mae Young Classic competitions. Standing there for too long, I finally asked for a bag of ice and treated my knee. The news was out that I had an issue. I also avoided pain meds at all costs, and, later, on my second total knee replacement on the same knee, I quit taking them within three days.

Then they asked me to wrestle, and it was only seven months after my total knee replacement. I suspect whoever asked me hadn't known about the NXT experience. My doctor said it was fine, but to be smart.

The WWE's doctor thought differently. At *Evolution*, at the Nassau County Coliseum on Long Island, New York, it was about an hour to go until the battle royal match, and I asked the doc to tape up my knee. He left to talk to someone and came back and said, "We are going to have to pass on you going out there." I said, "What are you talking about? I have a doctor's paper saying that it's okay. So I don't know what doctor you're talking to. But I have my surgeon saying it's okay. If you want me to sign another liability thing, that's fine." I went and got it, showed it to them, and they had me sign something else, and I went out there . . . and you can see the outline of my knee brace under my red leggings.

It was a real rush getting in the ring again, even if I didn't last very long and was eliminated by Nia Jax when she pushed me over the top rope to the floor. The hard-core Japanese fans probably appreciated my moment with Asuka, a throwback to my matches decades before with the legendary Lioness Asuka (no relation). Another veteran, Ivory, stayed in the battle royal until the final four, and, while I was happy for her, I knew that was the plan for me, but when they learned about the state of my knee, they didn't want to take a chance and rewrote the script.

My only other "wrestling" appearance with WWE came when I won the 24/7 title on a *Raw Reunion* night, in July 2019, pinning Candice Michelle, and then selling it to "The Million Dollar Man" Ted DiBiase before I trashed it. So, technically, one might argue that I'm still a 24/7 champion!

It's definitely my opinion that WWE could have done more with me while I was on a *Legends* deal. The second deal was different from the first, in that it only applied to Alundra Blayze and had no connection at all to the Madusa name — meaning I could do other things, like the NWA all-women's event, *Empowerrr*, in August 2021. I was a backstage producer and appeared on-screen to present The Hex (Allysin Kay and Marti Belle) with the relaunched NWA Women's tag team titles (and that was a match I helped produce), and I did commentary. I was so damn proud to be a part of an amazing organization that gave us creative control, to inspire the women to take the reins with their own creativity.

The NWA had me back, too, producing and announcing on other shows. Being an agent is interesting. You are the conduit between the matchmaker — Billy Corgan in this case, and, yes, that's the same Billy Corgan who is the founder and lead singer of The Smashing Pumpkins — and the talent. We'd find a spot for us all to talk about the goal of the match, who was winning, and then collaboratively figuring out how we'd get there. I was pleasantly surprised at how receptive to my ideas the young wrestlers have been, and, in turn, I've learned much from them. In WCW and WWE, I was usually just told what to do, but our matches were less planned out move-for-move the way things are today. Just before they go out to the ring, we loop in the referee and let the TV people know of anything specific that is planned, like a move outside the ring that needs to be caught on camera. The talent not only has to know how long they have in the ring and plan accordingly, but also be able to shave time if necessary, adapt on the fly. There's a shared moment of euphoria when the boys or girls come back after a match where everything went well, but there are always little things to critique. For example, in one bout I was the agent for, the wrestler did a good job selling his injured leg but forgot to do so after coming out of a Boston crab. Is it nitpicky? Sure, but it's part of making the match believable, which is the foundation of pro wrestling.

The complication going from, say, Thunder Rosa's all-women's Mission Pro Wrestling (where I have also helped out) to NWA is learning their lingo, what they need, and what they expect. You also have to figure out the new power brokers, who are telling you what to do. Every venue is different, every dressing room is different, even the people who time the matches backstage differ in how they do things.

Many of the women wrestlers of today reach out for advice, which I am happy to provide. That's not to say that I always understand their world. I was always taught that it was important to get over with the fans, and to many now, it's about being over on Instagram, OnlyFans, or Twitter, not with the live crowd. Yet, when I sit down with them or conduct a seminar, they listen. The presentation of pro wrestling might have changed, but it's still woman versus woman in that ring, telling a story.

In 2020, the publishers of *Pro Wrestling Illustrated* named me one of its Stanley Weston Award (Lifetime Achievement) winners. It arrived in the mail in the middle of the pandemic, so I wasn't in the mood to celebrate. The award, named after the *PWI* founder and longtime publisher, has been around since 1981, and it's a who's who of winners. I was only the second woman after The Fabulous Moolah. It makes up for not ever giving me my own solo cover!

As great as all the accolades have been, it's tough to compare to the Iron Mike Mazurki Award, which I was given in September 2021, by the Cauliflower Alley Club, named after the organization's founder. It's the top award in our wacky pro wrestling industry, and I was chosen by my peers for the honor. Plus, I had my husband, Alan, introduce me. He is such a great speaker and had the crowd in Las Vegas in the palm of his hand, even if he teased me sometimes in his speech.

"The nominee must be recognized as having achieved success in more than one field — recognition and success in more than one field. *Hmm*, wife, stepmother, author, philanthropist, entrepreneur, certified master dog groomer, poster model — anybody here have a copy of that poster? Anybody? I do! Actress, recording artist, and singer; although, we don't talk about that when we're at home. 'Who's Madusa?' It's so good. Look it up on YouTube, it's amazing," is what Alan said early at the podium, and then listed all my accomplishments — and if you are unfamiliar with them by now, then you skipped ahead to this chapter.

Wearing an elegant, sleeveless black dress that showed off all my arm tattoos (I forgot the matching shawl back in Florida, though!), it was my turn next. With so many friends and fans in the crowd, and not the pressure of live television, it was a way looser speech than what I delivered at the WWE Hall of Fame. I mean, I started out with a pot joke, since I had to follow notorious *high*-flyer Rob Van Dam — I wouldn't have done that on the USA Network. It was *on*! I laughed about having to pee in a cup on long rides, because the boys wouldn't stop for me to go, spray-painting Wahoo McDaniel's hair, and getting fired via FedEx by WWE executive JJ Dillon, who was a couple of tables over.

During the week, I learned so much about the Cauliflower Alley Club and its charitable arm, which helps wrestlers in need. I'd become a lifetime member before arriving, and Alan signed up in Vegas after seeing the loving fellowship everywhere we turned.

I worked hard on my speech, even if I jumped in and out of reading it, thinking of off-the-cuff stories about people in the room. I quizzed Kevin Sullivan on whether he had anything to do with that barbecue sauce match in WCW, for example.

Since it wasn't on a major television network and preserved on the WWE Network, I want to share my closing remarks here, as we come to the end of my book:

> I've had a wonderful week. As I close here, I have a message to anyone aspiring to be in the entertainment business, something I kept telling myself and just a little secret that can help you keep on path when you're feeling defeated.
>
> Integrity is the practice of being honest and showing a consistent and uncompromising adherence to strong moral and ethical principles and values. In ethics, integrity is regarded as the honesty and truthfulness or accuracy of one's actions. Never compromise your integrity.
>
> If there's one thing I can say to help encourage you, it is when you feel defeated, visualize your greatest strength. Your character is louder than words and your integrity defines you.
>
> And for me, I'm not done. I am forever growing. Do not think for one moment I would ever leave these

businesses. My heart is here. I will always be back to claim it. Here's to the past, to the present, and to the future. Thank you and good night. I love you all. Thank you so much! Thank you, thank you, thank you.

21.

THE TAKEAWAY

THERE, I'VE COME CLEAN. Some of my closest friends wouldn't have known the details that I just wrote about. It was an exhausting process, but exhilarating, too — and freeing.

For all that I've revealed, I still feel the need to remind y'all that this book is about *me* and *my* experiences. This book isn't about you, whether you were family, a fellow driver, an executive, a wrestler, a lover. It's about *me*.

Walking with Daisy.

This whole book is a story. It's life experiences. It's what I had to endure and overcome. It's the adversities and choices in life — and the paths not taken, too.

It's led me to where I am today, and I am confident that I am a better person now. And isn't that what life is about?

I'm appreciative of whatever you took away from my story, but I came to a couple of conclusions myself.

Women can drive just as well as the men.

For all the successes of women in monster trucks after my pioneering days, there are still those glass ceilings in the business. One day, that glass will be shattered.

Hiding pain is not easy.

To be heard, I had to be loud, brash, outspoken. A bitch. People thought that was cockiness, and that I was arrogant. Nope. I was scared inside, and it took a tremendous toll on me to appear to be strong. There were times I cried myself to sleep, just a fucking wreck.

I do not relax.

Looking back on my life, it's been a sequence of clearing one hurdle after another, and I have developed a fear of relaxing. Even now, two careers in the rearview mirror, I still have a craving for more. You do you, let me be me.

Wrestling was never good to me. I was good to wrestling.

This should be clear by now. I gave and gave and gave, and kept hitting roadblocks and stubborn people protecting their power rather than rocking the boat. What could have been?

I'm not looking for a handout or an apology. I am laying out my truths, knowing full well that so many of these people I have talked about think they are untouchable to this day.

And revealing all this, I know I will be seen as the heel, the villain. It takes a certain kind of person to jump into that raging river to get it started.

AFTERWORD

WHEN I READ THIS STORY, I sat trying to catch my breath and process everything. As I devoured each chapter, I found myself stunned, then laughing, then crying, and then cheering as I sifted through the details of Debrah's life. What an incredible roller-coaster ride of emotion, exposing in intimate detail the tragedy and triumph of a woman who, from the day she took her first breath, was destined to fail. But didn't.

Wedding day.

My name is Alan Jonason, and I'm Debrah's husband. Until I read this book, I had no idea of the depth of the trauma and adversity Debrah had experienced almost every day of her life. It's unfathomable to me how a woman could experience everything you've just read and somehow triumph and thrive *because* of it. She should be a statistic, yet somehow isn't. Debrah Ann Bergman has continuously championed for women, shattered glass ceilings, and challenged "The good ol' boys' club" — and persevered every step of the way. Her story is a rallying cry to those who have faced adversity, hardship, and misfortune. If you've ever felt overwhelmed and unsure and didn't think you could make it another day, her story screams, "YOU CAN GET THROUGH IT!"

As time has passed in our 12 years of marriage, I've managed to slowly chip away at the tough outer shell that surrounds Debrah. Early on I knew she loved me, but there was always a feeling like she would take off and leave at any given time — especially if there was any discord between us. She mentioned leaving me frequently during our disagreements, but I understand it all now. It was fight or flight. It came from years of abuse at the hands of the numerous people who supposedly loved and cared for her but didn't. I now understand why she's had a difficult time trusting or allowing anyone near her. The constant fear of being let down, cheated on, lied to, or left alone would make anyone wary. Despite all of this, Debrah is the most generous and loving woman I've ever known. I've never felt a love as beautiful as Debrah's, and I consider myself the luckiest man on earth for finding her. In the past, she has been incredibly self-deprecating and struggled with acknowledging her own beauty and success, but over the last few years she has finally become comfortable with herself, her beauty, and her legacy. Speaking of legacy, I'd like to just touch on a few but incredibly important events in Deb's life and career.

Debrah's accolades are far-reaching and extensive. I'd like to mention a few: 1988 *Pro Wrestling Illustrated*'s Rookie of the Year (the first woman to win the award); three-time WWE Women's champion; WCW

Cruiserweight champion; the first female Monster Jam World Champion, and the only one to win in both racing and freestyle.

Talk about shattering glass ceilings, Debrah destroyed the building! However, I would be remiss if I didn't address the elephant in the room — recognition, or lack thereof. To give you some perspective on how the lack of recognition continues, I'll discuss the two sports she is most recognized for.

The Monster Jam Hall of Fame was officially unveiled in 2021. Dennis Anderson of Grave Digger fame and Scott Douglass — the voice of Monster Jam — were inducted as part of the inaugural class. Both deserving. How is the only female to win a racing and freestyle championship not included in the inaugural enshrinement, or the one after? It boggles the mind.

On March 28, 2015, Debrah was inducted into the WWE Hall of Fame. I was incredibly proud of her, and her speech was inspiring. She received the red-carpet treatment all weekend and felt like she was part of the WWE family again. About a week after the ceremony, in an April 7, 2015, Facebook post, Mick Foley applauded Deb's WWE Hall of Fame speech and said: "For me, the speech was a landmark event — a turning point from which the term 'Diva' suddenly seemed worn and a little insulting. 'Diva' was a great marketing idea that feels in 2015 like it's outlived its usefulness."

Ironically, during her Hall of Fame speech, Deb spoke about how nice her "wrestling belt" looked in comparison to the current Divas belt and received incredible applause for the statement. Sure enough, WWE "trashed" the Divas title and resurrected the Women's title almost exactly one year to the day after Deb's speech. Who was given the prestigious honor of unveiling the new WWE Women's Championship? The last woman to hold the title? A woman from the era who actually held the title? *Nope.* Lita. Now, keep in mind that the era Deb wrestled in was sandwiched between the "Golden Era" and the "Attitude Era" and is basically the "Forgotten Era." To give perspective, The Fabulous Moolah and Mae Young appeared regularly on programming during the Attitude Era, and most, if not all, of the female wrestlers from the

Attitude Era make regular appearances today. Have you seen anyone from the Forgotten Era brought back? Again, little recognition of Deb or any of the women who wrestled during her era who held the women's title.

By the way, she still hasn't been defeated for that title.

— ALAN JONASON, MAY 2022

ACKNOWLEDGMENTS

DEBRAH: The conceptualization and compilation of this book is a concerted effort of various friends, family, business colleagues, and fans' conversations and memories.

First, my love, my husband, Alan, is truly a strength who has kept me grounded and has helped me become a better person. I love you.

Pets and nature have been my grounding since I was a child. I dedicate my mental existence to past, present, and future pets for helping me keep my sanity and loving me unconditionally when no one else was.

ECW Press publisher David Caron and editor Michael Holmes believed in the book, and the wonderful staff who put it all together.

Greg came recommended to me by John Arezzi. Thank you, John. Our morning coffee talks set the tone, and thank you to coffee because that fueled me. As you might have induced, I have some trust issues. But Greg and I got there. Probably the key moment was when, after a particularly emotional session, he wanted to make sure that Alan was home, that I wasn't alone. (I can't believe how he fanboyed for Eric Bischoff, though.) Greg truly went into character, becoming me to help me write this book and learned to understand me. I know it wasn't easy! Thank you, Greg, for not giving up when you could have, for all the times you and I went back and forth not seeing eye to eye but finding a middle ground. You listened to ideas that were way out there, and I could hear you shaking your head over the phone — but still you listened. But, most of all, you are blunt, to the point, and had some couth being constructive to the criticism. I couldn't have done it without you.

Leonard Caplan — the man, the myth, the legend — is one of my best friends and was with me at the beginning of my writing my book and always encouraged me to move forward with a publisher.

To Vince Russo (yes, you read that correct), thanks for sitting with me hours upon hours while in the WWF, recording what we thought would be a novel. Thanks for mailing back all my tapes. I don't care what people say about you; though, I still am pissed at a few of your booking decisions.

To everyone else who had a hand in making this possible.

Paul Heyman deserves his own lines of gratitude. He is a man who has helped so many and asks for nothing in return. Paul put me on the map in our business and continues to exude greatness with his effortlessly innate ability to see greatness in someone and invest his own valuable time to help them onto a path to either continue with the tools he set out or to fail. He helped me become the woman I am today: *The Woman Who Would Be King*. Thanks for the title, Paul! Love you.

Ky Michelson was my imagineer with a crazy idea, and Eddie Sharkey trained me. Hey, look what I did, guys! The Gagne family in the AWA were the first to believe in me, and later in WCW, I met many great people and was given the opportunity to change the trajectory of women's wrestling live on TV. My heart will always be in Japan. Thank you to my Japanese family for helping me become better at my craft, while talent had to suffer through my novice time. To every single athlete, thank you. AJWP, Rossy Ogawa, Fumi Saito, I couldn't have done it without you. You have heard my WWE stories, and yet they still had the intestinal fortitude to induct me into their Hall of Fame. And I have a new, amazing NWA family, led by Billy Corgan. Pat Kenny believed in me and saw me as a producer, even when I didn't, and he has revived my Madusa character, too. And can I say, "I love me some Jazz!" I have not seen a locker room so drama-free in a long time, and it speaks volumes to the quality of the boys when they let me be their agent. As for the wrestling fans? You are the reason I was able to do all this.

Sit down, strap in, and crank it up, because in the world of monster trucks, Mike Weber changed my life; Ann and Bob Trent let me drive

Bigfoot; my Fab Four friends, Damon, George, Cam, Lee, were there with me for some great times; Dennis Anderson will always be the greatest ever monster truck driver, and I learned much from him; Becky was my protege, a badass chick who listened well; RL and Lyle bucked the good ol' boys' club to help me. The voice of monster trucks is Scott Douglass, and he offered guidance through the years and has done so much good for the industry itself. My MTG Monster Truck Girls, the women who dared to be different, pushed the needle, and drove harder than most men. This is for you. A big shout-out to my MTG then, now, and future . . . never settle and push the pedal to the metal.

Team Madusa is a many-person operation. My manager, Codi Smith, has always believed in me, keeping the brand front and center, constantly protecting it, while having an organic vibe at the same time. There were publicists in wrestling and monster trucks who helped get me out there, but it was different having my own. Leslie McClure and I have had many canny conversations, dealing with my trust issues and forgetfulness; your patience has helped me continue to do my best.

Alan Pavlosky created my first website before websites were a thing, and Bill Trevor picked up where Alan left off and moved it into the future, and they both deserve credit for their patience with me. I've been fortunate with graphic designers such as Collette, Josh, Tom, Mark, and all the helpers.

"Madusa Rocks" came from Nomad & Lola, so thank you for the best entrance music ever, available on iTunes; DomD FromThaMO created a bad-ass song, "Dig Deep," for my documentary.

So many photographers made me shine through the years. Anthony Neste was the photographer who set up the regal cover shoot, though it was Mickey Fitzpatrick who shot the photo we chose, taken late on a 106-degree day. You are a blessing. Per Bernal was my first legit photo shoot before either of us was known in our businesses! Maybe we will continue to make magic if Dwayne "The Rock" Johnson allows you some time away. Thank you to WWE for allowing us to use some cool photos from my time as Alundra Blayze. If we missed crediting any images, like the fabulous shot on the back cover of me on my truck in Australia, I apologize.

Every step of the way, my lawyers, the cutting edge, movers and shakers, the late great John Taylor and David Lumsden, had my back, assisted by everyone at TFH legal. Bill Larson, a trademark attorney, helped me start my empire and trademarked MADUSA. My amazing wizard mathematician CPA Rik English and company kept me on course financially, yet still always paying taxes.

Where do I start personally? This is the part I am scared of because I don't want to forget anyone. So many have played a role in my life, though some were like seasons — they changed, but without them I would have never had the great stories, memories, or even heartaches. So to the ones reading, wondering why you were not named, this is for you (though some were intentionally left out).

Thanks and love to family members who are true to me, honest, and allow me to fail without judgment.

Much love to: my beautiful, active Chica's Forever, the amazing women in my life who have been my place of rescue, fun, and amazing sisters for life: Sheila, Judi, Rosie, Shannon, Merry Beth, Annie; the cool neighbors, Sylvia and Danny; the amazing staff at the Homosassa Springs Post Office; the awesome Dr. Morrison and staff; a big shoutout to Natalya Neidhart for setting the stage and letting me deliver a Hall of Fame speech of a lifetime and for introducing me to Mickey Fitzpatrick, the creative makeup artist with the magic and finesse that is fierce. Thanks, Mickey, for always painting a beautiful canvas on me, including on the cover.

Brandon Pender is the one who legitimized my career outside of wrestling, so thank you for taking a chance, teaching me, and helping me perform on the big screen. I am forever grateful. The acting bug never left, and Lamarze Smith and DT Bullock have let an older woman continue her dream. *Champion* rocks! The talented director Jason Braiser took a chance and gave me opportunities, but he also introduced me to Quinton Huckaby, and Quinton forced me to face fear and create an opportunity with my Twitch channel, and if I didn't do that, I wouldn't have my amazing Twitch family, the #MADMODSQUAD.

My one wish is that Marian, the beautiful dancer, and the father I never knew, Clyde David Bergman, were around to read this. I am so grateful to have found my missing links, my brother, David, and sister, Inger, though my time with David was too short.

When WWE called me for the Hall of Fame induction, I didn't expect it to change things so much; all of a sudden, I was back in demand for wrestling conventions, interviews, merchandise, and even as a producer behind the scenes.

WWE has often called me back for appearances, including the A&E show, *WWE's Most Wanted Treasures*, where I got to showcase the title I am never surrendering (spoiler alert). While we all know the people on the screen, for me, Sue Aitchison is a key one behind the scenes.

I still have so much more to offer. Keep an eye out for part two. Maybe we'll call it *The Woman Who Would Be Emperor — gaijin* style.

GREG: It was John Arezzi who put Debrah in touch with me, and, had that not happened, I wouldn't be able to use "monster-trucking" as a verb and know all kinds of variations on another word that rhymes with "trucking." Truthfully, it is still surreal getting calls from someone I'd watched on the AWA broadcasts in 1987 and 1988 while I was an impressionable teenage boy — that kid would not believe she is a treasured friend today.

Speaking of friends, Debrah has oodles of them, and so many of them took the time to talk to me about her. In no particular order, they are: Fumi Saito (who was key to the Japan stories), Heidi Lee Morgan, Dale Torborg (though we talked a lot of baseball), Missy Hyatt, Janie Engel, Lyle Hancock, Annie Fish, Evan Marriott, Arlene Strandmark, Judi McEvoy, Michael Weber, Kevin Williams, Kim Bard (Crosby), Vince Russo, Brandon Pender, Scott Douglass, Dennis Anderson, Lee O'Donnell, Leilani Kai, Keiko, Ky Michaelson, Merry Beth Graham, Eric Bischoff, Mike Muzik, Evan Karagias, Kenny Navitski, Leonard Caplan, RL Arace, Jeff Yager, Myranda Cozard, Cam McQueen, Chad Fortune, Nikita Lafleur, Inger Bergman, Jaker and Suzi, Alan Jonason, Gorgeous George, George Balhan, Becky McDonough, Ashley, Mark, David Bergman, Granny Vi (who I am surprised I got off the phone), and the ever-elusive Paul Heyman.

As for my own friends, John Powell and Bob Kapur and our staff at SlamWrestling.net helped out where they could; the amazing Jamie Hemmings was the first to read this manuscript start to finish and provided great insight — enough that I wish even more we'd done that women's wrestling book years ago; Brad McFarlin and his DMs; Chris Bergstrom helped with genealogical research into Clyde David Bergman; Mark Dillon dug up some vintage technology, so I could listen to Deb's old answering machine messages; the vital staff at Toronto Public Library, as I requested every book on monster trucks that they had — all of which were aimed at a young audience; my Browns wife Diana heard about this book so often I'm surprised she still talks to me; that goes double for my actual wife, Meredith Renwick, and our son, Quinn, who both managed to make small talk with the force of nature that is Deb until I could get to the landline; and since I left him out of the acknowledgments of John Arezzi's book, *Mat Memories*, thank you to David Bixenspan for calling out wrongs.

After writing about pro wrestling for 35 years, I thought I knew the circus, but I didn't. So I learned a lot from *Battle for the Big Top: P.T. Barnum, James Bailey, John Ringling, and the Death-Defying Saga of the American Circus*, by Les Standiford, and *The American Circus: An Illustrated History*, by John Culhane. And it's handy when an ex-boyfriend has a memoir out, too, as I roared through Steven Schussler's *It's a Jungle in There: Inspiring Lessons, Hard-Won Insights, and Other Acts of Entrepreneurial Daring*.

After months of intimate discussions, Deb and I finally met in person at the Cauliflower Alley Club reunion in September 2021, and that was a great moment, but even better was the time hanging out with her and her husband, Alan, in July 2022, in the Florida heat. In December 2021, I made a bunch of new friends, hanging out backstage at the NWA taping in Atlanta, watching Deb work as an agent, so thank you to William Patrick Corgan and Pat Kenney and their amazing crew for the open arms — and Trevor Murdoch for always putting me over.

ABOUT THE AUTHORS

Debrah Miceli is the WWE Hall of Famer Alundra Blayze and the two-time Monster Jam World champion Madusa. She is active as a producer of NWA wrestling, a motivational speaker and a gamer on Twitch. Miceli continues to tour on many platforms. She lives in Florida with her husband, Alan, and their dog, Daisy. For more information go to MADUSA.com.

Greg Oliver is the author or co-author of 19 books, from entertainment to professional wrestling, from hockey to kids books. He is the 2020 recipient of the James C. Melby Historian Award for his contributions to pro wrestling history. He lives in Toronto with his wife, Meredith, and their son, Quinn. Visit www.OliverBooks.ca for all his books and projects.

Paul Heyman, who wrote the book's foreword, is a current WWE Superstar and manager to the stars. He first met Madusa in the American Wrestling Association in July 1987 when he was Paul E. Dangerously, and they have been friends ever since. He is the creative genius behind ECW. Always busy, find him at www.heymanhustle.com.